The Booklover's Guide to
NEW ORLEANS

❧ SECOND EDITION ❧

The Booklover's Guide to
NEW ORLEANS

SUSAN LARSON

LOUISIANA STATE UNIVERSITY PRESS
BATON ROUGE

Published by Louisiana State University Press
Copyright © 1999, 2013 by Susan Larson
All rights reserved
Manufactured in the United States of America
First printing

Designer: Barbara Neely Bourgoyne
Typeface: Whitman
Printer and binder: Maple Press

Library of Congress Cataloging-in-Publication Data

Larson, Susan.
    The booklover's guide to New Orleans / Susan Larson. — Second edition.
        pages cm
    Includes index.
    ISBN 978-0-8071-5307-9 (pbk. : alk. paper) — ISBN 978-0-8071-5308-6 (pdf)
— ISBN 978-0-8071-5309-3 (epub) — ISBN 978-0-8071-5310-9 (mobi) 1. Liter-
ary landmarks—Louisiana—New Orleans—Guidebooks. 2. Authors, Ameri-
can—Homes and haunts—Louisiana—New Orleans—Guidebooks. 3. New
Orleans (La.)—In literature—Bibliography. 4. Bookstores—Louisiana—New
Orleans—Guidebooks. 5. New Orleans (La.)—Bibliography. 6. New Orleans
(La.)—Guidebooks. I. Title.
    PS267.N49L37 2013
    810.9'976335—dc23

                                    2013010590

With love and thanks to Casey and Dash, always

and

In memory, with love,

Julian Wasserman
Diana Pinckley
Stephen Ambrose
George Herget
Coleen Salley
Mark Zumpe

Contents

Illustrations

A Note on the Second Edition

I began writing the first *Booklover's Guide to New Orleans* to answer
the questions readers often asked of me in my role as book editor
for the *New Orleans Times-Picayune*. I explored parts of our local
literary history that were new to me, bridging the gaps in my own
knowledge. When that book was published in 1999, I celebrated
more than ten years as book reviewer for the *Picayune* and a sense
of having learned a lot in the process. But history would have more
lessons to teach over the coming years.

This new edition is a heartfelt response to more than another
decade of living life in New Orleans. Our literary scene has continued to grow and evolve in fascinating new directions, but most
important, it has simply endured. There have been changes—festivals have come and gone, bookstores have opened and closed,
writers have moved in or moved on, gained recognition or suffered
as one-book wonders. The New Orleans booklist has continued to
lengthen, and the exploration of our rich culture continues apace.

The biggest, most convulsive changes by far occurred in 2005.
What does a fragile literary culture, built on paper after all, do in the
wake of a monumental flood? Surprisingly, it proves to be one of
the most durable cultural treasures that our city offers the rest of
the world. So my purpose in writing this literary guidebook anew
is clear. Everything the literary tourist or literary hopeful, from
avid reader to wildly successful writer, would hope to find in New
Orleans is still here, still strong. We still have a vibrant festive culture, with excellent independent and antiquarian bookstores, and

literary landmarks that have withstood the test of time and flood-water. Come visit, come listen to our stories and see them unfold on our streets.

One thing remains the same—New Orleans, that sweet old Muse, has never been more seductive. I fall more in love with the place every day.

Susan Larson
September 2012

The Booklover's Guide to
NEW ORLEANS

Welcome!

Every March, in what has become one of New Orleans's most comical and endearing rites of spring, hundreds of people crowd into Jackson Square, below the long gallery of the Upper Pontalba apartment building, and reenact one of the signature scenes from New Orleans literature. Shouts of "Stanleeeeeeey!" and "Stellllll-laaaaa!" fill the air as actors, tourists, and ordinary folks step into roles from *A Streetcar Named Desire.* On the balcony above, judges from the Tennessee Williams / New Orleans Literary Festival— celebrity guests and local luminaries, usually including at least one slip-clad gorgeous woman—look down on the motley crew in amusement, finally selecting the very best from the crowd of strong-lunged, determined, and often inebriated people.

Few American cities have such a visible and inviting literary culture, played out on its streets every day. If you come to New Orleans after reading John Kennedy Toole's *Confederacy of Dunces,* you will see Ignatius Reilly everywhere, whether he takes the form of an eccentrically dressed local, a Lucky Dog vendor on a French Quarter corner, or a statue outside a hotel on Canal Street. Even supernatural literary scenes come to life for tourists who visit Anne Rice's former mansions or venture into the Quarter on Halloween or attend the annual vampire ball or stroll through the Uptown cemetery where Lestat took his long rest. Those readers who have taken Walker Percy's *Moviegoer* to heart will find themselves drawn to the yellow cottage on Milan Street where he began writing the novel, a place just down St. Charles Avenue from Loyola University, where Percy taught his one and only creative writing course and where Thelma Toole brought her son's manuscript to him for consideration. These days visitors crossing paths with Hollywood stars is a commonplace, just like Binx Bolling's encounter with William Holden in the French Quarter. Ride the streetcar, stroll through the Carrollton neighborhood, or visit quiet Gentilly's streets for a sense of Binx Bolling's existential dilemma. "Not to be onto the search is to be in despair," Percy wrote.

And the search is always on, in New Orleans, in literary terms. Readers come here looking for great stories, stories they've read or heard or seen in the movies, stories they want to experience up close and personal. Writers come to compose their stories or live out a dream. They're drawn here by desire, ready to seduce, to be seduced.

It's easy to be charmed by the Big Easy. Most residents stay in love with it, for better or worse, for life. Most tourists are half in love with the place by the time they get here, drawn by the chance to act out a fantasy, live a slightly larger life, don a disguise—or take one off. Sometimes writers even dream of coming here, as did Constance Adler, author of *My Bayou: New Orleans through the Eyes of a Lover.* In New York she had dreams in which a voice told her, "You know, if you moved to New Orleans you could become an interesting writer."

New Orleans's literary heritage has paved the way for such a love affair. Certainly, you've tasted our food, heard our music, and seen the many films set here. But stories set you free to imagine your own version. Every night, somewhere in the world, someone is watching the film of *A Streetcar Named Desire,* and rarely is it not being performed onstage in some location. On late-night TV, you'll catch the film of *Interview with the Vampire,* and resolve to reread the book. These recurring and ubiquitous cultural references have given most visitors a sense of easy familiarity with the city, as if they were stepping into the pages of a well-known, well-loved story-book or entering a theater or movie set. Often they literally do, as movie crews have become a fact of life here in Hollywood South, and the HBO series set here, *Treme,* pays homage to one of our old-est neighborhoods. Visitors often report a sense of déjà vu, present moment merging with imagined memory. The past collides with the present at every turn, whether you're dining at a century-old restaurant, sitting at a table in a corner at the Napoleon House, or stepping into a fragrant courtyard.

In this book we trace the footsteps and tell the stories of many famous literary figures, past and present. As Andrei Codrescu writes in his introduction to the anthology *New Orleans Stories: Great Writers on the City*, "If New Orleans went into the memorial plaque business for all the writers who ever lived here, they would have to brass-plate the whole town." Watch for those brass plates—at Faulkner House in Pirate's Alley, on the front of the Hotel Monteleone on Royal Street, on the Pontalba home of Sherwood Anderson, and yes, on the Toulouse and Dauphine Street digs of Tennessee Williams—they're there, lovingly placed, marking the lives lived in New Orleans that led to books.

Andrei Codrescu at Octavia Books
Photo by Tom Lowenburg

Why have so many writers come to New Orleans? The early European explorers came here three hundred years ago seeking wealth and fame. What they found—and wrote about—was a kind of natural wonderland. Historians and religious figures came later and reported their progress back to the Old World. It is possible to stand outside the Ursuline Convent in the Quarter and imagine the young nun Marie-Madeleine Hachard recounting her observations of her new home. The clashes of cultures—Spanish, French, African, Creole—were grist for the writing mill in what became one of the South's great cultural centers. Journalists came to investigate, reported, and led others to come and look for themselves.

Some writers were drawn here as part of voyages down the Mississippi. Samuel Clemens would never have become Mark Twain without that river trip, and *Life on the Mississippi* would be incomplete without a stop in this port city. Later, others made New Orleans a must-see on grand tours of the American continent. William Thackeray visited the city on his way to St. Louis, stayed at the grand St. Charles Hotel, and said, "At that comfortable tavern on Pontchartrain we had a bouillabaisse than which a better was never eaten at Marseilles." His opinion of the city may have been improved by parting gifts of two bottles of cognac, a dozen bottles of Médoc, and a case of light claret. Long before there were drive-through daiquiri stands, this was truly one for the road!

In more recent times Gertrude Stein and Alice B. Toklas came to New Orleans as part of their triumphant American tour, during which Stein was received as the celebrity she was. There are still locals who remember their appearance at Tess Crager's famed Basement Street Book Shop and a party given in their honor, where the two sat side by side on a sofa for two hours and said nothing to anyone else. Finally, Alice turned to Gertrude and said, "Well, Puss, time to go!"

After 2005, of course, writers came here to bear witness—journalists first, to be sure, reporting on what locals often call the "federal flood," resulting from the levee breakage following Hurricane Katrina. Books poured out from news organizations whose members had parachuted in to cover the stories. Photographic records of the destruction soon followed, and now, so many years later, serious fiction and poetry and drama have come along, part of the city's ongoing narrative of resilience, of imagining its future self.

Gertrude Stein (*seated right*) and Alice B. Toklas at the Basement Book Shop during their visit to New Orleans
Historic New Orleans Collection, acc. no. 1983.215.113

In 2012 Stephen King visited New Orleans for the first time to read from and discuss his book *11/22/63*, a novel of alternate history in which the protagonist tries to go back and stop the assassination of John F. Kennedy. King drew heavily on the Lee Harvey Oswald lore associated with New Orleans, and his visit here gave him the occasion to sample his first beignet. The reading was a remarkable occasion: the price of admission was the purchase of a book from indie Octavia Books, and as the crowd entered the auditorium at the Academy of the Sacred Heart Nims Center, it was a dazzling sight to see so many people—about twelve hundred—in one room, reading.

From the very beginning, many native writers have stayed in New Orleans all their lives. Grace King, historian, novelist, literary hostess, and one of the great southern women of letters, experienced Reconstruction in New Orleans and spent her life writing about her beloved city and state in such books as *New Orleans: The Place and the People* and *Balcony Stories.*

Other New Orleans–born writers find time away restorative. Walk through the shady streets of the Garden District to Anne Rice's former home at the corner of First and Chestnut, the model for the house at the heart of *The Witching Hour.* Rice lived some of the glory days of her career here, and tour groups make frequent stops, but the author has moved on to a home in California, though there are rumors of her possible return to New Orleans. But the neighborhood now boasts another literary landmark: across the street lives Julia Reed, author of *The House on First Street: A New Orleans Story.*

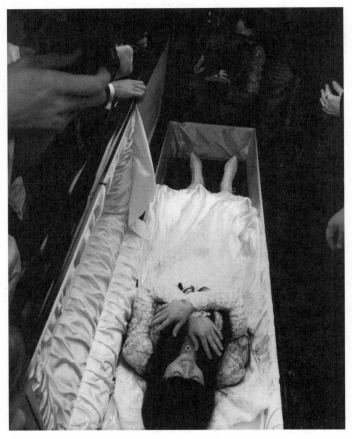

Anne Rice living it up at her jazz funeral
Courtesy New Orleans Times-Picayune, *photo by Bryan Berteaux*

Some native writers left for good but drew on their childhood memories for inspiration. When Lillian Hellman chronicled her girlhood days, she returned to that Prytania Street boardinghouse run by her aunts, the venue that inspired her play *Toys in the Attic.* The noted *New York Times* book critic Anatole Broyard, also a native, wrote about New Orleans summers in a wonderful essay called "Summer Madness." (When Broyard left New Orleans, he also left behind his racially mixed identity, revealed amid great controversy only after his death. His daughter, Bliss, also a writer, explored that heritage in *One Drop: My Father's Hidden Life—A Story of Race and Family Secrets.*)

Some writers come to New Orleans specifically to write. Walker Percy moved here in 1947, acting upon his simultaneous decision to marry, to write, and to become a Catholic. In his early days he lived near Audubon Park in a house that belonged to one of the founders of the *Double Dealer,* that famed literary magazine of the 1920s. Later he moved to the house on Milan Street, where he began working on *The Moviegoer,* that great New Orleans novel of the struggle against despair. Percy's legacy lives on today in the Walker Percy Center for Writing and Publishing at Loyola University, where Percy once taught a lone, legendary class that included such well-known writers as Tim Gautreaux, Kenneth Holditch, Walter Isaacson, and Valerie Martin.

Some writers even find a hiding place here. William S. Porter, a fugitive from embezzlement charges leveled by a Texas bank, fled to New Orleans, went to work for the newspaper, lived in a French Quarter apartment called the Rookery, and wrote several stories set in the city. Porter is, of course, better known by his nom de plume, O. Henry. Seth Morgan, fresh from a prison term after being found guilty of drug dealing, came to New Orleans to make a new start, then published the brilliant novel *Homeboy.* Easy prey for his addictions in this city of temptation, Morgan died in a horrific motorcycle crash on the St. Claude Avenue Bridge, leaving behind a promising start to a novel about New Orleans.

Some writers drift in and out of town. Richard Ford has owned several houses here—one in the Garden District, one in the French Quarter—and comes and goes, a New Orleanian but not quite. For a long time Barry Gifford was in and out of town, and several of his *Sailor and Lula* books are set here. These days best-selling novelist Laura Lippman is in residence while her husband, David Simon, shoots new episodes of *Treme.* Although she has yet to set any books here, many of her novels feature an affectionate nod to post-Katrina New Orleans.

And many writers find, as Tennessee Williams did, a spiritual home here. Williams, one of the writers most strongly identified with the city, made it uniquely his own. Every writer who takes New Orleans as a subject does so in the shade of his evocation of the place, specific as it is—so specific, in fact, that visitors still ask where they can find a streetcar named Desire, which stopped running in 1948. In his *Memoirs*, Williams referred to New Orleans as a transformative place, one in which he discovered a certain "flexibility in his sexual nature." Williams would return here again and again when he faced challenges in his life or setbacks in his writing, and he would be consoled and healed by the city.

But what is it about the city that draws writers so surely, so steadily? The exoticism? The freedom? The locals' casual acceptance of celebrity? The cityscape steeped in history? The sultry air?

The world's most famous streetcar in its preretirement days
Historic New Orleans Collection, acc. no. 1974.25.37.103

The great food? The constant music? The festive calendar? Perhaps it is living in a place where words and stories—just like food and music—are the currency of daily life, a place where the writing life is valued and understood. In New Orleans being a writer is, indeed, one of the oldest and most honorable professions.

The past remains alive and well, even in this post-Katrina era. The horse-drawn carriages that still convey tourists through the French Quarter often resound with folk history. "Over there, that's where Tennessee Williams lived when he wrote *Streetcar*," the driver will proclaim, and a reverent hush will fall over the group. Tourists who venture down the seductive little stretch of Pirate's Alley between the Louisiana State Museum at the Cabildo and St. Louis Cathedral will find Faulkner House Books, an elegant store now occupying the place where Faulkner lived and worked during his brief but transformative time in the city.

The literary life of the present is equally vital. There are successful and aspiring writers doing good work here as well as a number of best-selling authors who are from here; a strong culture of independent bookstores that support local writers; and entertaining and educational literary festival and conferences. There are strong offerings in creative writing at the New Orleans Center for Creative Arts for high school students as well as at the University of New Orleans. The creative writing program at Louisiana State University is one of the oldest in the country.

And no place does festivals like Louisiana. Which brings us back to that afternoon in Jackson Square that takes place every spring during the Tennessee Williams / New Orleans Literary Festival. It's the true beginning of the literary year, followed by the New Orleans Jazz and Heritage Festival, which offers great music. Authors come to town to work and play then, and the book tent at the festival is the place to meet them. Summer brings the Essence Music Festival, the "party with a purpose," which includes appearances by leading African American writers. And fall brings the Pirate's Alley Faulkner Society celebration, "Words and Music: A Literary Feast in New Orleans."

But the literary life unfolds every day of the week. Any Sunday afternoon you can amble into the Maple Leaf Bar in Carrollton, scene of the longest-running reading series in the South, settle in for a few beers, and hear writers perform their latest work. Or duck into the Gold Mine Saloon in the Quarter any Thursday night, where the 17 Poets! Literary and Performance series draws a loyal following. The New Orleans Healing Center in the St. Claude Arts District offers literary programming along with musical evenings. Some bookstores, such as McKeown's Books and Difficult Music, sponsor musical performances in store. That's New Orleans style.

Best of all, literary offerings in New Orleans are relatively inexpensive and open to everyone. Make a pilgrimage to your favorite writer's house and pay your respects. Stop by a local bookstore and see what strikes your reading fancy, then eavesdrop on the literary conversation. Check out the city's many archives and browse through literary treasures for free. Or join in the caffeine culture of New Orleans—that writer scribbling at the next table or tapping out the Great American Novel could be you.

After the flood of 2005, a popular bumper sticker slogan was "Be a New Orleanian wherever you are." But nothing beats being a New Orleanian here. Come on down. Stroll the streets. Ride the streetcar. And listen. New Orleans tells her stories all the time. One of them is meant just for you.

Tales of the Crescent City

A LONG AND WONDERFUL HISTORY

Writers are often drawn by the literary mystique of a place. There's the lure of another writer's vision or presence, a seductive land-scape, an attractive lifestyle. But it takes a literary infrastructure to build a literary mystique, and first and foremost comes a literary history, a writing tradition. Every literary city requires prominent authors whose work defines the place, whether they speak for the place or from it; books that come to represent it in the popular consciousness; histories chronicling significant events; novels, plays, and poems that interpret its spirit. Then it's important to add in the network of bookstores, literary salons and festivals, writers' conferences, educational programs, and media support that energizes successful writers and helps establish new ones.

What New Orleans offers writers is a chance to engage with the city as much or as little as they choose. Some writers live very social lives here; others prefer isolation. Some watch the culture; some are active participants. The resulting literature is as varied as human nature. And if, occasionally, writers feel the long shadow of their predecessors, they are still busy stepping into the light of the present. And after 2005 what New Orleans *really* offers writers is a city in which every citizen has a story and values the telling of it.

IN THE BEGINNING (1718–1860)

From the very beginning, many of those who came to New Orleans were driven to write. The first writers were explorers of the New

Gayarré Place, named after Louisiana historian Charles Gayarré
Photo by Dennis Persica

World, driven to push westward and report back about their discoveries. The first history of Louisiana, published in 1758, was written by Antoine-Simon Le Page du Pratz, who found the place not to his liking and returned to France. Other early accounts include François Xavier Martin's history of Louisiana, published in 1827; Charles Gayarré's four-volume *History of Louisiana,* issued from 1848 to 1866 in French and English; and Alcée Fortier's four-volume history of the same name, published somewhat later, in 1904.

Some particularly endearing early writings are those of Marie Madeleine Hachard, the young Ursuline nun who came to New Orleans in 1727 and recorded her impressions in letters to her family, which were eventually published in France and reissued by Louisiana State University Press as recently as 2007. In one she wrote: "There is a popular song sung here which says that this city is as beautiful as Paris. However, I find a difference between this city and Paris. Perhaps the song could convince people who have not seen the capital of France, but I have seen it, and the song does not persuade me to the contrary." Centuries later writer Hamilton Basso would refer to New Orleans as "Paris in my own backyard," perhaps demonstrating the difference between the immigrant and the native sensibility.

The city's early literature owes its greatest debt, naturally, to the French, particularly the French Romantics. After finding it a disappointing investment, France ceded New Orleans to the Spanish in 1762, took it back briefly at the start of the 1800s, and sold it to the United States through the Louisiana Purchase of 1803. But the French heritage lingered. (The influence also worked in reverse, as Louisiana inspired writers in the home country. The French writer Chateaubriand set two novels, *Atala* [1801] and *René* [1802], in the colony.)

By 1850 Charles Testut could include fifty-two writers in his *Portraits littéraires de la Nouvelle Orléans*. Poets and brothers Dominique and Adrien Rouquette, who lived at 413 Royal Street (you can still see the letter R in the wrought-iron work), were the best-known writers of this period. Dominique published two collections of poems, *Meschacébéennes* (1839) and *Fleurs d'Amérique* (1856). Adrien became a missionary to the Louisiana Choctaws; his best-known work, a novel called *La Nouvelle Atala* (1879), grew out of that experience.

After the Civil War the French influence largely declined. The notable exception was Alfred Mercier, who, after his education in France, returned to New Orleans to practice medicine and write. His novel, *L'Habitation Saint-Ybars* (1881) was an important contribution to Louisiana literature, though little read or known today. Mercier was also instrumental in the 1876 founding of the French literary society L'Athénée Louisianais and edited its journal, *Les Comptes-rendus*.

Drawn to this bend in the river, writers just kept on coming—and the words just kept on flowing. The landscape inspired them; so did the confluence of cultures. Writers were drawn by the Mississippi River, the early days of the French opera here, the exoticism of the place. Writers have always been here, writing. And against all odds! The humid climate, the location largely below sea level—these are not conducive to the preservation of paper artifacts that are holy relics of literary culture. And then New Orleans, from the very beginning, was known for low amusements rather than high culture—as a wild, wicked, and, yes, illiterate place.

Early Bookselling

In the article "Books and Booksellers in New Orleans, 1730–1830," published in the *Louisiana Historical Quarterly* in 1937, writer Roger Philip McCutcheon quotes a Frenchman's 1803 observation that in New Orleans there were "no booksellers . . . and for a good reason, that a bookseller would perish of hunger there in the midst of his books, unless these taught the fascinated reader the art of doubling his capital in a year's time."

In the face of such a gloomy view McCutcheon points out that people were nevertheless reading in New Orleans, with fifty-six booksellers or stores operating between 1804 and 1824. So prominent a personage as Judah Touro, the famed philanthropist, sold books. In 1816 merchant Vincent Nolte, the author of *Fifty Years in Both Hemispheres* (1854) as well as the inspiration for Hervey Allen's *Anthony Adverse* (1933), was offering imported books for sale, as were many others. There were reading rooms and rental libraries throughout the city. The first public library was founded in 1808. The French printer and bibliographer Antoine Louis Boimare had a rental library of some ten thousand volumes. The first bookseller advertised himself as Mermet, "marchand libraire," in 1808 and had a shop on Royal Street in 1811.

Les Cenelles

The city's complex racial heritage has always been reflected in its literature. Perhaps the most significant local publication of the mid-nineteenth century was *Les Cenelles* (1845). Edited by Armand Lanusse, it was the first anthology of poetry by African Americans to be published in the United States. Containing eighty-two poems by seventeen poets, *Les Cenelles*, "The Hawthorns," grew out of an 1843 magazine called *L'Album littéraire*. Three of the contributors— Pierre Dalcour, Victor Séjour, and Camille Thierry—received fur-

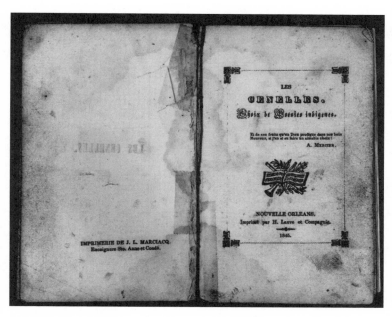

Title page of *Les Cenelles*
Historic New Orleans Collection, acc. no. P7.632.RL

ther recognition in France. The book is very rare today (only a few copies are known to exist in the city—in the Historic New Orleans Collection, the Tulane University Library, the Xavier University Library, and one private collection) and commands enormous prices.

Visiting Writers before the Civil War

Although relatively few writers were writing in English in New Orleans before the Civil War, some of them are now extremely well known. John James Audubon earned fame primarily as an artist, but writing was an integral part of his life. The great painter's journals from 1821 and 1822 describe his daily life in New Orleans; he lived in Louisiana until 1830. His residences included 706 Barracks Street and 505 Dauphine Street. Audubon Park bears his name today. He spent some time at Oakley Plantation near St. Francisville as a tutor to a family's young daughter, a period in his life that has inspired at least two books, *Audubon's Watch: A Novel,* by John Gregory Brown (2002) and *A Summer of Birds: John James Audubon at Oakley House,* by Danny Heitman (2008).

Walt Whitman wrote for the *New Orleans Crescent* in 1848, and his "I Saw in Louisiana a Live Oak Growing" is perhaps the greatest poem associated with the state. The place on Washington Avenue where Whitman stayed no longer exists, but you can follow the avenue (past the contemporary landmark of Commander's Palace, just off Prytania Street), enjoying the magnificent live oaks, down to the river, imagining what he saw there.

Samuel Langhorne Clemens traveled to New Orleans frequently between 1857 and 1861 as a young riverboat pilot and—according to at least some of his biographers—acquired his pen name, Mark Twain, here. He described all this in *Life on the Mississippi* (1883); he would later return as a best-selling author.

THE LATE NINETEENTH CENTURY

The Centennial Exposition of 1884

The late 1800s ushered in a golden age of literary activity, begun partly by such visitors as Edward King of the influential magazine *Scribner's,* who came to New Orleans in 1873. The single greatest influx of writers occurred with the New Orleans World's Fair—officially, the "World's Industrial and Cotton Centennial Exposition"—in 1884. Joaquin Miller covered the fair for New York papers, Julia Ward Howe headed the Women's Department, and editors Richard Watson Gilder of *Century Magazine* and Charles Dudley Warner of *Harper's* arrived to take in the extravaganza and absorb the local culture. These visitors and others like them provided important links to the larger work of New York publishing, thereby offering new opportunities for New Orleans writers, increasing readers' interest in the city and engendering more demand for pieces about it. Many names from this period have endured; some are enjoying a critical revival and reassessment—George Washington Cable, Lafcadio Hearn, and Grace King among them.

Cable, King, Hearn, Chopin

George Washington Cable's tales of Creole life gained national attention after his short story "'Sieur George" was published in *Scribner's* magazine in 1873. Although Cable, a native New Orleanian, has often been dismissed as a local-color writer, a new generation of readers is now discovering the city through his eyes as his works are reprinted. Many French Quarter buildings—Madame John's Legacy and Lafitte's Blacksmith Shop, for example—are exactly as he described them more than a century ago. His Garden District home was a popular destination for visiting writers.

Cable's books include *Old Creole Days, The Grandissimes, Dr. Sevier,* and the nonfiction work *The Creoles of Louisiana.* Then, as today, New Orleanians disliked criticism, even from within, and especially when they recognized the truth of it. An early civil rights activist, Cable inspired a storm of outrage, so much so that he moved to Northampton, Massachusetts, where he continued to associate with the literati of his day, and he wrote a charming little book, *The Amateur Garden,* in which he described with sweet nostalgia the gardens of New Orleans in winter.

The LeMonnier house, setting for George Washington Cable's "'Sieur George" *Historic New Orleans Collection, Vieux Carré Survey Sq. 42*

Grace King's career as a writer began in direct response to Cable's popular success and his depictions of racial injustice. In the course of becoming a Creole apologist, she also became one of New Orleans's great women of letters. Her 1886 short story "Monsieur Motte" is still taught today. Some of her other well-known works are *Balcony Stories* (1892); *New Orleans: The Place and the People* (1907); and *The Pleasant Ways of St. Medard* (1916). King's elegant mansion on Coliseum Square was occupied by members of her family until recently.

One of the most interesting chroniclers of New Orleans during this period was the romantic, enigmatic Lafcadio Hearn. Born in the Greek isles to an Irish father and a Greek mother and raised in Greece, Ireland, Britain, and France before immigrating to the United States, he arrived in New Orleans in 1877 from Cincinnati and lived here for ten years. Hearn wandered about the city, watching (though he was blind in one eye), reporting, and taking part in the life of the place. He captured unique aspects of Creole life and dialect because, as an outsider, he was open to them. After having left behind his wife, a woman of color, he was rumored to have had an affair with Marie Laveau.

During his decade here Hearn produced remarkable writing for local newspapers—he was the first literary editor of the *Item*, and he wrote for the *Times-Democrat*. He is the author of such Louisiana classics as the novel *Chita* (1889) and *"Gombo zhèbes"* (1885), a charming collection of Creole proverbs he gathered on his peregrinations throughout the city. A food lover, Hearn also opened a restaurant on Dryades Street called Hard Times and wrote *La Cuisine creole*. He also wrote one of the guidebooks to the 1884 Centennial Exposition. He eventually settled in Japan, where he became a cult figure in the city of Matsue; he spent the rest of his years writing about Japanese culture for an American audience. (Today Matsue and New Orleans, bound by their shared adopted son, are sister cities.) Jonathan Cott's 1991 biography, *Wandering Ghost: The Odyssey of Lafcadio Hearn*, led to something of a Hearn revival, but as long ago as 1949, Malcolm Cowley called Hearn "the writer in our language who can best be compared with Hans Christian Andersen and the brothers Grimm." (I often imagine an Andrew Lloyd Webber musical called *Lafcadio!*)

The feminist movement led to a rediscovery of the work of Kate Chopin, and her 1899 novel *The Awakening* is now taught as an

Lafcadio Hearn
Historic New Orleans Collection, acc. no. 1974.61.10

American classic. Chopin lived in New Orleans from 1870 to 1879, and much of her time here was occupied with her duties as a wife and mother. She spent summers on Grand Isle, where the dramatic conclusion of *The Awakening* takes place. She also resided for a time in the Louisiana plantation country of Cloutierville and Natchitoches, although most of her life was spent outside of Louisiana. Her experience in New Orleans, however, was the basis for most of her published work. Strollers on Esplanade Avenue can still see Creole cottages that resemble Edna Pontellier's home in *The Awakening*. Chopin lived the relatively privileged life of the wife of a cotton factor (broker for rural planters), but she was quick to see the strictures of New Orleans society and to envision another, more liberated existence for women.

Mollie Moore Davis came to New Orleans in 1879; her husband was the editor of the *Daily Picayune*. She wrote primarily novels, short stories, and plays. In a charming little book, *Keren-happuch and I,* published in 1907, she told stories about the famous guests at her salon on Royal Street—Eugene Field, Booth Tarkington, Lafcadio Hearn, George Washington Cable, and Grace King among them.

Alice Moore, who became better known as Alice Dunbar-Nelson, grew up in Uptown New Orleans and published her first book, *Violets and Other Tales,* in 1895. She married poet Paul Laurence Dunbar and, in New York City, knew many of the leaders of the Harlem Renaissance. A second collection of her short stories, *The Goodness of St. Rocque,* was published in 1899. Dunbar-Nelson was rediscovered in the 1980s, when scholar Gloria Hull edited *Give Us Each Day: The Diary of Alice Dunbar-Nelson,* as well as her collected works.

Poetry and Advice in the Newspaper

In these days of declining and failing newspapers, it's hard to believe that newspapers once took the space to publish poetry. Over the nineteenth century New Orleans newspapers nurtured and provided employment for writers. Eliza Jane Poitevent, who grew up on a plantation near Pearl River, Louisiana, became the literary editor of the *Daily Picayune* in late 1860, at a weekly salary of twenty-five dollars. She was the first woman on staff, and she married editor Colonel A. M. Holbrook in 1872. When he died, she took over the paper herself, becoming the first woman publisher of a daily city newspaper in the United States. She married newspaperman George Nicholson in 1878, and the Nicholson family owned the newspaper for another eighty years. She wrote poetry under the pseudonym Pearl Rivers, and under her editorial leadership, poems began to appear occasionally on the *Daily Picayune*'s front pages. She hired her friend Elizabeth M. Gilmer, whom she knew from summer vacations in Bay St. Louis, Mississippi, to come to work at the paper. Gilmer would gain national fame as a journalist and advice columnist, writing under the pseudonym Dorothy Dix.

THE *DOUBLE DEALER* AND THE 1920S

The next notable period in New Orleans literature began in the 1920s, when the renowned literary journal the *Double Dealer* launched its five-and-a-half-year run under the editorial leadership

Front cover of the *Double Dealer,* October 1921
Courtesy the author

of Albert Goldstein and Julius Friend. It began as a response to
H. L. Mencken's criticism of the South as a "Sahara of the Bozart."
In a 1951 article in *Dixie Roto* magazine (the Sunday supplement
to the *Times-Picayune-States*), after *Dealer* contributor William
Faulkner had received the Nobel Prize, founder Albert Goldstein
recalled the magazine's origins: "Four young men—Julius Friend,
John McClure, the late Basil Thompson, and I—had put our heads
together and dreamed up an ambitious project. We conceived a

serious literary magazine. Its chief aim was to encourage budding writers; incidentally, it would show critic H. L. Mencken, at that time plagued with the notion that the South was culturally stagnant, that he didn't know what he was talking about." Youth and lack of funds were no obstacles for the determined editors, and as Goldstein wrote, what "started as 'A Magazine for the Discriminating,' soon became 'A National Magazine from the South.'"

Sherwood Anderson, already firmly established in America's literary pantheon, attached himself to the *Double Dealer* crowd and wrote an article for the magazine, ambitiously titled "New Orleans, *The Double Dealer,* and the Modern Movement in America." The essay celebrates the city and Anderson's experience here: " I am in New Orleans and I am trying to proclaim something I have found here and that I think America wants and needs."

Some of his words seem eerily applicable today: "At any rate, there is the fact of the 'Vieux Carré'—the physical fact. The beautiful old town still exists. Just why it isn't the winter home of every sensitive artist in America, who can raise enough money to get here, I do not know. Because its charms aren't known, I suppose. The criers-out of the beauty of the place may have been excursion boomers." Of course, Anderson may have been especially charmed by his own apartment in the Pontalba buildings, those lovely structures flanking Jackson Square and named for Micaela Almonester, Baroness Pontalba, who oversaw their construction in the mid-nineteenth century.

Anderson's residency in 1922 and 1924 attracted other writers to New Orleans, including the young William Faulkner. Other visitors to Anderson's apartment included John Dos Passos, Carl Sandburg, Gertrude Stein, and Anita Loos. Anderson spent his first winter in New Orleans working on *Many Marriages* and *Horses and Men.*

Defiantly literary (and financially unsuccessful), the editors of the *Double Dealer* sought out and published some of the most remarkable names in American literature. William Faulkner's and Ernest Hemingway's first published works appeared in the magazine. Goldstein wrote, "Dig into the old files, and you find Faulkner, Hemingway, Thornton Wilder, Mark Van Doren, Richard Aldington, Gilbert Seldes, Ben Hecht, Mary Austin, Louis Untermeyer, William Alexander Percy, Howard Mumford Jones, Robert Penn Warren, John Crowe Ransom, Edmund Wilson, Ezra Pound, Burton

Rascoe, Jean Toomer, Robert Graves, Lola Ridge, Henry Bella-
mann, Lord Dunsany, Allen Tate, Maxwell Bodenheim, Carl Van
Vechten, Hamilton Basso, David Cohn, Llewlyn Powys, Witter
Bynner, Elizabeth Coatsworth, and dozens more of that ilk."

The editors achieved their goals and even convinced Mencken
that, as Goldstein put it, the magazine was "delivering Southerners
from what he called their cultural swamp": "After nearly six years
of publication—a long life as a 'little magazine' went—*The Double
Dealer* was discontinued. Not because it had failed; to the contrary. It had been a constructive force in the postwar movement,
which sought to kick over the traces of a decayed literary tradition. It bowed out mainly because its work was done." Its editors
and writers went on to other things. John McClure, for example,
became the editor of *Scribner's* magazine, providing an important
link between New Orleans and the New York publishing world.

Even in its heyday, the *Double Dealer* was not the only game in
town. Other writers were at work on other projects in New Orleans in the 1920s. Roark Bradford began his fourteen years here
as a newspaper reporter but eventually turned to fiction. *Ol' Man
Adam an' His Chillun* (1928) was the basis for Marc Connelly's 1929
play *The Green Pastures,* which won the Pulitzer Prize for drama in
1930. That year another Quarterite, Oliver La Farge, received the
Pulitzer Prize for fiction for his novel, *Laughing Boy.*

La Farge taught at Tulane University with noted archaeologist
Frans Blom and took his meals with William Faulkner and the
artist William Spratling in their French Quarter apartment on Pirate's Alley, now Faulkner House Books. At the same time Hamilton Basso, a New Orleans native, was beginning his long career as
a journalist (he is perhaps best known for *The View from Pompey's
Head,* published in 1954). Today Basso's books have been reissued,
and he is the subject of a 1999 biography, *The Road from Pompey's
Head: The Life and Work of Hamilton Basso,* by Inez Hollander Lake.

Faulkner, who lived in the city for six months in 1924 and 1925,
wrote articles for the *Times-Picayune* and the *Double Dealer* that
were eventually published as *New Orleans Sketches.* Later works
with New Orleans settings were the novels *Mosquitoes,* a wicked
satire of Quarterites on a boating expedition on Lake Pontchartrain; *Pylon,* based on the opening of the Shushan Lakefront Airport; and *Soldier's Pay,* a novel about a returning war veteran.

William Spratling's drawing of
himself and William Faulkner from
*Sherwood Anderson and Other
Famous Creoles*
*Historic New Orleans Collection,
acc. no. 73.320.6*

Many who knew Faulkner in his New Orleans days remember
him as an unpleasant little man who drank a lot and kept an observant eye on everyone. That eye became all too obvious in a satirical work published in 1926 called *Sherwood Anderson and Other
Famous Creoles*. Faulkner collaborated with his roommate William
Spratling on this book, which consisted of caricatures by Spratling
and captions by Faulkner. One representative example was "Oliver
LaFarge, from Harvard, a Kind of School near Boston," indicating, as Spratling put it, "Bill's lack of respect for Yankee culture."
The final caricature depicts the two collaborators, complete with
empty bottles under the writer's chair and the BB gun the two
friends would occasionally fire from their window at French Quarter passersby (even nuns, Spratling says in his 1967 autobiography, *File on Spratling*). The first edition of this little curiosity is
now rare and expensive, though the book has been reissued by the
University of Texas Press. A charming 2012 book by John Shelton
Reed, *Dixie Bohemia: A French Quarter Circle in the 1920s*, traces the
lives of the "famous Creoles."

THE WORKS PROGRESS ADMINISTRATION
AND THE 1930S

Literary activity continued at a high pitch in the 1930s with the
Federal Writers' Project, a New Deal WPA program designed to
provide employment for writers and artists. In Louisiana the project was led by the remarkable Lyle Saxon. Saxon, "Mr. French
Quarter," was a seminal figure not only in literature but in historic
preservation. In October 1935 he became the state director of the
Federal Writers' Project in Louisiana; later he served as regional
consultant for projects in other southern states. The program
ended in 1942. Among the important works produced by the project in Louisiana were *The New Orleans City Guide* (1938), *The Louisiana Guide* (1941), and *Gumbo Ya-Ya* (1945), a folklore collection
that is still a local classic.

Saxon asked Marcus Christian, the "poet laureate of New Orleans Negroes," to direct the Negro unit—separate in those days of
segregation—of the Louisiana Federal Writers' Project. Christian
succeeded the first director, Lawrence Reddick, a Dillard University history professor. From 1936 to 1943 the group included such

Master mixologist Joe Gilmore (*left*) and writer Lyle Saxon
Historic New Orleans Collection, acc. no. 1983.215.9

amazing writers and artists as Arna Bontemps, Elizabeth Catlett, Octave Lilly, Benjamin Quarles, and Margaret Walker. Novelist Frank Yerby, who later wrote *The Foxes of Harrow* (1946), was also a professor at Dillard at that time. "The History of Black Louisiana" in manuscript (it was never published in book form, alas) is part of the Marcus Christian Collection at the University of New Orleans (UNO), along with many poems, including Christian's epic Whitmanesque "I Am New Orleans."

A wonderful era in New Orleans bookselling began in 1928, when Tess Crager opened her Basement Book Shop along the 7700 block of St. Charles Avenue. The store was moved in 1932 to 7221 Zimple Street, where it remained for fifty years. Crager and her husband, Robert Crager, formed a publishing company in 1947 and published John Chase's landmark history of New Orleans street names, *Frenchmen, Desire, Good Children,* and reprinted the work of Lyle Saxon. Tess Crager was the agent not only for Saxon and Chase but also for New Orleans authors Charles "Pie" Dufour and Robert Tallant. Authors who visited the store over the years include W. H. Auden, André Maurois, Stephen Spender, Gertrude Stein, Edna St. Vincent Millay, T. H. White, and Alexander Woollcott. The Historic New Orleans Collection / Williams Research Center has a collection of photos from the shop, and they are lovely to look at.

Katherine Anne Porter lived in the lower Pontalba apartments on Jackson Square in 1937; she was in love with and later married Albert Erskine, business manager of the *Southern Review* and later a famed editor at Random House. Robert Penn Warren and his wife rented a room around the corner on Royal Street so they could come down from Baton Rouge, where Warren was managing editor of the *Southern Review,* and visit Porter on weekends.

THE 1940S AND 1950S

Two of the greatest literary figures associated with New Orleans, both playwrights, received national acclaim in the 1940s and 1950s. Lillian Hellman's *The Little Foxes* was produced in 1939 and followed by *Another Part of the Forest, Watch on the Rhine,* and *Toys in the Attic;* the latter's setting was based on the Prytania Street

Contemporaneous photograph of the house on St. Peter Street where
Tennessee Williams wrote *A Streetcar Named Desire*
Historic New Orleans Collection, Vieux Carré Survery Sq. 62

boardinghouse belonging to Hellman's aunt. And Tennessee Williams won Pulitzer Prizes for *A Streetcar Named Desire* in 1948 and
Cat on a Hot Tin Roof in 1955.

Novelist Frances Parkinson Keyes led an active literary career
from the 1920s to the 1970s, but her most famous novel, *Dinner at
Antoine's,* was a national best seller in 1948. Newspaperman Har-

nett Kane enjoyed a long career writing about Louisiana; he was such a tireless promoter of his work that finding an *unsigned* book of his is a rarity.

The Beat Generation made a brief, early foray into New Orleans in 1948 and 1949, when William S. Burroughs, drawn to the drugs and decadence of the city, was living in Algiers. Jack Kerouac and his sidekick and muse, Neal Cassady, visited Burroughs in 1948, and the opening of *On the Road* celebrates their arrival. Another link to the Beat movement was poet Bob Kaufman (1925–86), a New Orleans native who is said to have invented the term *beatnik*. Born to an African American Catholic mother from Martinique and a Jewish German father, he left home at thirteen to join the Merchant Marine, in which he served for twenty years. He later became a fixture as "The Original BeBop Man" on the San Francisco poetry scene.

THE 1960S AND 1970S

The 1960s and 1970s were a time of intense and diffuse literary activity in New Orleans. Writer Jon Webb moved here with his wife, "Gypsy" Lou Webb, in 1954 (the Webbs had earlier lived in New Orleans circa 1940, when Jon was writing his first novel, *Four Steps to the Wall*). He determined to publish a magazine called the *Outsider* in 1960. Poet Walter Lowenfels provided an introduction to Henry Miller, and the first issue included the work of such other Beat icons as Gregory Corso, Lawrence Ferlinghetti, Allen Ginsberg, and Gary Snyder. The four issues of the *Outsider* are now collector's items. The Webbs' Loujon Press also produced exquisite editions of work by Miller, Ginsberg, and Charles Bukowski, who visited the couple here.

The Free Southern Theater, founded by John O'Neal and Gilbert Moses, and originally based in Mississippi, moved to New Orleans in 1964. The next year Tom Dent, son of Dillard University president Albert Dent, returned to New Orleans from New York to continue his career as a poet, playwright, and activist. Now the Tom Dent Literary Forum honors his memory every year. With Kalamu ya Salaam the theater established a writing workshop, BLKARTSOUTH, which began publishing a journal in 1968. That journal, *Nkombo*, included work by such contemporary writers as

Norbert Davidson, Tom Dent, Quo Vadis Gex-Breaux, Nayo (Barbara Malcolm), and Kalamu ya Salaam. The Congo Square Writers Workshop began in 1972, founded by Dent and Lloyd Medley.

Another literary circle revolved around the *New Orleans Review,* based at Loyola University and founded by Miller Williams (the poet who wrote the poem for President Clinton's 1996 inauguration and father of singer Lucinda Williams) and short story writer and novelist John William Corrington. The *New Orleans Review* first appeared in 1968 and continues to the present; it published the first chapters of John Kennedy Toole's 1980 novel *A Confederacy of Dunces.*

Other literary reviews include the *New Laurel Review,* founded by Paul and Alice Moser Claudel in 1972 and still published periodically under the editorial direction of Lee Meitzen Grue. The *Xavier Review,* begun in 1961 as *Xavier University Studies*, is now published annually (after ceasing publication from 1971 to 1980) and has contained writing by Tom Dent, Jerry Ward, Al Young, and others as well as interviews with James Baldwin, Andre Dubus, Ernest Gaines, Alex Haley, and Walker Percy.

A publishing party in New Orleans, 1969: *from left,* Walker Percy, Kay Archer, T. Harry Williams, Turner Catledge, Tess Crager, and Paul Rossiter
Historic New Orleans Collection, acc. no. 1983.215.28

Recognition for more New Orleans writers came in the 1960s. Shirley Ann Grau, a graduate of Tulane's Newcomb College, turned to writing after the university would not accept her as a graduate student and won the Pulitzer Prize for fiction in 1965 for her novel *The Keepers of the House*. Walker Percy won a National Book Award for *The Moviegoer* in 1962. Percy, for many years a kind of elder statesman for young writers, encouraged Sheila Bosworth and Nancy Lemann in their work. (Ironically, during the same period John Kennedy Toole was teaching at nearby Dominican College but would never meet Percy, who eventually saw Toole's work through to posthumous publication.)

In 1970, another banner literary year for the region, Louisiana State University historian T. Harry Williams won both a Pulitzer Prize and a National Book Award for his biography *Huey Long*. Lillian Hellman won a National Book Award for her memoir *An Unfinished Woman*, and former New Orleanian Robert Stone won a National Book Award for his novel *Dog Soldiers*. In 1976 New Orleans native Anne Rice, then living in San Francisco, became a best-selling novelist with the publication of *Interview with the Vampire*.

The Maple Street Book Shop, founded by Mary Kellogg and her sister Rhoda Norman in 1966 and subsequently owned by Kellogg's daughter, Rhoda Faust, is still a haven for local writers and prominently identifies with several of them, including Ellen Gilchrist and the late Walker Percy. Currently it is owned by Donna Allen, who has expanded its reach with several branches throughout the city. George DeVille opened his elegant double-decker bookshop on Carondelet Street in 1977. Now one of the country's oldest gay bookstores, Faubourg Marigny Books was founded by Tom Horner in the mid-1970s, was later run by Alan Robinson and now belongs to Otis Fennell.

THE 1980S AND 1990S AND INTO A NEW CENTURY

The 1980s and 1990s and the early years of the twenty-first century saw an extraordinary rise in the profile of New Orleans writers and literary culture. The decade of the 1980s started out strong when literary recognition came to several New Orleanians. In 1981 John Kennedy Toole won a posthumous Pulitzer Prize for *A Confederacy of Dunces,* and Ellen Gilchrist received a National Book Award for *Victory over Japan: A Book of Stories. A Confederacy of Dunces,* one of the greatest of all New Orleans novels, captured the imagination of the country with its outrageous protagonist and its hilarious yet realistic portrayal of life in New Orleans, far beyond the stereotypical Garden District elegance and French Quarter decadence. And then, of course, journalists were drawn to the tragic history of the book's author, who committed suicide in 1969.

Several factors contributed to the consolidation of the city's literary reputation in the 1980s and 1990s. Many prominent literary figures of that period were newsworthy and colorful. Stephen Ambrose wrote biographies of Presidents Eisenhower and Nixon, achieved best-sellerdom with his *D-Day: June 6, 1944,* and followed that up with the popular successes of *Undaunted Courage: Meriwether Lewis, Thomas Jefferson, and the Opening of the American West* (still my favorite of his books), *Citizen Soldiers,* and *Band of Brothers* (for which he also won a Golden Globe for the HBO series). His authoritative presence and mastery of his subject matter led television journalists and producers to seek his thoughts on subjects ranging from Nixon's funeral to the D-Day anniversary and the film *Saving Private Ryan.* For a time Ambrose was truly America's historian, as he commented upon important events and his books became best sellers, though he was dogged by accusations of plagiarism near the end of his life.

Douglas Brinkley began his rise to fame as Ambrose's protégé at the Eisenhower Center at the University of New Orleans, then moved to Tulane, then on to Rice University. Brinkley has written on subjects as diverse as Walter Cronkite, Rosa Parks, Ronald Reagan, Theodore Roosevelt, and Hunter S. Thompson.

Walter Isaacson, former managing editor of *Time,* wrote the best-selling biographies *Kissinger: A Biography* (1993), *Benjamin Franklin: An American Life* (2003), and *Steve Jobs,* which was a record-setting best seller in 2011. Nicholas Lemann, staff writer for the *New Yorker,* became the dean of the Columbia School of Journalism and wrote about such diverse topics and standardized testing and the idea of the meritocracy in American life, the great black migration, and the last battle of the Civil War. Isaacson, Lemann, and Michael Lewis, who have often joked about themselves as the "State Street School of Writers" (Lemann and Lewis grew up Uptown, while Walter Isaacson grew up in Broadmoor), became public figures, but they never forgot their New Orleans roots. Lewis followed up his phenomenal debut best seller, *Liar's Poker* (1989), with a string of best sellers, including *The Blind Side* (2006) and *Moneyball* (2003), both made into highly successful feature films, as well as books about the changing financial markets; he always seems to be ahead of the curve, right at the cutting edge.

New Orleans also produced notable political commentators. Cokie Roberts, a native and daughter of Lindy Boggs, also launched a career as a best-selling author, writing about women in history as well as her own family life. Donna Brazile, who managed Al Gore's presidential campaign, had a best seller with *Cooking with Grease: Stirring the Pots in American Politics* (2005), which not only illuminated her career but also drew on her New Orleans childhood; she is now a columnist for *O* magazine. James Carville is another prominent commentator with long ties to the city; a native of Carville, he lives in an Uptown mansion with his wife, Mary Matalin, and teaches at Tulane University. Another standout on the best-seller lists was Ellen DeGeneres, who catapulted to fame with her daily talk show, *Ellen*.

James Lee Burke (*right*) at the Garden District Book Shop with owner Britton Trice in the 1990s
Photo by Earl Perry

Novelists who had already launched successful careers either stayed the course or took off in new directions. James Lee Burke continued to win awards and a huge following for his novels featuring Cajun detective Dave Robicheaux. Richard Ford was living in New Orleans when he won the 1996 Pulitzer Prize for *Independence Day*. Anne Rice might have moved to California and turned to Christian fiction for a time, but she continued to make the bestseller lists.

In short, the literary scene in New Orleans had a lot going for it in the summer of 2005. Writers were hard at work, indie booksellers were hanging in, festivals were well established, if feeling the economic pinch but planning ahead. There were publishers here, creative writing programs, writers and readers groups, libraries, as well as a dedicated core of individuals who make things happen, the things that writers need and readers want—before the storm New Orleans had them all.

KATRINA

Carnival historian Henri Schindler has a wonderful line in his book *Mardi Gras New Orleans:* "New Orleans has a climate that is notoriously unkind to paper and velvets." We were about to discover the truth of that as never before.

New Orleans writers are accustomed to evacuating for hurricanes, taking enough essentials to tide them over three or four days before the return. I always take along whatever I'm writing as well as a big bag of books (this was pre-Kindle, of course, and I can go through *a lot* in four days).

Slowly, as book people watched the news unfold of our flooding city, we began to realize what we were losing—homes, personal libraries, public libraries, papers, books—a way of literary life. Writers who stayed behind in New Orleans had varied experiences. Niyi Osundare, the great Nigerian poet, and his wife would have to be rescued by boat from their Lakeview attic, the flooded rooms below filled with his books and papers. When he ended up at Franklin Pierce University (then Franklin Pierce College) in New Hampshire, a school official presented him with a flash drive, and for quite a while he wore his works in progress around his neck on that small lifeline.

Here are some of the challenges writers faced after Katrina: first came the terrible choice, whether to stay or go. After the storm we lost surprisingly few writers, Douglas Brinkley being a notable exception. Later many writers had to face the shock of prolonged dislocation as well as the choice of whether to write about Katrina or something else entirely. Then there was the problem of how to claim such a large story. Brinkley, for example, focused on that first dramatic week after the storm. Then–*Times-Picayune* journalist Jed Horne chose to tell the story through the lives of a diverse group of people. Mark Schleifstein and John McQuaid focused on environmental issues in *Path of Destruction,* building on *Times-Picayune* reporting they had done over a period of years. LSU's Ivor van Heerden discussed scientific issues that were at the heart of his life as an academic. Then came books from trusted news organizations and trusted individuals as well as benefit anthologies.

Oral historians quickly got to work to capture the storm experience as well as the importance of New Orleans culture. McSweeney's *Voices from the Storm: The People of New Orleans on Hurricane Katrina and Its Aftermath* examined the human rights crisis. The Katrina Narrative Project at the University of New Orleans resulted in two volumes of oral histories, *Voices Rising 1* and 2.

This being New Orleans, some writers of course responded with humor. Artist Tom Varisco took aim at the messages left on the refrigerators placed outside people's homes with *Spoiled,* a beautifully designed little photo book that came encased in a plastic bag. (To explain: returning residents faced the common ritual of dealing with spoiled food after a month or more away. Usually, it was best not to open the refrigerator at all; hence, the huge numbers of duct-taped appliances left at the curb.) The writers of NOLA-Fugees began a satirical website, its title riffing on way evacuees were called refugees. "We're the canary in the coal mine of the American empire" was and is their motto. Just because it's funny doesn't make it any less true.

Others responded with reasoned fury. Tom Piazza's *Why New Orleans Matters* addressed House Speaker Dennis Hastert's question about whether the city should be rebuilt. Written at top speed and published in the fall of 2005, it was voted book of the year by the New Orleans Gulf South Booksellers Association.

Rebuilding issues placed new importance on books about urban issues, environmental issues, and geography. Writers such as Peirce F. Lewis (*New Orleans: The Making of an Urban Landscape*), Tulane's Richard Campanella (*Geographies of New Orleans: Urban Fabrics before the Storm*), and LSU's Craig Colten (*Perilous Place, Powerful Storms: Hurricane Protection in Coastal Louisiana* and *An Unnatural Metropolis: Wresting New Orleans from Nature*) were much in demand. Katrina turned every New Orleanian into a geographer!

Journalists passing through turned out books. Most notable among the early ones was Anderson Cooper's *Dispatches from the Edge*, which gave New Orleanians a new mantra: "Hope is not a plan." Much later would come Dan Baum's *Nine Lives: Death and Life in New Orleans*, which began as *New Yorker* blog coverage.

Public intellectuals often weighed in, with varying results. Michael Eric Dyson's analysis of the racial implications of the flood's aftermath in *Come Hell and High Water* completely ignored the fact that, in the final analysis, black and white people died in equal numbers here.

There were intensely personal accounts by doctors, politicians, and people in law enforcement, some self-justifying, some deeply generous—even finally, one by the hurricane recovery czar Ed Blakely, whose derogatory remarks about the city caused such an outcry that his publisher defended the book in the letters to the editor section of the *Times-Picayune*. There were scholarly collections of essays resulting from Katrina conferences around the county.

Photographers determined early on to document the tragedy and published such books as Robert Polidori's *After the Flood*, Chris Jordan's *In Katrina's Wake*, which moved me to tears, and Thomas Neff's *Holding Out and Hanging On: Surviving Hurricane Katrina*. Many photographers were accused of opportunism in having their works used for commercial purposes, most notably Polidori; still others who photographed ruined interiors and people's wrecked possessions were seen as taking advantage.

By the third anniversary—not surprisingly, if one allows time for writing and the publishing cycle—there was a spate of personal memoirs: Ian McNulty's *Season of Night*, about his early days back in the darkened city; Julia Reed's *House on First Street: My New Orleans Story*, about her storm experiences; and Phyllis Montana-LeBlanc's *Not Just the Levees Broke*, by the woman who stole the show in Spike Lee's documentary *When the Levees Broke;* and stories of St. Bernard Parish, recounted in Ken Wells's 2008 title *The Good Pirates of Forgotten Bayous.*

Patty Friedmann, a writer who never leaves home for hurricanes, stayed in her home in Carrollton and was flooded in. She left town by boat and later used her experiences as the basis for one of the first Katrina novels, *A Little Bit Ruined.* Christine Wiltz and her husband, Joe Pecot, stayed in their home in Carrollton as well and managed to avert a considerable amount of damage there as they coped with roof leaks, then left town as the scene became more dangerous. Wiltz wrote about her experiences for the *New Yorker* and the *Los Angeles Times.* Then they took shelter in James Lee Burke's New Iberia home. Later, she would imagine the landscape of post-Katrina New Orleans in an e-book called *Shoot the Money.*

Publisher Joshua Clark, known for the landmark anthology *French Quarter Fiction,* published by his Light of New Orleans Publishing, stayed in the Quarter throughout the storm and its aftermath. His memoir, *Heart like Water: Surviving Katrina and Life in a Disaster Zone,* was a 2008 National Book Critics Circle nominee in the category of memoir/autobiography.

Writers became cultural first responders with such works as Tom Piazza's *Why New Orleans Matters,* published in the fall of 2005. John Biguenet chronicled his return to the city as the *New York Times*'s first guest columnist and later turned his formidable playwriting talents to a Katrina trilogy—*Rising Water, Shotgun,* and *Mold.*

Some writers faced uncomfortable success. John Barry's masterpiece *Rising Tide: The Great Mississippi Flood of 1927 and How It Changed America* (1997) became a best seller again, but the reason for his success made him unable to truly enjoy it. He joined the ranks of prominent writers who came forward to address New Orleans's place as a great American city—along with Richard Ford, Walter Isaacson, Nicholas Lemann, Michael Lewis, and Anne Rice, who wrote impassioned pieces in the *New York Times* in the immediate aftermath.

In the pages of the *New Orleans Times-Picayune* writers did an incredible job chronicling the lives lost and the challenges ahead. Columnist Chris Rose gained a huge following in print and online for his impassioned columns, which were eventually collected in *1 Dead in Attic,* which became a national best seller.

Writers stepped into new, important civic roles. Walter Isaacson served as a cochair of the Louisiana Recovery Authority. John Barry became the president of the Levee Board. Julia Reed stepped up to be president of the board of the Ogden Museum of Southern Art.

Residents rejoiced in the opening of each bookstore, the return of each festival. Before long, poets were showing up at Carrollton's Maple Leaf Bar on Sunday afternoons, just as they have for decades, or going down to the French Quarter's Gold Mine Saloon, where Dave Brinks and Megan Burns were keeping their own lights on for poetry. Literary journals such as the *New Orleans Review* and the *New Laurel Review* returned to print.

Changing a Literary Narrative

The arc of published Katrina books followed a pattern comparable to that of the books that came out after the terrorist attacks of September 11, 2001. First came volumes of compilations from news organizations, there on the scene with vast resources in writing, photography, and publishing. There were instant histories from organizations such as CNN and the television networks and newspapers.

Writers and artists also sprang into action with relief anthologies—gorgeous books such as *Do You Know What It Means to Miss New Orleans?*, a lovely little volume edited by David Rutledge and published by Chin Music Press. Rosemary James of Faulkner House Books edited the anthology *My New Orleans: Ballads to the Big Easy by Her Sons, Daughters, and Lovers*, which sold out of a 20,000-copy first printing.

Then came works of photography, with the artists looking for color and terrible beauty in the damage. Poetry came early too, with its immediate and vivid response to such visual stimuli. But fiction—fiction takes time. How did authors adapt to such a changed landscape? Fiction writers had to reckon with historical reality and the new normal. How did they do it? Many reprised familiar characters, giving readers the chance to experience these stories through known eyes; others went in completely new directions. Some despaired, thinking that reality had finally trumped fiction.

Post-disaster fiction offers a curious set of challenges. First off, it's hard to write if you're preoccupied with the business of daily life—restoring a home, putting a life back together. And then there are the technical concerns. How do you make fiction stronger than reality? What about works already in progress? Do you adjust for the events of Katrina or make your work historical in outlook?

Then there is the marketplace. How many readers are there for works set during an event readers may feel they know too much about already? Is there Katrina fatigue for fiction? Are there readers? Only time will tell. The best Katrina fiction may come in ten or even twenty years. But here's a look at how some of our novelists—and editors—have handled it so far.

Many of the first novelists to write about Katrina and its aftermath were crime novelists, who turned to familiar characters as a way of giving readers perspective and used crime plots set against the storm as background. Best-selling novelist James Lee Burke is the author of what was the first well-received post-Katrina novel, *The Tin Roof Blowdown,* in his series featuring Cajun detective Dave Robicheaux. He is also the author of a story collection, *Jesus Out to Sea,* which includes two stories set in post-K Louisiana. Both books were published in time for the second anniversary of the storm.

Although his New Iberia home was undamaged, Burke took New Orleans's devastation to heart. "For a long time I didn't even think about writing. I just couldn't do it," he said. "I was depressed for a long time, not just over Katrina, but the way the whole Southern rim of states was gone. Then someone called me up on a Friday and asked if I'd do a story, and I said I'd think about it. And the next day I went to church, and as Pearl and I walked through the door, I remembered a story of a drowned priest in the Ninth Ward." And then he was off and writing.

For Burke, who was seventy then, his fiction reflected the political reality of the American landscape. "Louisiana is the future unless we change our ways of doing things," he said. "Louisiana is the microcosm of the macrocosm. Other people look upon it as an aberration. But everything that has happened in the United States has occurred in Louisiana, only it's more visible here. We had the biggest slave market in the Western Hemisphere on the banks of the Hudson River, and it's beyond belief what was done to blacks in the North, but slavery just ended there sooner. The New Orleans accent developed just as it developed in neighborhoods in

New York City . . . But maybe more important in the Dave Robicheaux books, to my mind, and this is not good, Louisiana represents the future unless we change."

Christine Wiltz, known for her Neal Rafferty mysteries, a novel about the city's racial politics (*Glass House*), and a biography (*The Last Madam: A Life in the New Orleans Underworld*), has turned her attention to a post-Katrina novel. Her chilling story "Night Taxi," in *New Orleans Noir*, is a riveting portrait of Lakeview after the storm. "I have no desire to write about the unnatural disaster that is known as Katrina," she said. "One story and a few articles knocked the idea of a novel right out of me. Now, the question of why we stay plays with my imagination far more than the question of why we leave."

"I wanted to write a love story to the city," Wiltz said, "so I'm writing about three bad girls who are also good guys and who love this city even though a lot of people say it's going to hell." *Shoot the Money* was published in paperback in 2013.

For Tom Piazza, who published *Why New Orleans Matters* in the first months after the storm, writing fiction about Katrina has been a matter of following the muse. His novel *City of Refuge* was published in 2008. "I knew it was the book I had to write," he said. Piazza's story centers on a Ninth Ward African American family and a Carrollton white family who face different stresses during and after the storm. Its timeline takes them through evacuation, exile, and return.

While inspiration was swift and sure, execution brought its challenges, not the least of which was finding himself away from New Orleans, doing residencies in various writers' colonies. "Spending time away from New Orleans was hard," Piazza said. "One difficulty was just finding myself back in the emotional and logistical constellation that was Hurricane Katrina for all of us. Having to imaginatively put myself back in the emotions I was feeling two years ago was the hardest thing I've ever had to do."

But the reason for doing it, the path forward, was always clear. Piazza speaks for many of his confederates when he speaks of his hoped-for audience in an eloquent explication of why fiction writers write anything at all: "You hear novelists say how writing a serious novel changes you and if it doesn't change you, it's not a serious novel. It's like a great love or a serious friendship. If you go through life and you're not changed by love and friendships, you're not really alive. The pilgrimage you make from beginning to end is a transfiguring process—the small victories you make, the transcendence you're able to achieve—that should come through to a serious reader."

And, according to Piazza, fiction will always have its place. "We don't read a novel the same way we read history," he said. "A novel does things history and journalism can't do. A novel can bring together the inner and most private questions that a person has to confront. A novel can go into the most private places in the human heart. And a novel can see the external life of communities, whether by community you mean a block, a city, or a nation . . . So what the novel does is, it mediates between the most private emotional transactions conceivable and the most public, social transactions we know of. That's its peculiar strength."

Books, Literally

The loss of books during the 2005 flood was immeasurable. Not only were personal libraries and collections lost in ruined houses, but many were books that had incredible value to their owners—family Bibles, beloved editions of *Harry Potter* (so J. K. Rowling generously included New Orleans on her American reading tour in 2007), and cookbooks. Especially cookbooks. Cookbooks are the best-selling category of books in New Orleans bookstores and gift shops across the board. The emotional cost of losing family recipes was incalculable.

As *Times-Picayune* food editor Judy Walker realized when people began to request newspaper reprints of recipes they'd lost, recipes bind our city and our families together. She began the Recipe Recovery Project, asking readers to send in favorite family recipes and searching out requested items from the *Times-Picayune* archive. The project resulted in *Cooking Up a Storm: Recipes Lost and Found from the New Orleans Times-Picayune,* which was a finalist for a prestigious James Beard Award.

Some people set about rebuilding personal libraries; others did not. That was one of the side effects of the aftermath—a new relationship to material possessions. An underground economy of books swirled around the city, with a renewed emphasis on the Symphony Book Fair and the Friends of the Library book sales.

POST-KATRINA: THE RETURN OF NEW ORLEANS

Writer Jarret Lofstead once quoted James Baldwin to me: "The determined will is rare." It was certainly not rare in post-Katrina New Orleans, where citizens were determined to return to their city and to rebuild better and smarter. And it was certainly not rare in literary culture, where writers and organizers and librarians got to work immediately.

Festivals

Louisiana has a reputation for letting the good times roll, and festivals are an important part of that reputation. These communal rites, especially the literary ones, reinforce our sense of community and provide an important sense of reunion each year. In 2006 things came back, if smaller, then better. And in those early days, writers provided an important perspective on the Katrina experience; almost every festival sponsored some event relating to that shared history. The festivals also served the important purpose of showcasing New Orleans to the world; writers came, went home, and wrote about their time here.

As engines for tourism, these festivals were up and running when needed. The literary calendar was virtually complete in 2006, with the Tennessee Williams / New Orleans Literary Festival in March, the NOLA Bookfair and the Louisiana Book Festival in October, and "Words and Music: A Literary Feast in New Orleans" in November. All of these ventures have continued, though the Louisiana Book Festival was canceled twice—in 2005, after Katrina, and again in 2010, due to state budget cuts. As then president of the Tennessee William / New Orleans Literary Festival Patricia Brady said, "We were going to have that festival if we had to stand there and shine flashlights at the stage." Fortunately, there was no need for that, and the festival went on to celebrate its twenty-fifth anniversary in 2011, bigger and better than ever.

Libraries

Librarians struggled to deal with the unbelievable damage wreaked by floodwater and sustained power loss; in Orleans Parish eight out of thirteen branches were destroyed or damaged. The Main

Library was federalized as a FEMA facility, and visitors went past Blackwater security agents every time they went there for either FEMA or library services. With the near collapse of city government and the funding crunch, the library staff was reduced by 90 percent, leaving a mere twenty librarians to try to move the struggling system back to functionality (for more information, see the chapter "Literary Resources").

In 2012 the system was on its way. In one historic spring week the New Orleans Public Library opened three new libraries and four branches total for the year. The system still faces considerable funding challenges in keeping all its branches operating at top capacity, but there is hope.

Library interest has been renewed, largely thanks to the warm welcome New Orleanians found at libraries across the country during the long evacuation period. Libraries were refuges, and librarians were invaluably helpful to New Orleans citizens in desperate need of information—about the fate of their homes, their friends, their city.

Publishing

New Orleans boasts many small independent publishers—many created for the sole purpose of publishing one book—but its backbone has long been Pelican Publishing, owned by Dr. Milburn Calhoun, who died in 2012, and his family. Daughter Kathleen Calhoun Nettleton took over the business after her father's death, and the company remains strong.

"I think in many ways the literary community post-K reflects the current civic climate—if you want things to happen you have to help make them happen yourself, " Anne Gisleson of the New Orleans Center for Creative Arts (NOCCA) said. "The average citizen has taken an interest in preserving, sustaining, rebuilding and creating culture, and that's very exciting. NOLA Bookfair is so inspiring because these are projects coming up from the street: NOLAfugees.com, Hot Iron Press, Neighborhood Story Project, *Meena* magazine, not ones that are heavily funded or socially connected. Very DIY." Gisleson is part of a publishing collective, Press Street, that includes fellow writers Ken Foster and Case Miller and artists Brad Benischek and Susan Gisleson.

Andy Young, who teaches at NOCCA, created a new literary

journal. "I think it is also important that we not fall into complete isolation, feeling like we are cut off from the rest of the world's experience and suffering. *Meena*, the Arabic/English literary journal I co-edit with poet Khaled Hegazzi, which is based in Alexandria, Egypt, and New Orleans, is about linking us to a wider culture. 'Meena' means 'port' in Arabic, and we hope that we've created a kind of literary port-of-entry between two cultures that, while disparate and diverse, have plenty in common."

Bookstores

In bookselling changes have been both interesting and dramatic. While Barnes & Noble in adjacent Metairie remained closed for many months due to storm damage, customers often found their way to local independents, which quickly found their business returning to pre-storm levels.

There were some serious losses along the way—most notably Mary Price Dunbar's store, Beaucoup Books, and Michele Lewis's two Afro-American Book Stop stores. The two women shared the Beaucoup space for a time in an innovative collaboration, but both left retail to devote more time to family and to continue bookselling on the Internet and through special author events and book fairs. Lewis opened a new store on Read Boulevard in 2007. Beth's Books opened in the Bywater (it has since closed), and McKeown's Books and Difficult Music on Tchoupitoulas Street began hosting readings and signings. Blue Cypress Books opened in Carrollton.

Tom Lowenburg and Judith Lafitte of Octavia Books were the first booksellers to reopen after the storm, and they are busier than ever. "We've never seen such gratitude, such crowds for writers like Tom Piazza and Anderson Cooper," Lowenburg said. "Personally, it's deepened my commitment to stay here."

In mid-March 2006 Barnes & Noble marked its Metairie reopening with a celebration that was the literary equivalent of Mardi Gras, with profits supporting the Jefferson Parish Library. The store provides an important venue for author appearances and reading groups as well as partnering with such events as "Words and Music: A Literary Feast in New Orleans." A short-lived Borders Books and Music, in the old Bultman Funeral Home on St. Charles Avenue, opened in 2009 and closed when the chain declared bankruptcy two years later, as did a nearby Metairie location.

A New Understanding, a Teachable Moment

Fresh literary energy emerged from the fact that every New Orleanian had a story—perhaps a tale of complete loss or a chronicle of exile and return. We began to see our lives as individual strands in the great collective epic of New Orleans. Which may account for the hundreds—literally—of self-published Katrina memoirs and narratives and children's books and the huge crowds that turned out for readings and literary events post-Katrina. In this new era we are all self-declared writers, all avid readers.

Of all the Katrina books two moved me the most. One was *Katrina, Our Teacher,* a sweet book from students at St. Angela Merici School in Metairie. The aptly named Faith Kyame got her first graders to tell their Katrina stories, describe their experiences, and then talk about what they'd learned—good life lessons all. The other was *Hurricane Katrina,* the volume assembled by the *Times-Picayune* staff, a stunning example of committed journalists who were determined to cover the story of their lives. As I write this, the *Times-Picayune* has announced it will cut back publication to three days a week. The effect on our communal reading life will be dire.

New Literary Dilemmas

The flood of Katrina material—"Katriniana," I call it—created dilemmas for publishers as well. While documentation was important, was there a market for it? Was publishing these books a moral responsibility? Eventually, the market held sway, as it always does. There were dilemmas for local book buyers as well—to buy these books online and save money or support local independent bookstores?

And last but not least, readers had tough choices. To read or not to read? To collect or ignore? Many, many people complained of not being able to read at all after the flood for a variety of reasons—no time, posttraumatic stress, lack of concentration, too much emotion. Many people obsessively collected Katrina books without reading them. Many others read every word. Still other readers escaped into books but could only read light material. It was a difficult time, when many sought human companionship rather than the solitude of a book.

There were, to be honest, dilemmas for the reviewers as well, at least this one. As a New Orleanian, it was difficult to discourage the hopeful self-published author, hard to read every word, difficult to control the fury at books that got things wrong. Reading was an emotional rollercoaster. And more than that, so many of these books were and are IMPORTANT. As Katrina brought home to us, there is no safe place to live in America. All of us are at the mercy of weather or geography. The scale of our city's devastation is the measure of American vulnerability, no matter where you live.

Going Forward

I write these words on a desk stacked high with books. Tonight my friend Chris Wiltz and I will go to a gathering at the New Orleans Center for Creative Arts. I will be interviewing that great Louisiana enchanter William Joyce at a party for the film and children's book *The Fantastic Flying Books of Mr. Morris Lessmore,* his Katrina-inspired work, which also celebrates the life of our friend, storyteller Coleen Salley.

Last evening I went to a talk and a book signing by Ninth Ward native Ruth Salvaggio, author of *Hearing Sappho in New Orleans: The Call of Poetry from Congo Square to the Ninth Ward.* She spoke in Octavia Books, which is located in a building across the street from where her mother was born. This Sunday afternoon she'll make an obligatory stop at the Maple Leaf Bar, celebrating the way poetry ebbs and flows here and some things endure.

Next week Richard Ford will be in town to read from and sign *Canada.* He pops up from time to time, unexpectedly at the Tennessee Williams / New Orleans Literary Festival last year, stopping by the WWNO studio for an interview while in town to see the dentist. Part of his heart is here. And maybe part of a tooth!

I just finished setting up an interview with James Lee Burke to talk about *Creole Belle,* the nineteenth in his Dave Robicheaux series which takes place in the aftermath of the BP oil spill. Like Ford, he and I have been talking over the years as their books came out, and it has been a pleasure and a privilege to hear their thoughts.

The stack of books nearby also includes a fair number devoted to Katrina and its aftermath; as the seventh anniversary approaches, for New Orleans readers the onslaught of seasonal book titles is both expected and difficult to bear. I spent some time this morning calling authors to get them to come to the opening of the Algiers Regional Library and finding them more than willing to tell their stories, cook their dishes, give of their time, at such a meaningful celebration.

Now, more than ever, we are a literary community. We are bound by our choices to live here, to write here, and to read here. It is an amazing thing to live in a city where everyone acknowledges their stake in the communal life. The great challenge of the present is to make sure we are a literate community, to spread the love of reading to those who don't already have it.

Going Forward Together

What are the elements that ensure the literary future of our city, our state? There are so many—the storied physical charms of New Orleans, the rich history, the survival of our independent bookstores, the strength of our creative writing programs, the determination of volunteers who keep festivals and libraries going.

One of the things that reassures me the most about our literary future is the presence of so many writing families in New Orleans. James Lee Burke once said, "They say if you drink from the Bayou Teche, you'll never leave." (I was never sure whether he meant that the pollution would kill you or that the water would work a magic charm.) Publisher John Travis titled a recent anthology of short fiction *There's Something in the Water*. Whatever—writers abound here, and the number of whole families living literary lives abound.

The largest extended family of writers is the Burke/Dubus clan. James Lee Burke—many people think he's a Louisiana native, but truly, he was born in Houston—is the father of thriller writer Alafair Burke. He's also the cousin of the late novelist and short story writer Andre Dubus, who's the father of Andre Dubus III, the award-winning novelist and memoirist. Elizabeth Nell Dubus is a playwright and novelist, the elder Andre's cousin and mother to Delaune Michel, who is the author of two novels herself. Mandeville writer Pamela Binnings Ewen is one of the Burke/Dubus cousins. One year five family members published books!

Anne, Stan, and Christopher Rice are another amazing writing family. Stan was the first—sometimes people forget that he was a poet and taught creative writing at San Francisco State University before Anne published her first book. When the family moved to New Orleans in 1989, he continued to write and publish poetry, but he also concentrated on his striking paintings, which serve as jacket illustrations for his poetry collections. Christopher Rice began to write almost immediately after high school and launched his own successful career as a writer of thrillers.

Another well-known family of writers is the Lemann family. Nicholas Lemann's sister Nancy is a well-known novelist. Novelist Sheila Bosworth is married to their father, attorney Thomas Lemann.

Rodger Kamenetz, poet, memoirist, and dream therapist, is married to novelist, short story writer, and painter Moira Crone. Their daughter Anya is also a writer of nonfiction; their daughter Kezia edited her high school literary magazine.

Other literary parent-child duos are former congresswoman and ambassador to the Vatican Lindy Boggs and her daughter, best-selling author Cokie Roberts. The late *New York Times* book critic Anatole Broyard, a New Orleans native, is the father of memoirist Bliss Broyard. Poet Peter Cooley is the father of Nicole Cooley, a poet and novelist. Kalamu ya Salaam is a poet and essayist; his daughter, Kiini Ibura Salaam, has just published her first book of short stories.

Spouses James Carville and Mary Matalin moved to New Orleans after the storm; Carville teaches at Tulane University. Another high-profile literary couple is David Simon, writer and producer of the HBO series *Treme* and a best-selling author, and his wife, best-selling crime novelist Laura Lippman; they live here when the series is filming. Errol Laborde is the editor of *New Orleans Magazine* and *Louisiana Life* and a Carnival historian; his wife, Peggy Scott Laborde, is the author of several popular histories and the producer of documentary films. Literary novelist Valerie Martin is married to literary translator John Cullen. Photographer Josephine Sacabo is the author of many literature-inspired books; her husband, Dalt Wonk, is a journalist and fabulist. Together they operate Luna Press. Thriller writer Bill Loehfelm, who won the Amazon 2008 Breakthrough Award for his novel *Fresh Kills*, is married to writer AC Lambeth. Poet Gina Ferrara is married to poet/novelist Jonathan Kline, and novelist Sarah Inman to NOLA-Fugeewriter Joe Longo.

Other literary spouses include poet Andy Young and Khaled Hegazzi, who run the literary journal *Meena*, and Nancy Dixon and poet-publisher Bill Lavender. And Joseph and Amanda Boyden, who met in the UNO creative writing program, have gone on to great acclaim; Joseph won Canada's prestigious Giller Prize for *Through Black Spruce,* and Amanda is the author of *Babylon Rolling.* Novelist Joyce Corrington is the widow of noted novelist, short story writer, and screenwriter John William Corrington.

The Sancton family brought a commitment to writing fiction and memoirs. The late Tom Sancton was a legendary reporter of the civil rights era; his late wife, Seta, was Eudora Welty's best friend and an author as well. Son Tom Sancton is the author of a New Orleans classic, *Song for My Fathers: A New Orleans Story in Black and White,* as well as a fine musician.

All of which may seem like an incredible version of "Who's your mama?" New Orleans style, but it's pretty remarkable to add it all up.

In a *New York Times* piece published in 2005, Richard Ford wrote: "I write in the place of others, today, for the ones who can't be found. And there is a blunt ending now, one we always feared, never wished for, and do not deserve. Don't get me wrong. We would all turn the days back if we could, have those old problems, those old eccentricities again. But today is a beginning. There's no better way to think of it now. Those others surely will be writing soon."

And so they are. And will be.

A Literary Address Book

One of New Orleans's great charms is the diversity of its neighborhoods, from the classic elegance of the Garden District to the funky ambiance of the Bywater and Marigny, from the street life of the Tremé to the European atmosphere of the French Quarter. Places and architectural styles may vary, but one thing is true: writers live in every part of this city, from the Ninth Ward to Uptown, from Lakeview to Algiers.

The places in this chapter are located all around town. Many of the great literary places are still in the Quarter, but be sure to venture out of those blocks to see more of the city, its bookstores and libraries. The people included in the list that follows are primarily historic figures. The only addresses given are historic ones (as we all know, writers need privacy to work).

ALGIERS

William S. Burroughs House
509 Wagner St.

It seems inevitable that one of the great literary outlaws of the twentieth century would eventually make his way to New Orleans, and Burroughs (1914–97)—best known for *Naked Lunch* and *Junkie* and his script for the movie *Blade Runner*—lived at 509 Wagner Street in Algiers during 1948 and 1949. Jack Kerouac and Neal Cassady visited Burroughs and his wife, Joan, here, a trip that Kerouac immortalized in *On the Road*. Burroughs came to New Orleans after being arrested in Texas for public indecency and drunk driving, but New Orleans was full of temptation. He cruised Lee Circle and Exchange Alley, notorious drug hangouts at the time, and eventually he was arrested for drug possession; he fled to Mexico rather than stand trial in New Orleans and face a two-year stint in Angola.

Burroughs House marker
Photo by Dennis Persica

BAYOU ST. JOHN

Bayou St. John

The neighborhood takes the name from the bayou itself, but don't miss the chance to walk around the bayou and see the kayakers and houses around this lovely body of water, which some regard as the heart of the city. This neighborhood is the setting for Constance Adler's terrific memoir, *My Bayou: New Orleans through the Eyes of a Lover,* and much of Ian McNulty's memoir, *Season of Night,* also takes place here; it is also the neighborhood that is the setting for Barb Johnson's *More of This World or Maybe Another.* The neighborhood is a subdistrict of the Mid-City District Area; its boundaries as defined by the City Planning Commission are Esplanade Avenue to the north, North Broad Street to the east, St. Louis Street to the south, and Bayou St. John to the west.

Degas House
2306 Esplanade Ave.
(504) 821-5009
degashouse.com

This house was built for Michel Musson, a cotton dealer who was the uncle of French artist Edgar Degas. Degas came for a New Orleans visit from All Saints' Day 1872 through Mardi Gras 1873. He painted his famous *The Cotton Market, New Orleans* during that time. Christopher Benfey's *Degas in New Orleans* is a great look at the city during that time.

CARROLLTON

Maple Leaf Bar
8316 Oak St.
mapleleafbar.com

Home of the longest-running poetry reading series in the South, founded by Everette Maddox and now continued by Nancy Harris, the Maple Leaf Bar holds readings every Sunday at 3 p.m. In the old days there were washing machines in the back, and you could multitask.

The Maple Leaf is portrayed in many books and stories by New Orleans writers. It is thinly disguised as "The Raintree Street Bar" in the Ellen Gilchrist short story "The Raintree Street Bar and Washerteria." There are poems about it in books and chapbooks such as *Mirror Wars* and *Shards*, by Nancy Harris; *Body and Soul* and *Rhythm & Booze*, by Julie Kane; and *The Everette Maddox Song Book, Bar Scotch*, and *American Waste* by Everette Maddox. There have also been three anthologies of poets who have read their work at the Maple Leaf: *The Maple Leaf Rag, The Maple Leaf Rag 15th Anniversary Anthology,* and the *Maple Leaf Rag III.*

Everette Maddox (1945–89) called the Maple Leaf Bar "the only place where you can hear poetry, wash your clothes, and get drunk at the same time." A native of Montgomery, Alabama, Maddox came to New Orleans in 1975. He taught at Xavier University and the University of New Orleans and founded the still ongoing Sunday reading series at the Maple Leaf Bar. He was coeditor of *The Maple Leaf Rag: An Anthology of New Orleans Poetry.* He published three collections of his poems—*The Everette Maddox Songbook, Bar Scotch,*

The Maple Leaf Bar
From John Travis, ed., The Maple Leaf Rag: 15th Anniversary Anthology *(New Orleans: Portals Press, 1994), drawing by Jennie Kasten*

and *American Waste*; a posthumous collection, *I Hope It's Not Over, and Good-By,* was edited by Ralph Adamo and published in 2009.

CENTRAL BUSINESS DISTRICT

The Double Dealer
201 Common St.
203 Baronne St.

This magazine of the 1920s had offices at 201 Common Street and 203 Baronne Street in the Central Business District. All the noted writers of the era hung out here.

Joel Chandler Harris Home
Rampart and Canal Sts.

The creator of Uncle Remus, Joel Chandler Harris (1848–1908) first came to New Orleans in October 1866, when, a mere teenager, he took a job as the private secretary to William Evelyn, the editor of the magazine *Crescent Monthly*. He lived at the corner of Rampart and Canal Streets, "in a small room at the top of a French board-inghouse under the shadow of a great cathedral."

Evelyn did not support Harris's literary ambitions, so the young man returned home to Georgia. After achieving great success with his stories, he returned to New Orleans in May 1882 to discuss a proposed lecture tour with Mark Twain. While they were here, Harris and Twain visited George Washington Cable. Twain and Cable later toured together, as Harris was too shy for such an undertaking.

Lafcadio Hearn Homes
228 Baronne St.
39 Constance St.
278 Canal St.
68 Cleveland St.
516 Bourbon St. (French Quarter)

Hearn (1850–1904) originally came here as the *Cincinnati Commercial*'s political correspondent. When he arrived in 1878, the cheapest lodging he could find was in a rooming house at 228 Baronne Street. He later lived with a Creole family at 39 Constance Street, then at 278 Canal Street, then in a boardinghouse at 68 Gasquet (now Cleveland) Street, and still later at 516 Bourbon Street, opposite the old French Opera House.

Hearn lived in New Orleans for ten years. He was the assistant editor of the *Item* as well as its first book critic and later became the *Times-Democrat*'s first literary editor and translator. His published works include the charming *"Gombo zhèbes": A Little Dictionary of Creole Proverbs;* a cookbook, *La Cuisine Creole;* and *Chita: A Memory of Last Island,* a novel based on a real event, a hurricane that struck Louisiana's Ile Dernière in 1856, taking the lives of hundreds of vacationers and residents. Hearn later emigrated to Japan and became famous for his writings about that country.

CENTRAL CITY

Buddy Bolden House
2309 Freret St.

The famous jazz musician moved to 2309 Freret Street in Central City when he was ten years old; he lived here until 1904. Built in

1871, it's typical of a shotgun double. Read Michael Ondaatje's *Coming through Slaughter* for an atmospheric look at Bolden's life.

COLISEUM SQUARE

Grace King Home
1749 Coliseum St.

Grace King (1852–1932) was the quintessential southern woman of letters of her time. Her writing career began as the result of a challenge. When King voiced her disapproval of George Washington Cable's writing about the Creoles, Richard Watson Gilder, the editor of *Century Magazine,* who was visiting New Orleans, asked her, "Why, if Cable is so false to you, do not some of you write better?" The very next day King began writing her first short story, "Monsieur Motte." Her literary work would expand to include some thirteen volumes of fiction and history.

As a friend and protégée of the great Louisiana historian Charles Gayarré, to whom she dedicated her 1895 work, *New Orleans: The Place and the People,* King remained a conservative in her writing, much of which concerns New Orleans during the difficult period of Reconstruction, a time in which her own family suffered considerable losses. Although she ultimately revised her opinion of Cable's work, she remained a champion of the white southern cause all her life.

King's home at 1749 Coliseum Street, on Coliseum Square, where she lived with her brother and two sisters, was the site of a famous literary salon. There King played hostess to visiting writers such as Julia Ward Howe, Joaquin Miller, Mark Twain, and Charles Dudley Warner.

THE FRENCH QUARTER

Antoine's
713 Louis St.
(504) 581-4422
antoines.com

Open since 1840, this historic restaurant is the setting for Frances Parkinson Keyes's *Dinner at Antoine's.* If you stop in for a meal or a drink at the Hermes Bar, try to sneak a peek at the fabled Rex Room, a shrine to the glories of Carnival.

John James Audubon Homes
706 Barracks St.
505 Dauphine St.

"At New Orleans at last!" That was how the naturalist and painter John James Audubon (1785–1851) announced his arrival January 7, 1821, in his journal. He lived first in a ten-dollar-a-month room at 706 Barracks, which was between two grocery stores. In June 1821 he left for Oakley Plantation near St. Francisville, where he had been engaged to tutor Eliza Pirrie, the fifteen-year-old daughter of the house. That short-lived arrangement lasted until October 1821, when he returned to New Orleans and rented a house at 505 Dauphine Street. In spring of 1822 he departed for Natchez. He passed through New Orleans two more times—in 1830 and 1837. His time at Oakley has inspired at least two books, and there are many biographies of the artist.

Hamilton Basso Home
1200 block of Decatur St.

Basso (1904–64), a New Orleans native, grew up over a shoe factory in the 1200 block of Decatur Street. His family moved from the Quarter across Canal Street to the city's American Sector when he was nine. He became a newspaper reporter in New York and New Orleans and married a New Orleans girl, Etolia Moore Simmons, who edited the wonderful anthology *The World from Jackson Square.* They lived in North Carolina and New York, where Basso wrote for many leading journals. He is the author of *Beauregard: The Great Creole* and three novels with a New Orleans setting: *Relics and Angels, Cinnamon Seed,* and *Days before Lent.* His 1954 novel, *The View from Pompey's Head,* was his first best seller.

Beauregard-Keyes House
1113 Chartres St.
(504) 523-7257
bkhouse.org

This important French Quarter landmark is open to the public for tours, by admission. The home was built in 1826 for the grandmother of Paul Morphy, the famous chess champion, and was the residence of Confederate general P.G.T. Beauregard from 1866 through 1868. Mrs. Keyes, the legendary hostess and novelist best known for *Dinner at Antoine's,* published in 1948, restored the house between 1944 and 1950. It is now available for rent as a party venue.

Roark Bradford Home
719 Toulouse St.

Bradford (1896–1948) lived in the Pontalba building while working as an editor at the *New Orleans Times-Picayune.* Later he and his wife, Mary Rose, had a literary salon at their French Quarter home at 719 Toulouse Street, where they frequently entertained such guests as William Faulkner, Sinclair Lewis, and John Steinbeck. Bradford is the author of *How Come Christmas;* his *Ol' Man Adam and His Chillun* was later adapted as Marc Connelly's 1930 Pulitzer Prize–winning play *Green Pastures.* His son, Richard, lived here until the late 1960s; he is the author of several novels, the best known of which is *Red Sky at Morning.*

John Dos Passos Home
510 Esplanade Ave.

John Dos Passos (1896–1970) lived at 510 Esplanade Avenue in February and March 1924, while he was finishing *Manhattan Transfer.* His novel *Number One,* published in 1943, was an indictment of demagoguery, based on his fascination with Huey Long. Later novelist Wilton Barnhardt lived in this building while finishing *Gospel.*

Faulkner House
624 Pirate's Alley
(504) 524-2940
faulknerhousebooks.net

The home and bookshop of Rosemary James and Joseph DeSalvo Jr., this French Quarter mecca is a designated National Literary Landmark by Friends of American Libraries. The lovely bookshop features fine rare and new volumes, and the owners have entertained such star boarders as Jim Bennett, Roy Blount Jr., Robert Olen Butler, Elizabeth Dewberry, Tom Franklin, William Gay, Barry Gifford, Barry Hannah, Bret Lott, Willie Morris, Elizabeth Spencer, William Styron, A. J. Verdelle, and Joan Williams as well as actors

Entrance to the Faulkner House
Photo by Dennis Persica

Patricia Arquette, Delta Burke, Nicolas Cage, Jeremy Irons, John
Malkovich, Sharon Stone, and Cicely Tyson.

A FAULKNER HOUSE TIMELINE:

1924—Faulkner came to New Orleans, attracted by the literary fer-
ment around the *Double Dealer* magazine, which had published his work in 1922. His friends Sherwood Anderson
and his wife, Elizabeth, were living in the nearby Pontalba
building at the time.

1925—Faulkner moved into Pirate's Alley with artist and writer
William Spratling.

1926—*Soldier's Pay,* a novel he had worked on in New Orleans,
was published.

1927—*Mosquitoes* was published; this novel was inspired by the New
Orleans arts colony and a day Faulkner spent on Lake Pontchartrain in the company of Anderson and Lillian Friend,
one of the *Double Dealer*'s founders, as well as others.

1935—*Pylon* was published; this novel was partly inspired by the
opening of Shushan Lakefront Airport and the death of a
young aviator at that event.

1949—Faulkner won the Nobel Prize for Literature.

1958—Faulkner's collection of writing about New Orleans, *New Orleans Sketches*, was published.

1990—Faulkner House Books opened on the writer's birthday, September 25.

Galatoire's Restaurant
209 Bourbon St.
(504) 525-2021
galatoires.com

Friday lunch at Galatoire's, a famed New Orleans tradition that's been known to extend into the dinner hour, is sure to feature a writer or two. And Galatoire's has been known to furnish the backdrop for many a fiction writer, in addition to being the subject of *Galatoire's: Biography of a Bistro*, by Marda Burton and Kenneth Holditch.

Charles Gayarré Home
601 Bourbon St.

Gayarré (1805–95), the foremost Creole intellectual of his era, lived in the cottage at 601 Bourbon Street (now a bar) in the late nineteenth century but moved to a plantation in Mississippi after the loss of his family fortune during Reconstruction. He was Grace King's mentor as a historian and a bitter enemy of George Washington Cable. His four-volume history of Louisiana is still a major source of information. He was the third president of the Louisiana Historical Society, and his lectures and papers spanning twenty-eight years are collected in two of these volumes.

Gold Mine Saloon
701 Dauphine St.
(504) 586-0745
goldminesaloon.net

Owned by poets Dave Brinks and Megan Burns, this is the spot to go for poetry every Thursday night for the 17 Poets! Literary and Performance series.

Hermann-Grima House
820 St. Louis St.
hgghh.org

This house/museum may have inspired Lermontant's home in Anne Rice's *Feast of All Saints.*

Ignatius J. Reilly Statue
French Quarter Hyatt
819 Canal St.

Bronze statue of Ignatius Reilly at the former location of D. H. Holmes on Canal Street
Photo by Dennis Persica

A Confederacy of Dunces's Ignatius Reilly, one of New Orleans's most famous literary characters, comes to life in bronze, right where the D. H. Holmes clock used to be. It was installed in 2002 and is removed temporarily every year for Mardi Gras.

Oliver La Farge Home
714 St. Peter St.

La Farge (1901–63) came to New Orleans in early 1925 as an assistant in ethnology at what is now Tulane's Middle American Research Institute, an appointment that lasted until July 1927. His French Quarter apartment at 714 St. Peter Street was known as the Wigwam and was a gathering place of artists, writers, and scientists. He was invited by the renowned archaeologist Frans Blom to be assistant director of the first Tulane expedition to Central America. La Farge's first novel, *Laughing Boy,* was published in 1929 and received the Pulitzer Prize in 1930.

LeMonnier House
640 Royal St.

Famous as the setting for George Washington Cable's 1873 story "'Sieur George," this house is attributed to the architect Barthélémy Lafon and is often called "The Skyscraper."

Madame John's Legacy
632 Dumaine St.

This building, French colonial in style though constructed under the Spanish regime, is one of the oldest in New Orleans, built in 1788 after a great fire that destroyed most of the city. It was the setting for George Washington Cable's story "'Tite Poulette," about a quadroon woman who received the house as a legacy of her white lover. If the West Indies–style gallery looks familiar, it's probably because you saw it in the film version of Anne Rice's *Interview with the Vampire.*

William March Home
613 Dumaine St.

"William March" was the pen name of novelist and short story writer William Edward March Campbell (1893–1954), who lived in the

Quarter at 613 Dumaine Street from 1950 to 1954. March came here after suffering a nervous breakdown in New York and established a salon in the Quarter, where he achieved enough stability to complete the long promised novel *The Bad Seed*, about a murderous child, during the last year of his life.

Hotel Monteleone
214 Royal St.

This comfortable hotel is now the home of the Tennessee Williams / New Orleans Literary Festival. Its long history as a literary landmark goes back much earlier, for the hotel has hosted such literary patrons as William Faulkner, Richard Ford, Winston Groom, Ernest Hemingway, Eudora Welty, and Tennessee Williams (and his grandfather!). Don't forget to stop by the remodeled Carousel Bar, which, yes, really does revolve.

Truman Capote (1924–84) liked to say he was born at the hotel, but he was born Truman Streckfus Persons on September 30, 1924, at Touro Infirmary; his parents, Arch and Lillie Mae Persons, were visiting New Orleans and staying at the Monteleone at the time. He later lived in the Quarter at 711 Royal Street in 1945 while he was writing *Other Voices, Other Rooms* and liked to hang out with

Hotel Monteleone plaque
Photo by Dennis Persica

the female impersonators at Gunga Den, a nearby bar. In George Plimpton's oral biography of Capote, socialite Slim Keith described Capote's famous Black and White Ball, given November 28, 1966, at the Plaza Hotel in New York: "I think it was something a little boy from New Orleans had always dreamed of doing. He wanted to give the biggest and best goddamned party that anybody had ever heard of."

Napoleon House (Girod House)
540 Chartres St.

A popular watering hole—don't pass up a Pimm's Cup!—the Napoleon House was built in 1814 for Nicholas Girod, mayor of New Orleans from 1812 to 1815. Girod planned to offer the house as a refuge to the defeated Napoléon Bonaparte, hence the name and decor.

Old Ursuline Convent
1100 Chartres St.
(504) 529-3040
stlouiscathedral.org/convent.html

This convent is the oldest building in New Orleans and the only one to have survived from the period of French domination. It was built in 1745.

Le Petit Salon
620 St. Peter St.

Originally known as the Victor David House, named for the hardware merchant for whom it was built in 1838, this building next to Le Petit Théâtre du Vieux Carré was purchased in 1925 by Le Petit Salon, a ladies' literary group founded by Grace King. The group restored the house, and members still meet there. (Note the three different styles of ironwork on the three balconies.)

The Pontalba Buildings
Jackson Square

These gorgeous buildings overlook the Stanley and Stella Shouting Contest every spring during the Tennessee Williams / New Orleans

Literary Festival. Read Christina Vella's *Intimate Enemies: The Two Worlds of the Baroness de Pontalba* to learn the fascinating story of their creator.

Among the famous residents of the Pontalba are Sherwood Anderson (1876–1941) and his third wife, Elizabeth Prall Anderson, who lived in an apartment in the Pontalba at 540-B St. Peter Street in 1924. It was designated a Literary Landmark by the Friends of the Library USA in 1997.

Anderson was already well known by the time he arrived here; *Winesburg, Ohio* had been published. He worked on *Dark Laugher* in New Orleans and was inspired to write one of his best-known short stories, "A Meeting South," while living here. In that story Anderson describes taking William Faulkner to meet a former madam, Aunt Rose Arnold, who lived at 625 Chartres Street.

The Andersons entertained many famous guests, some welcome, some not—including Faulkner, Ring Lardner, Carl Sandburg, Edmund Wilson, and publisher Horace Liveright. He influenced the writing of Faulkner, Hemingway, and Gertrude Stein and was helpful to younger writers. When Anderson's wife, Elizabeth, asked him to help Faulkner get *Soldier's Pay* published, he agreed—on the condition that he didn't have to read it. Anderson fell out with Faulkner after the 1926 publication of *Sherwood Anderson and Other Famous Creoles*, in which Faulkner mercilessly parodied his mentor.

Another well-known Pontalba resident was Katherine Anne Porter (1890–1980). Porter was thirteen when her family moved to New Orleans, and she remembers her education in the Ursuline Convent. She liked to say that she ran away from New Orleans and got married at sixteen, but that may have been adapted from her aunt's history.

Porter came to live at 543 St. Ann in the Pontalba in September 1937, after falling in love with Albert Erskine, at the time the business manager of the *Southern Review*. Many of Porter's early short stories—"Old Mortality" and "Pale Horse, Pale Rider" among them—were published in the *Southern Review*. She and Erskine married in 1938, with Robert Penn Warren and his wife as witnesses.

A Lake Charles native, writer and photographer Clarence John Laughlin (1905–85) is another Pontalba character. He is probably best known for *Ghosts along the Mississippi*, which depicts the decaying remains of plantation culture. He lived in the Pontalba, and his work was revived and celebrated in *Haunter of Ruins: The Photography of Clarence John Laughlin.*

Alan Rinehart Home
1022 Dumaine St.

The noted book publisher once lived at 1022 Dumaine Street in the Quarter. His mother was the mystery writer Mary Roberts Rinehart.

Adrien and Dominique Rouquette Home
413 Royal St.

The Rouquette brothers lived at 413 Royal Street in the Quarter. Adrien (1813–87) was a poet and nature lover who became a missionary to the Louisiana Choctaws; he is best known for *La Nouvelle Atala.* Dominique (1810–90) was also a poet. Look for the *R* in the ironwork on the balcony of the building.

St. Louis Cathedral
Jackson Square
Mailing address:
Cathedral-Basilica of Saint Louis King of France
615 Pere Antoine Alley
New Orleans, LA 70116-3291
(504) 525-9585
stlouiscathedral.org

This beautiful church is truly the great heart of the city. Stop in, light a candle, say a prayer.

Lyle Saxon (1891–1946) Homes
612 Royal St.
536 Royal St.
627 St. Peter St.
620 St. Peter St.
534 Madison St.

Lyle Saxon was one of the most beloved of all French Quarter residents of his time. He was also one of the most important of all Louisiana writers, responsible for the production of the enduring WPA guides to New Orleans and to Louisiana. He would also be a guest at my ideal dinner party!

Saxon came to New Orleans to write for various newspapers, spent a year in Chicago as a reporter, then returned to New Orleans in 1918 and eventually began writing for the *Times-Picayune.* He was a pioneer in his love for the Quarter. When he first moved there, his friends were horrified; it was a dangerous, rundown neighborhood. But he persevered, and others soon followed his lead. His first home in the Quarter was at 612 Royal Street; he rented sixteen rooms for the sum of sixteen dollars a month. He loved the old streets and wrote about them beautifully.

He covered the fire that destroyed the French Opera House on December 4, 1919, and described sitting on a curb, watching the destruction with artist friend Alberta Kinsey. "The heart of the old French Quarter has stopped beating," he wrote in the *Times-Picayune* in a story that is included in his book *Fabulous New Orleans.*

Other French Quarter addresses associated with Saxon include 536 Royal Street, a building he acquired in 1920 and lived in intermittently. He sold it in 1925 before moving to New York. He lived in an apartment at 627 St. Peter in early 1925 and moved into a third-floor apartment at 620 St. Peter in 1926. At that time Roark Bradford and Oliver La Farge were also living on St. Peter Street.

Perhaps Saxon's most famous French Quarter address was his final one. In 1937 he bought the house at 534 Madison Street, still one of the loveliest French Quarter streets. The courtyard was a frequent setting for drinks prepared by Saxon's legendary manservant, Joe Gilmore, celebrated as one of the best bartenders in town. Saxon began work on *The Friends of Joe Gilmore,* a loosely structured, hilarious autobiography that was also a tribute to his great friend, but he died before completing it. Edward Dreyer, Saxon's longtime friend and collaborator on *Gumbo Ya-Ya,* the collection of Louisiana folklore published in 1945, finished the work by adding a section entitled "And Some Friends of Lyle Saxon."

Gwyn Conger and John Steinbeck were married in this house in March 1943. Saxon sold it the next year, repairing to his beloved St. Charles Hotel.

Jon Edgar Webb and Louise Webb Homes
638 Royal St.

618 Ursulines St.
1109 Royal St.

The Webbs, two of the most colorful characters to grace the New Orleans literary scene, first came here from the Midwest in the 1930s, migrated elsewhere, then settled here again from 1954 to 1967. In the 1960s the Webbs operated the Loujon Press at 638 Royal Street and 618 Ursulines Street in the French Quarter, publishing four beautiful books and one of the period's leading avant-garde magazines, the *Outsider*. They also lived at 1109 Royal Street. Louise, or Gypsy Lou, sold her paintings at the corner of St. Peter and Royal by day and helped Jon with the publishing venture at night.

Jon Webb (1905?–71), a former newspaperman, was the author of a novel, *Four Steps to the Wall*, based on his prison experiences. (No one ever really understood how such a hardworking man with such high literary aspirations became involved with the armed robbery of a Cleveland jewelry store. He served three years in the Mansfield Reformatory, where he edited a prison newspaper.)

The first issue of the *Outsider*, published in 1961, reads like a who's who of the Beat generation, with work by William S. Burroughs, Edward Dorn, Allen Ginsberg, LeRoi Jones, Henry Miller, Charles Olson, Gary Snyder, and Colin Wilson. The first issue also included "A Charles Bukowski Album," eleven poems, indicating how strongly Webb was committed to Bukowski's work. Loujon Press published two of his books, *It Catches My Heart in Its Hands* (1963, in two limited editions) and *Crucifix in a Deathhand* (1965, in conjunction with New York publisher Lyle Stuart). The press also published Henry Miller's *Order and Chaos Chez Hans Reichel* and *Insomnia, or The Devil at Night*.

The Webbs moved to Tucson in 1967, seeking a healthier climate. The final two issues of the *Outsider* and the Henry Miller books were published there. Jon Webb died in 1971. Gypsy Lou lives near New Orleans today. "Where did we go?" she said of her life with Webb. "What did we do? Everything!"

Barbet Schroeder's 1987 film *Barfly* was based on Bukowski's (1920–94) life. The poet visited New Orleans briefly in 1942. The city became important to him when Jon and Gypsy Lou Webb began publishing his work in their magazine. Bukowski later said that that most of the poems in *Crucifix* were written during "one very hot, lyrical month in New Orleans in 1965."

The Webbs have been the subject of renewed interest, with the documentary directed by Wayne Ewing, *The Outsiders of New Orleans: Loujon Press,* and a history by Jeff Weddle, *Bohemian New Orleans: The Outsider and Loujon Press.*

Thornton Wilder Home
623 Bourbon St.

In 1939 Wilder (1897–1975) rented a room in the house at 623 Bourbon Street, more recently the former residence of former congresswoman and U.S. ambassador to the Vatican Lindy Boggs. Boggs is also an author of a terrific memoir, *Washington through a Purple Veil.*

Tennessee Williams Homes
620 Chartres St.
722 Toulouse St.
710 Orleans St.
632 St. Peter St.
1014 Dumaine St.

No one has captured the heartbreak and romance of New Orleans better than Tennessee Williams (1911–83), who often fled to the city to heal his personal wounds. A number of French Quarter addresses are linked with America's most famous playwright. In the 1930s Williams lived at 620 Chartres and would often go down the street to Victor's Café and listen to the jukebox and drink brandy Alexanders. (Victor's went out of business in the 1960s.)

In 1939 Williams rented rooms at 722 Toulouse Street, now a part of the Historic New Orleans Collection museum complex. In 2011 a historical marker was placed on the building in honor of the centennial of Williams's birth, observed during the twenty-fifth annual Tennessee Williams / New Orleans Literary Festival. While living here, Williams wrote the slogan for his landlady's restaurant ("Meals for a Quarter in the Quarter") and occasionally helped out as a waiter. *Vieux Carré* is set in this building.

At 710 Orleans Williams lived in a second-floor apartment with a view of St. Anthony's Garden in the back of St. Louis Cathedral. Williams wrote *Ten Blocks on the Camino Real* here in January 1946.

Most famously, 632 St. Peter Street, an 1842 townhouse that was once the home and studio of artist Achille Peretti, is where

Williams lived from October 1946 through March 1947, while writing *A Streetcar Named Desire*.

The playwright's final Quarter address was the house at 1014 Dumaine. In a 1970 interview with New Orleans writer Don Lee Keith, Williams said: "In New Orleans, I found the kind of freedom I had always needed. And the shock of it against the Puritanism of my nature has given me a subject, a theme, which I've probably never ceased exploiting."

Touring the French Quarter in 1971, Williams recalled his time here for a piece by Rex Reed in *Esquire* magazine: "This place has so many memories. I came here in 1939 to write. I was heartbroken over my sister Rose's confinement in a psychiatric hospital and I suffered a breakdown myself. In New Orleans I felt a freedom. I could catch my breath here. See that bar over there? That used to be called Victor's. I lived just around the corner in a large room on top of an old house where I worked under a skylight at a large refectory table writing *A Streetcar Named Desire*. At that time, I was under the impression that I was dying. I didn't feel much like eating, but in the evening after working all day my only close friend would bring me a bowl of oyster stew and in the afternoons I would go around the corner to Victor's Café and have myself two Brandy Alexanders. Without that sense of fatigue and that idea of imminently approaching death I doubt I could have created Blanche DuBois."

GARDEN DISTRICT

George Washington Cable Homes
632 Dumaine St. (French Quarter)
1313 Eighth St.

Cable was born here in 1844 in an old frame house on Annunciation Square, the fifth child of George Washington Cable and Rebecca Boardman. He attended the Boys High School on Laurel Street near First Street, but when his father died, George, then in his early teens, took over his father's job in the customhouse to help out the family.

After New Orleans fell to Union forces, during the Civil War, the family moved to Mississippi rather than declare loyalty to the

United States, and Cable enlisted in the Confederate cavalry. After the war ended, he returned to New Orleans and married Louise Bartlett in 1869. They lived at 632 Dumaine Street, then settled in a lovely Garden District home, 1313 Eighth Street.

Cable began his literary career at the *Picayune* in 1869, and he began writing for *Scribner's Magazine* in 1873, where his story, "'Sieur George" was published. Today Cable is primarily remembered for his books *Old Creole Days* and *The Grandissimes,* both of which were received by "old" New Orleans society as critical statements on the racial status quo as well as their mores and speech. Cable was great friends with Lafcadio Hearn, and thanks to his national reputation, many of the great writers of the time—Joel Chandler Harris, William Dean Howells, Harriet Beecher Stowe, Mark Twain, Charles Dudley Warner, and Oscar Wilde—were guests at his home on Eighth Street.

His provocative stand on racial issues and his continued advocacy of the freedman led to increasing social ostracism. Illustrator Joseph Pennell once said that Cable was "the most cordially hated little man in New Orleans, and all on account of *The Grandissimes.*" Eventually the family moved to Northampton, Massachusetts. In his lifetime Cable was compared to Nathaniel Hawthorne and Victor Hugo; today his books are not widely read. He died in 1925.

Kate Chopin Homes
443 Magazine St.
1413 Louisiana St.

Chopin (1851–1904) lived here from 1870 to 1879. Her husband, Oscar, was a cotton factor with offices on Union Street; their first child, Jean Baptiste, was born here in 1871. Early residences included a first home at 443 Magazine Street; it was a double cottage shared with the family who lived next door at 445, just like the Pontelliers' residence in *The Awakening.* By 1874 the family had moved Uptown to a house at the corner of Constantinople and Pitt that no longer exists. They moved to 1413 Louisiana Street, originally 229 Louisiana, in the Garden District, in 1876, where they lived until 1879.

Chopin lived in Louisiana—in New Orleans and then in Cloutierville and Natchitoches—for only fourteen years, from 1870 to

1884, but that time marked her work forever. Two of her three novels and more than half of her works of short fiction are set in Louisiana.

The Awakening is the best known of her books. It depicts the life of Edna Pontellier, a married society woman who longs for more out of life. "I don't mind walking," Edna says. "I always feel so sorry for women who don't like to walk; they miss so much—so many rare little glimpses of life; and we women learn so little of life on the whole." Chopin walked about the city a good bit, listening and observing, picking up the material that would inform her later work. Much of her life here was consumed by the demands of her large family; summers were spent on Grand Isle, that coastal resort where Edna takes her fatal swim in *The Awakening*.

Columns Hotel
3811 St. Charles Ave.
(504) 899-9308
thecolumns.com

This inviting hotel on the St. Charles streetcar line was the setting for the movie *Pretty Baby*. Settle in for a drink on the wide veranda or in the side garden, and you might just spot a writer or two. Built in 1883, the building was designed by architect Thomas Sully.

Stan Rice, Anne Rice, and Christopher Rice Homes
1237 First St.
1020 Philip St. (Irish Channel)
2524 St. Charles Ave.

The lovely lilac-colored Garden District mansion at 1237 First Street was famously home to New Orleans's best-known literary family— Anne and Stan Rice and their son, Christopher. Anne Rice (1941– present), born Howard Allen O'Brien, is a New Orleans native who has immortalized her hometown in *The Vampire Chronicles*, beginning in 1976 with the phenomenally successful *Interview with the Vampire*. Rice, known for her passionate novels of the supernatural, says that the house at First and Chestnut, called Rosegate, chose her. Haunted by the house itself, she used it as the setting of her best-selling saga *The Witching Hour*, about a family of Garden District witches and the male spirit, Lasher, who torments and tempts them across generations. The Rices moved to the house in 1989; *The Witching Hour* was published the following year.

Stan Rice (1942–2002), who was head of the creative writing department at San Francisco State University before he and Anne returned to New Orleans in 1988, was a poet who died of cancer at the age of sixty. He published eight volumes of poetry. He was also a painter whose brilliant colors and primitive vision won him a following in the art world. A book collecting his work, *Paintings*, was published in 1997.

Christopher Rice (1978–present) attended Brown University and the Tisch School of the Arts but left both to pursue his writing. He moved to Los Angeles, where he lives today. Rice published his first novel, *A Density of Souls*, loosely based on his experiences at the Isidore Newman School, in 2000, when he was twenty-two.

The First Street house was built in 1857 by Charles Pride, designed by James Calrow for Albert Hamilton Brevard, in a mixture of Greek Revival and Italianate styles. From 1947 to 1972 it was the home of the renowned federal judge John Minor Wisdom.

Another New Orleans residence associated with Anne Rice is 2524 St. Charles Avenue, in the Garden District, where she lived when she was fourteen. The setting for her highly autobiographical novel *Violin*, it was owned by the Catholic Church and had been a school, a convent, and a rectory before she purchased and restored it in 1995.

When the Rices first moved back to New Orleans in 1988, they lived at 1020 Philip Street in the Irish Channel. Rice has said that she wanted to be near the place where she grew up, and this house is at the very heart of the landscape of her childhood. It is near Redemptorist School, and from her bedroom window she could see the steeples of the churches of St. Alphonsus and St. Mary's Assumption, important landmarks in her early life.

The other Uptown property associated with the Rice family is St. Elizabeth's Children's Home, 1314 Napoleon Avenue. This complex was built in the 1830s as an orphanage operated by the Daughters of Charity. The central part of the building was constructed as a school for girls in the 1860s and became an orphanage again in 1870. The brick wings were added in the 1880s. Stan Rice had his gallery on the Prytania Street side of the building.

After Stan's death, Anne moved to a gated community in the

suburb of Kenner, then to California to be near her son. She now lives in California, but there are rumors of a return to New Orleans. Her writing career has been rich and varied, including a spiritual memoir, *Called Out of Darkness*, a remarkable memoir of growing up Catholic in New Orleans; a series of novels depicting the life of Christ; and recently *The Wolf Gift*, in which she seems to be returning to her earlier fictional concerns.

Edward Larocque Tinker Home
1407 First St.

Tinker (1881–1968), a New York lawyer, came to New Orleans to marry native Frances McKee Dodge. The couple lived in the Garden District at 1407 First Street. Tinker developed a deep interest in Louisiana and became an authority on its history. He wrote many books, including *Creole City, Gombo: The Creole Dialect of Louisiana,* and *Old New Orleans.*

Walt Whitman Home
Washington Ave.

Whitman (1819–92) came to New Orleans in 1848; he and his brother lived at the Fremont Hotel, across from the St. Charles Hotel. He wrote editorials for the *New Orleans Crescent* for a few months, then wrote occasional pieces for the *Picayune.* For a while he lived on Washington Avenue in the Garden District, near the river, but the building no longer exists. "I Saw in Louisiana a Live Oak Growing," from *Leaves of Grass,* is one of the most famous poems associated with the state.

LOWER GARDEN DISTRICT

Henry Morton Stanley Home
1729 Coliseum Square

New Orleans was the boyhood home of adventurer Henry Morton Stanley (1841–1904), as in "Dr. Livingstone, I presume." He was adopted by cotton merchant Henry Hope Stanley and his wife, who befriended him after young Henry, a runaway Welsh cabin boy, jumped ship. His house was originally located at 906 Orange Street but has been moved to 1729 Coliseum Square.

GENTILLY

John Chase Home
4635 Music St.

An editorial cartoonist for the *New Orleans States,* Chase (1905–86) wrote the definitive, charming history of New Orleans street names, *Frenchmen Desire Good Children,* and was a coauthor of, with four other writers, *New Orleans Yesterday and Today.* He lived at 4635 Music Street in Gentilly.

NINTH WARD

House of Dance and Feathers
1317 Tupelo St.
Open by appointment
(504) 957-2678
houseofdanceandfeathers.com

If you have a car, by all means travel to the Lower Ninth Ward to see this backyard museum of African American life, with its collection of Mardi Gras Indian memorabilia and histories of the city's many social and pleasure clubs, which sponsor second-line parades. The life and work of Ronald Lewis is chronicled in the museum catalog, *House of Dance and Feathers,* published by the Neighborhood Story Project, and in Dan Baum's *Nine Lives: Life and Death in New Orleans.* Call before you go and donate as generously as you can.

St. Claude Avenue Arts District
New Orleans Healing Center
2372 St. Claude Ave.
(504) 940-1130
neworleanshealingcenter.org

This is an anchor of the St. Claude Arts corridor. This attractive building features a branch of the Maple Street Book Shop, managed by writer Ken Foster; the Isle of Salvation Botanica, run by voodoo priestess and author Sallie Ann Glassman; Café Istanbul, run by performance poet Chuck Perkins; as well as a host of other businesses. Well worth a visit.

UPTOWN

Stanley Clisby Arthur Home
1309 State St.

Arthur (1880–1963), a director of the Louisiana State Museum, lived at 1309 State Street, Uptown. He is probably best known for *Old New Orleans* and *Famous New Orleans Drinks and How to Mix 'Em*, still in print.

Dorothy Dix [Elizabeth Meriwether Gilmer] Homes
1617 Jackson Ave.
1225 General Pershing St.
6334 Prytania St.

Newspaper columnist Dorothy Dix (1861–1951)—at one time a household name in America, was born Elizabeth Meriwether. She came to New Orleans in 1878 to work for the *Picayune* for the salary of five dollars a week, thanks to her friendship with the paper's publisher, Eliza Nicholson. For a time she lived at 1617 Jackson Avenue. She took the name Dorothy Dix, perhaps patterning herself after Nicholson, who wrote poetry as "Pearl Rivers." Gilmer wrote theater reviews, edited the women's page, and began a syndicated advice column, then covered murder trials for the *New York Journal* for sixteen years. She returned to New Orleans in 1917 and lived in a house at 1225 General Pershing Street. During her later years she served as president of Le Petit Salon and as a member of the board of directors of the *Times-Picayune*.

During the latter part of her life she lived in the top floor of a gracious duplex facing Audubon Park at 6334 Prytania Street. In 1936 *Time* marked the fortieth anniversary of her newspaper column, which was published until 1949. Harnett Kane wrote an endearing, affectionate biography of her called *Dear Dorothy Dix*.

F. Scott Fitzgerald Home
2900 Prytania St.

In 1930 Fitzgerald (1896–1940) briefly rented rooms—found with the help of Sherwood Anderson—at 2900 Prytania Street. He seems not to have liked New Orleans much, but he did develop a liking for Sazeracs, the famous cocktails made at the Roosevelt Hotel's

Sazerac Bar (still the place to sample one today); one biographer tells of the time the writer drove all the way to Montgomery with a pitcher of drinks to see his beloved Zelda.

Here's a Sazerac recipe from Kerri McCaffety's classic *Obituary Cocktail:*

> 1 jigger cognac (or rye whiskey)
> crushed sugar cube
> 3 dashes Peychaud's bitters
> 2 dashes Angostura bitters
>
> Chill in shaker and strain into a glass laced with Pernod or Herbsaint. Garnish with a twist of lemon peel.

Lillian Hellman Homes
1718 Prytania St.
1829 Valence St.

Max and Julia Hellman were living in a boardinghouse at 1718 Prytania Street when Lillian was born in 1905 It was run by Hannah and Jenny Hellman, Max's sisters, who are the basis for characters in Hellman's play *Toys in the Attic.* The two women later moved to 1463 Prytania Street, operating another boardinghouse there.

In 1910 Max moved the family to 1829 Valence Street, a sign of his growing prosperity in a shoe manufacturing business he had established. The business failed, and the family moved to New York the following year, although Hellman returned to Orleans, Persephone-like, for half of every year until she was sixteen. Hellman's most evocative account of her young life is found in *An Unfinished Woman;* when she wrote of her childhood, she wrote mainly about New Orleans.

Hellman last visited New Orleans in 1977, when she spoke at Tulane along with her friend Peter Feibleman. At one remarkable moment she set her tissue on fire with the ash from her cigarette and seemed not to notice. The audience was alarmed, but Feibleman sprang to attention and quickly put it out. She died in 1984.

Harnett Kane Home
5919 Freret St.

Kane (1910–84) was a newspaperman and historian whose best-known work is *Louisiana Hayride: The American Rehearsal for Dicta-*

torship, 1928–1940. He also wrote a biography of his colleague, *Dear Dorothy Dix,* as well as many other books. *Have Pen, Will Autograph* is a humorous account of an author tour, circa 1959. Indeed, he signed so many books that the joke is that the really valuable Kane book is an unsigned copy! He lived near Loyola University.

Walker Percy Homes
1450 Calhoun St.
1820 Milan St.

Bunt and Walker Percy moved to an Uptown house at 1450 Calhoun Street in September 1947, shortly after their marriage. At the time Walker Percy (1916–90) was receiving religious instruction from the Jesuits at Loyola University; his conversion informed all of his fiction. The Percys lived here until 1948.

The Calhoun Street house has its own literary history. It was owned by Julius and Elise Friend. Julius had been an editor of the *Double Dealer,* which had published the work of William Alexander Percy, Walker's uncle, perhaps best known for his reminiscences, *Lanterns on the Levee.*

From fall 1957 to fall 1959 Percy and his wife lived part-time in an Uptown cottage at 1820 Milan Street. They came here from nearby Covington to be close to their daughter's audiologist; Mary Percy Moores was receiving frequent treatment at the time, and the long drive back and forth was taking its toll on the family.

This neat, one-story, two-bedroom house is a typical Louisiana home, with a small sunroom in the back. What happened here has captured the imagination of generations of readers. It's the place where Percy conceived of and began his National Book Award–winning novel, *The Moviegoer,* published in 1961.

In a 1980 interview, "Why I Live Where I Live," for *Esquire* magazine, Percy said: "New Orleans may be too seductive for a writer. Known hereabouts as the Big Easy, it may be too easy, too pleasant. Faulkner was charmed to a standstill and didn't really get going until he returned to Mississippi and invented his country. The occupational hazard of the writer in New Orleans is a variety of the French flu, which might also be called Vieux Carré Syndrome. One is apt to turn fey, potter about a patio, and write feuilletons and vignettes or catty romans a clef, a pleasant enough life but for me too seductive.

"On the other hand, it is often a good idea to go against demographic trends, reverse the flight to the country, return to the ruined heart of the city. When the French Quarter is completely ruined by the tourists—and deserted by them—it will again be a good place to live. I'm sick of cutting grass. Covington lies at the green heart of Louisiana, a green jungle of pines, azaleas, camellias, dogwood, grapevines, and billions of blades of grass. I've begun to hear the grass growing at night. It costs $25 to get my lawnmower fixed. If my wife would allow it, I would end my days in a French cottage on Rue Dauphine with a small patio and not a single blade of grass."

Robert Tallant Home
3324 Carondelet St.

Tallant (1909–57) was a native New Orleanian who became a folklorist. He worked under Lyle Saxon for the Federal Writers' Project in the 1940s and wrote *Voodoo in New Orleans* and *Mardi Gras as It Was* and the wonderfully comic *Mrs. Candy* novels as well as the classic *Romantic New Orleanians.*

John Kennedy Toole Homes
390 Audubon St.
7632 Hampson St.

Toole (1937–69) lived in the upstairs front apartment at 390 Audubon Street, Uptown. He found this place for his family when he was sixteen years old and starting at Tulane, knowing that his parents would want to be close to the school and that they expected him to live at home. After graduating from Fortier High School, Toole wrote his first novel, *The Neon Bible,* the subject of a bitter court case after he died and finally published in 1990. He wrote *A Confederacy of Dunces* while he was stationed in Puerto Rico during a tour of duty in the army. He was twenty-six years old when he completed the book, but he failed to find a publisher during his lifetime. He committed suicide in 1969.

For many, *Confederacy* ranks as the best novel of modern New Orleans. The perambulations of Ignatius Reilly, sometime medievalist and purveyor of hot dogs, and his ensuing meditations are all written about with a broad and wicked humor. The real sounds and smells and flavors of the streets of New Orleans are in this book, along with its many dialects.

In 1967, while teaching at Dominican College, Toole moved to the cottage at 7632 Hampson Street, his final residence. After a pilgrimage to Flannery O'Connor's home in Milledgeville, Georgia, Toole took his life in Biloxi, Mississippi.

After Toole's death, his mother, Thelma Toole, determined to get her son's work published. She pursued Walker Percy's attention doggedly, until finally he agreed to read the manuscript, was impressed, and encouraged Louisiana State University Press to publish the novel. It won the Pulitzer Prize in 1981, more than a decade after his death. Ironically, Percy's *Second Coming* was also nominated that year; Percy lost the prize to a book that he was largely responsible for bringing to publication.

In recent years Toole has been the object of renewed attention, with a new documentary, *John Kennedy Toole: The Omega Point,* by Joe Sanford, and a new biography, Cory MacLauchlin's *Butterfly in the Typewriter.*

WAREHOUSE DISTRICT

National World War II Museum
945 Magazine St. (entrance on Andrew Higgins Dr.)
(504) 528-1944
nationalww2museum.org

One of New Orleans's greatest sources of civic pride and most notable tourist attractions, the National World War II Museum was originally the idea of University of New Orleans historian and Illinois native Stephen E. Ambrose (1936–2002), who gave generously of his own money to make it happen. When Ambrose originally began collecting the narratives of the members of "The Greatest Generation," he knew that eventually they would need a home, and this is the end result of that effort. In addition to world-class exhibits, the museum offers an amazing range of programming in conjunction with anniversaries and holidays as well as ongoing library events with historians and scholars.

A Literary Datebook

SPRING

Tennessee Williams / New Orleans Literary Festival
938 Lafayette St.
Suite 514
(800) 990-3378
(504) 581-1144
tennesseewilliams.net
info@tennesseewilliams.net

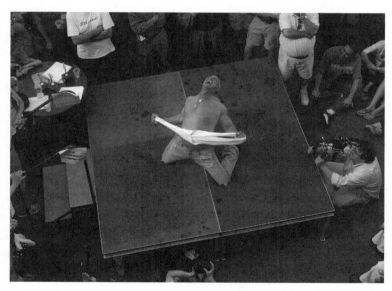

Bryan Buckles, runner-up in the 2012 Stella Shouting Contest
Photo by Earl Perry, courtesy of the Tennessee Williams Festival

Nicole Martin, winner of the 2012 Stanley Shouting Contest
Photo by Earl Perry, courtesy of the Tennessee Williams Festival

This festival, a highlight of the spring season, celebrates the literary heritage of the city in the name of one of its best-known former literary residents. From its founding in 1987, this grassroots community festival has steadily grown into an international event, with a full schedule of events at various French Quarter venues.

The festival usually takes place during the weekend in March closest to Williams's birthday (March 26) and includes plays, literary panels and readings, addresses by noted writers, a book fair, literary walking tours, and the usual New Orleans parties. It culminates in the signature Stella and Stanley Shouting Contest on Sunday afternoon, and contestants are judged on passion, volume, and originality. It's one of the great moments in which the city's literary past really comes alive in the present, leaving a trail of torn T-shirts along the way.

Past festivals have featured such luminaries as Edward Albee, Elizabeth Ashley, Alec Baldwin, John Berendt, Robert Olen Butler, Zoe Caldwell, Richard Ford, Ernest Gaines, Tim Gautreaux, John Guare, Anne Jackson, Wally Lamb, Terrence McNally, Marian Seldes, John Patrick Shanley, Eli Wallach, and John Waters.

The festival includes a series of master classes at the Historic New Orleans Collection, aimed at facilitating interactions with authors, poets, journalists, agents, editors, and other literary professionals. The Tennessee Williams Scholars' Conference brings together academic specialists in the playwright's life and work and sponsors the Tennessee Williams Annual Review. The festival also sponsors fiction and poetry contests judged by outstanding writers as well as an annual playwriting contest.

Symphony Book Fair
Warehouse: 8605 Oak St.
(504) 861-2004
symphonyvolunteers.org

The city's largest book fair benefits the Louisiana Philharmonic Orchestra and is held each spring at various locations. The sale includes art, sheet music, records and CDs, and some very rare books. The fair accepts donations of books, art, and sheet music all year round at its warehouse. From June 5 to August 31 the warehouse is open from 9 a.m. until 1 p.m. on Tuesdays and Fridays. From September 1 to May 31 the warehouse is open from 10 a.m. until 2 p.m. on Tuesdays and Fridays.

Saints and Sinners Literary Festival
938 Lafayette St.
Suite 514
(504) 581-1144
sasfest.org
saintsandsinnola@aol.com

The Saints and Sinners Literary Festival, founded in 2001, began as a way to reach out with information about HIV/AIDS and has grown into one of the country's largest festivals celebrating lesbian, gay, bisexual, and transgendered literature. It is usually held over four days in May and features panel discussions, master classes, and various social events in the French Quarter. Over the years the festival has played host to such luminaries as Dorothy Allison, Mark Doty, Val McDermid, and Radclyffe.

Friends of the New Orleans Public Library Book Sale
fnopl.org

As part of the Katrina recovery efforts, the Friends of the New Orleans Public Library began holding twice-weekly book sales in the carriage house behind the Latter Library at 5120 St. Charles Avenue. New Orleanians came here to donate books they no longer needed or to restock personal libraries. Now it can be a great treat for visitors as well—a chance to pick up some new books at very reasonable prices and take a peek at one of New Orleans's treasured landmarks. At this writing hours are Wednesday and Saturday, 10 a.m.–2 p.m.

Friends of the Jefferson Public Library Book Sale
friends of jeffersonlibrary.org

The Friends of the Jefferson Public Library sponsor a semiannual book sale and operate a store in the East Bank Regional Library, 4747 W. Napoleon, in Metairie.

New Orleans Jazz and Heritage Festival Book Tent
nojazzfest.com

The New Orleans Jazz and Heritage Festival, which takes place the last weekend in April and the first weekend in May, brings a feast of music and food to the New Orleans Fairgrounds. In between bites of cochon de lait and crawfish pie and music from blues to zydeco, stop by the book tent sponsored the New Orleans Gulf South Booksellers Association. Staffed by knowledgeable volunteers, the book tent offers a broad selection of books about Louisiana music and culture and food. Proceeds go to various literacy projects. Watch for celebrity autographings by such notables as

Buddy Guy, Dr. John, and Wynton Marsalis. Information is available at independent bookstores in the area or on the website, nojazzfest.com. Lagniappe for booklovers: this is a great place to take refuge if rain pops up as well as a wonderful place to chill with younger readers.

SUMMER

Essence Music Festival
essence.com/festivals

This "party with a purpose," celebrating the best in African American music, takes place over the Fourth of July weekend. In addition to pure entertainment, the festival offers a series of empowerment seminars featuring leading African American authors as well as a festival marketplace offering a broad selection of books and crafts.

Bayou Soul Writers and Reader's Conference
bswconference.com

Founded in 2011 by novelist Clarence Nero, the Bayou Soul Writers and Reader's Conference offers impressive literary opportunities for those who are attending the Essence Music Festival. This event features a good range of writers, editors, and agents as well as a number of authors, with advice for beginning writers as well as those already established.

San Fermin in Nueva Orleans
nolabulls.com

San Fermin in Nueva Orleans is a local adaptation of the running of the bulls in Pamplona, Spain. It's a summer weekend during which locals take to the streets and run from the Big Easy Rollergirls, who skate among them, chasing them with plastic bats. It's *very* New Orleans. In homage to Papa Hemingway the weekend concludes with Pobre de Mi, an event that includes a Hemingway impersonators contest, readings, and sketches inspired by his work. (Not for children.) You really have to see this to believe it. And then, trust me, you'll wear your "Death in the Afternoon Drinking Society" T-shirt with pride.

Tales of the Cocktail
talesofthecocktail.com

Tales of the Cocktail, a festival devoted to cocktails, cuisine, and culture, could only have started in New Orleans. Begun in 2002, it takes place every July and features five days of seminars, dinners, competitions, and tastings as well as an incredible range of presentations by writing mixologists and cocktail historians.

AUTUMN

New Orleans Bookfair & Media Expo
neworleansbookfair.com

New Orleans boasts a vibrant alternative literary scene, and the NOLA Bookfair is a rowdy gathering of alternative presses and publishers that takes place each fall. Founded in 2001 by G. K. Darby of Garrett County Press, the fair offers everything from gorgeous artists' books to underground comics to anarchist literature. In 2009 best-selling author John Berendt appeared as the keynote speaker. There are organizational meetings throughout the year, and everyone is welcome. Don't miss the wonderful letterpress demonstrations by John Fitzgerald.

New Orleans Children's Book Festival
Latter Library
5120 St. Charles Ave.
nolabookfest.org

This festival, sponsored by the New Orleans Public Library and the Ruby Bridges Foundation, takes place in October on the Latter Library grounds on St. Charles Avenue. The event features storytelling, book giveaways, and activities and crafts. It was founded in 2010.

Louisiana Book Festival
The Center for the Book at the State Library of Louisiana
701 N. Fourth St., Baton Rouge
louisianabookfestival.org

Sponsored by the Center for the Book at the State Library of Louisiana, the Louisiana Book Festival began in 2002 and has now grown into one of the largest in the country, usually including more than two hundred authors at more than one hundred literary events. It's a great day to find New Orleans writers all in one place! It takes place every fall (the actual date varies according to the LSU football schedule) on the grounds of the State Capitol in Baton Rouge and features writing workshops, author appearances, a book fair, numerous events for children, food, and music. It's well worth the drive from New Orleans, with the additional attractions of the State Museum and the State Library. The festival is free; food and drink are available at reasonable prices.

Literary Halloween

Thanks to the novels of Anne Rice, New Orleans has become a travel destination for celebrating Halloween. And now that the Voodoo Music Experience is the same weekend, there are even more reasons to visit the city in the fall. The Anne Rice Fan Club holds its traditional Halloween ball that weekend; for information check out the website neworleansvampireball.org.

Jewish Community Center Book Festival
Jewish Community Center, Uptown
5342 St. Charles Ave.
nojcc.org

This annual event, usually in November, at the Jewish Community Center has featured such well-known authors as Madeleine Albright, Walter Isaacson, Steve Roberts, Dennis Ross, and Judith Viorst. Events over the week include a special luncheon for booklovers, events for children and families, and a bookstore with an incredible selection of titles of Jewish interest run by local indie Octavia Books.

Words and Music: A Literary Feast in New Orleans
c/o Pirate's Alley Faulkner Society
624 Pirate's Alley
wordsandmusic.org

The Pirate's Alley Faulkner Society, founded by Joseph DeSalvo Jr. and Rosemary James, owners of Faulkner House Books, in order to "celebrate the written word," hosts this event in the fall, usually headquartered at the Hotel Monteleone and with events taking place at various French Quarter venues. Authors who have previously appeared include Robert Olen Butler, Julia Glass, Oscar Hijuelos, Dennis Lehane, and Ted Turner. Taking place over several days, Words and Music includes writing workshops, literary lunches, music events, and the celebration of the winners of the prestigious Pirate's Alley William Faulkner–William Wisdom Creative Writing Competition.

READING SERIES

The longest-running poetry series in the South (more than thirty years) keeps on trucking every Sunday at the Maple Leaf Bar, 8316 Oak Street. Readings begin at 3 p.m. Drop by, knock back a few, and bring your own poems for the open mike. More information is at mapleleafbar.com.

Another local favorite is the 17 Poets! Literary and Performance Series, which takes place every Thursday at 8 p.m. at the Gold Mine Saloon, 705 Dauphine Street. Poet Dave Brinks, who owns the bar, is also the author of *The Caveat Onus,* a great post-Katrina poem cycle. Check out www.17poets.com

The 1718 Reading Series, which takes its name from the date of the city's founding, is a joint effort by Loyola and Tulane writing students. It takes place monthly, September through May, at the Columns Hotel, 3811 St. Charles Avenue. Check out 1718aneworleansreadingseries@blogspot.com.

FOR THE VISITOR

Check out entertainment listings in the *Times-Picayune* and in *Gambit,* the weekly newspaper, as well as nola.com and bestofneworleans.com. Or listen to the weekly radio show *The Reading Life* at wwno.org for information about visiting authors and local events. Veteran blogger Mark Folse (author of *Carry Me Home* and *A Howling in the Wires*) does a great job with literary listings in his blog *Odd Words,* at toulousestreet.wordpress.com, as does Nathan Martin at press-street.com.

New Orleans Bookshops

New Orleans has a long tradition of independent, specialty, and antiquarian bookshops, and some of our booksellers are great local characters who can give advice on everything from the best new title to the best neighborhood restaurant. The New Orleans–Gulf South Independent Booksellers Association can be reached through Britton Trice at Garden District Book Shop at the address that follows. And if you're in town during the New Orleans Jazz and Heritage Festival, stop by the book tent, sponsored by area booksellers, which features a broad range of local titles.

INDEPENDENT BOOKSHOPS

Garden District Book Shop
2727 Prytania at the Rink
(504) 895-2266
gardendistrictbookshop.com

This charming, airy building takes its name from its previous use; the Rink originally housed the ice-skating rink for the 1884 World's Fair. In 1979, after three years at a location on Jackson Avenue, owner Britton Trice opened this shop in the Garden District. It is a frequent stop for local and national authors—everyone from Pat Conroy to Anne Rice to James Lee Burke has appeared here. Check out the gallery of author photos in the store. The stock is an eclectic selection, with special strengths in gardening, interior design, and regional titles, and the staff is always welcoming and

Pat Conroy at the Garden District Book Shop
Photo by Britton Trice/Garden District Book Shop

knowledgeable. Other shops in the Rink are charming as well, and with a nearby coffee shop, you're set for a morning or afternoon, and Commander's Palace is right around the corner. Tours of the nearby cemetery at Washington and Prytania also meet here.

Maple Street Book Shop
7529 Maple St.
(504) 866-4916
(504) 861-2105
maplestreetbookshop.com

Maple Street Used and Rare
7523 Maple St.
(504) 866-7059

Founded in 1964, the flagship store is in a funky old house in the University area, at 7529 Maple, and is a local favorite. Originally founded by Mary Kellogg and Rhoda Norman, the store passed to Mary's daughter, Rhoda Faust, who owned Faust Publishing Company and was a longtime friend of novelist Walker Percy, some of whose work she published. In 2007 Faust sold the store to Donna Allen, who renovated it with care and attention and established new neighborhood branches. The 7529 Maple Street building was for many years the children's bookshop; now it has been reclaimed as a store for new books, and a used bookshop is next door, at 7523 Maple. Staff favorites are always a good bet here, especially from Cindy Dike, longtime manager of the children's shop. Both shops are near restaurants and coffee shops.

Octavia Books
513 Octavia St.
(504) 899-READ (7323)
octaviabooks.com

Husband-and-wife team Tom Lowenburg and Judith Lafitte opened this gorgeous shop Uptown in 2000. It was very quick to reopen after Katrina and hosted a landmark book signing for Tom Piazza's manifesto, *Why New Orleans Matters,* that was one of the most significant homecoming events for the literary community post-Katrina. The beautifully designed, light and airy space features comfortable browsing areas and is home to an adorable working dog named Pippin. The stock offers an eclectic and generous range of titles, with especially gorgeous gift books and an extensive selection of children's books. Frequent author appearances and book clubs are also part of the shop's offerings; be sure to sign up for their newsletter. Locals often combine a visit here with a trip to the Laurel Street Bakery around the corner; a yoga studio is next door. The shop is featured in John Klingman's beautiful book about modern architecture in the city, *New New Orleans Architecture.*

SPECIALTY SHOPS

African American Books

Afro-American Bookstop
7056 Read Blvd.
(504) 243-2436
e-mail: afrobooks2@aol.com

Owner Michele Lewis (named Blackboard's bookseller of the year for 1998) owned three stores in a small chain of shops until the flood of 2005 washed away both businesses and home. But this store, which opened in 2008, caters to the local community with African American cards, books by and about African Americans, games, puzzles, and Kwanzaa supplies. Most leading African American authors visit this store or the Community Book Center on their New Orleans tours. Watch for special events during the Essence Music Festival and the Bayou Classic football game between Southern University and Grambling during Thanksgiving weekend.

Community Book Center
2523 Bayou Rd.
(504) 948-7323
communitybookcenter.com

This is the oldest African American bookstore in New Orleans, begun more than twenty-five years ago when owner Vera Warren Williams used three hundred dollars to invest in titles for a book fair. Now she and store manager Jennifer Turner have fussed over and mothered a generation of New Orleans readers and authors. The store functions as a real community center, sharing space with several other organizations, with a coffee shop across the street. They carry a good selection of books, cards, games, puzzles, and Kwanzaa supplies and have a strong inspirational section.

The Community Book Center
Photo by Dennis Persica

Art Books

A Gallery for Fine Photography
241 Chartres St.
(504) 568-1313
agallery.com

Photographer Josh Pailet has assembled an impressive selection of prints, covering luminaries such as Henri Cartier-Bresson and Robert Mapplethorpe and showcasing such locals as George Dureau and Josephine Sacabo. Pailet, who is the author of a book on the 1984 World's Fair, augments the art with a fine selection of new and used books.

New Orleans Museum of Art Shop
New Orleans Museum of Art
City Park
noma.org

This shop features unusual gift items and jewelry as well as a fine selection of art books and exhibition catalogs and sponsors a monthly book club that discusses art-related books.

Cookbooks

Kitchen Witch Cookbooks
631 Toulouse St.
(504) 528-8382
kwcookbooks.com

Philipe LaMancusa and Debbie Lindsey operate this French Quarter charmer, with its emphasis on all things foodie. They'll have good recommendations, too, and do searches for out-of-print books. Ask about their book group for classic New Orleans cookbooks.

Gay and Lesbian Books

FAB (Faubourg Marigny Art and Books)
600 Frenchmen St.
(504) 943-3700

Specializing in gay and lesbian literature and art, FAB, founded in 1978, is one of the oldest gay bookstores in the country. The store holds frequent signings and carries periodicals, CDs, and gift items, in addition to books and figurative art. Owner Otis Fennell is also a good source of information about the local gay and lesbian community. The store stays open late to capitalize on the lively foot traffic in this interesting neighborhood—check out the action at the various music venues and restaurants on the street.

Louisiana Specialties

The Historic New Orleans Collection Shop
533 Royal St.
(504) 598-7147
hnoc.org

This bookstore offers a large selection of books on Louisiana history and culture, architecture, and the Civil War as well as first editions and a great selection of unusual gifts; it also carries books and reproductions from the collection's holdings. The collection is a frequent host to concerts and scholarly conferences; be sure to check out the calendar when you're here.

Religious Books

Catholic Book Store
3003 S. Carrollton Ave.
(504) 861-7504
cbstorenola.com

Opened in 1939, this store is fully stocked for Catholic readers, with books, Bibles, music, and religious articles. It serves as the bookstore for the adjacent seminary but appeals to the layperson as well. Flooded in 2005, the store operated in a trailer for several years, before its grand reopening. For handicapped accessibility there's an elevator at the rear of the store.

Lifeway Christian Store
3939 Gentilly Blvd.
(504) 282-2626

This large store, on the campus of the New Orleans Baptist Theological seminary, carries Bibles, devotional texts, hymnals, music, and more.

USED AND ANTIQUARIAN BOOKSHOPS

Arcadian Books and Art Prints
714 Orleans Ave.
(504) 523-4138

This store, in business since 1981, has a good selection of French-language items and current material on Louisiana history as well a nice selection of out-of-print books. This is a bookstore for Francophiles and would be a memorable stop for French tourists. Owner Russell Desmond is the go-to guy for Francophone info.

Beckham's Book Shop
228 Decatur St.
(504) 522-9875

It's easy to lose yourself in this multistory shop, which offers one of the most interesting selections of used books in the city, The store, open seven days a week, has operated in this location since 1970. Owners Cary Beckham and Alton Cook are French Quarter icons and can lead you to interesting selections.

Blue Cypress Books
8126 Oak St.
(504) 352-0096
bluecypressbooks.blogspot.com

Elizabeth Barry Ahlquist has assembled an interesting collection of mostly used (and in good condition) books on this Carrollton thoroughfare. The store has some interesting specialties (sustainable agriculture books support the interests of the many local farmers' markets and backyard gardeners), and owner Ahlquist, the mother of three, has a good stock of used children's books. There's good shopping and eating nearby as well.

Crescent City Books
204 Chartres St.
(504) 524-4997
blackwidowpress.com

This two-story shop specializes in world history and art and features a broad range of scholarly used and antiquarian books as well as interesting prints. Open seven days a week. The shop sponsors the monthly Black Widow Literary Salon. Manager Michael Allen Zell is also a novelist.

Dauphine Street Books
410 Dauphine St.
(504) 525-1215

Owned by Steve Lacy, this shop specializes in modern literature, jazz and local history, and art and photography. The building was also the home of the first elegant parlor house owned by legendary madam Norma Wallace, subject of Christine Wiltz's book *The Last Madam: A Life of the New Orleans Underworld*. A good place to spend some time while waiting for your reservation at Bayona, next door, but beware, it's easy to get lost here.

Maple Street Book Shop sign
Photo by Dennis Persica

Faulkner House Books
624 Pirate's Alley
(504) 524-2940
faulknerhouse.net

This small, elegant shop is a must-see for literary tourists, one of the most famous landmarks in the city. Faulkner lived and worked here while in New Orleans, and the ground floor is now home to a store with fine southern literature in rare and first editions as well as a carefully chosen selection of new titles. Owner Joseph DeSalvo Jr. is a Boswell buff; he and his wife, Rosemary James, are cofounders of the Pirate's Alley Faulkner Society, which produces "Words and Music: A Literary Feast in New Orleans" every fall.

Librairie Book Shop
823 Chartres St.
(504) 525-4837

A sister store to Beckham's Book Shops, this shop has been in operation since 1967.

Maple Street Used and Rare Book Shop
7523 Maple St.
(504) 866-7059

This charming Uptown shop occupies the former location of Maple Street Book Shop, which moved next door. In addition to used books, the store offers a good selection of magazines, cards, and blank books.

McKeown's Books and Difficult Music
4737 Tchoupitoulas St.
(504) 895-1954

Maggie McKeown's shop certainly has one of the most alluring titles in town, doesn't it? Browse her interesting stock (she's the only bookstore on Tchoupitoulas Street), and you may be surprised to drop in on a musical performance. And there's a snowball stand across the street!

McLaughlin Books
512 Terry Pkwy., Ste. F
Terrytown, LA 70056
(504) 367-3754

This shop, open since 1978, features used hardbacks and paperbacks.

Front of McKeown's Books
Photo by Dennis Persica

UNIVERSITY BOOKSTORES

Dillard University Bookstore
Henson Hall
2601 Gentilly Blvd.
(504) 816-4299

Loyola University Bookstore
Loyola University
6363 St. Charles Ave.
Danna Center
(504) 865-3262

Tulane University Bookstore
29 McAlister Dr.
Lavin-Bernick Center for Student Life
(504) 865-5913

University of New Orleans Bookstore
University Center
2000 Lakeshore Dr.
(504) 280-6373

Xavier University of Louisiana Bookstore
University Center
4980 Dixon St.
(504) 520-7300

CHAIN STORES

Barnes & Noble Booksellers
3721 Veterans Memorial Blvd.
Metairie, LA 70002
(504) 455-4929

Barnes & Noble–Westbank
1601B West Bank Expressway
Harvey, LA 70058
(504) 263-1146

BOOK WHOLESALERS

Forest Sales and Distributing Company
139 Jean Marie St.

Reserve, LA 70084
(985) 479-1456

This wholesale distributor of regional interest books and cookbooks has served the region since 1967.

Literary Resources

LIBRARIES

Admit it—there are certain tourists who make a point of visiting libraries. There are even some for whom libraries are destinations themselves. And like any city with a long history, New Orleans has treasure troves tucked away in libraries and research centers. The city's public library system became a focal point of interest in the library world after 2005, when so much was lost in the federal flood. At this writing the New Orleans Public Library system is on its way back, though it faces the same funding struggles that public libraries do across the country. Eight out of thirteen branches were closed after Katrina, eight out of fifteen in nearby Jefferson Parish, and St. Tammany and St. Bernard Parishes suffered great damage as well. The price of lost materials in Orleans Parish alone was $6.8 million, most of which was covered by FEMA funds.

One interesting note: New Orleanians learned firsthand the value of public libraries during the diaspora of 2005. Where did they go for computer access? Public libraries. Where did they go for assistance in getting valuable information? Public libraries. We were welcomed across the country by librarians who only wanted to help. And when we returned home, it was to expectations of libraries with new standards of service, in new incarnations. The main library of the New Orleans Public Library system was federalized and became a center for FEMA. Libraries were up and running in trailers as soon as humanly possible. In Jefferson Parish the lights of the East Bank Regional Library were a beacon to citizens, and the library took the lead in offering programming in disaster relief, mold remediation, all the tools citizens needed to survive in a landscape recovering from a flood. The East Bank Regional Library hosted a reading by Rick Bragg and Sonny Brewer in November 2005, one of the great literary homecomings. Bookmobiles and FEMA trailers were pressed into service as branch libraries throughout south Louisiana.

And librarians became heroes in another way. The first convention to return to New Orleans was the 2006 meeting of the American Library Association (ALA). Not only did these librarians come bringing much-needed tourist dollars; they brought sweat equity as well, putting in tough volunteer hours restoring two city branches—Alvar and the Children's Resource Center.

According to an America Library Association statistic, thirty-five public libraries in Louisiana were closed, and the cost to rebuild them and their collections came to an estimated $63 million, and that figure did not include school and higher-education library repairs. Libraries in eleven parishes suffered serious damage.

The system made a great leap forward in 2012, with the opening of five new branches—Rosa F. Keller, Norman Mayer, Robert E. Smith, the East New Orleans Branch, and the Algiers Regional Branch. The Jefferson Parish system also opened a beautiful new Lakefront library. These were amazing civic celebrations.

Today the New Orleans Public Library serves all kinds of researchers—scholars, fiction writers, Carnival historians, filmmakers, set designers and decorators, genealogy buffs, lawyers, and politicians—with vast resources available just for the asking.

The main website is neworleanspubliclibrary.org, but also check individual branches' Facebook pages.

Main Library
219 Loyola Ave.
(504) 529-READ

The New Orleans Public Library is unique in that the city charter mandates that the library be the repository of the official city archives. The Louisiana Division is a reference resource devoted to the state of Louisiana and the city of New Orleans. In addition to the city archives, which date from 1769 to the present (and which also includes the pre-1927 records of the civil courts and the pre-1932 records of the criminal courts of Orleans Parish), the Louisiana Division offers an extensive genealogy collection, the African American collection, the Carnival Collection, manuscripts, maps, newspapers, periodicals, microfilms, photographs, slides, motion pictures, sound recordings, videotapes, postcards, and ephemera of every sort, including restaurant menus and postcards. For best service let the archivist know you are coming.

Algiers Regional Branch
3014 Holiday Dr., Algiers
(504) 596-2641

This beautiful new branch opened in summer 2012.

Alvar Branch
913 Alvar St.
(504) 596-2667

This branch in the Bywater neighborhood, a WPA structure, opened to the public in 1940. It took on about a foot of water during the flood and was one of the branch libraries that were the focus of relief efforts during the 2006 ALA convention.

Central City Branch
2405 Jackson Ave., Building C, Room 235
(in the Mahalia Jackson Center)

This branch is a perfect example of the library's partnership with community centers.

Children's Resource Center
913 Napoleon Ave.
(504) 596-2628

This Uptown branch was one of New Orleans's original Carnegie libraries; it opened in 1908 as the Napoleon Branch but was repurposed to serve neighborhood children.

Cita Dennis Hubbell Branch
725 Pelican Ave., Algiers
TEMPORARY LOCATION:
225 Morgan St. (the Algiers Courthouse Carriage House)
(504) 366-0657

The library at 725 Pelican Avenue first opened in 1907. The Algiers Branch, as it became known, was one of five libraries in New Orleans established with money from Andrew Carnegie. The others were the main library on Howard Avenue, the Napoleon and Royal branches, and several years later the Dryades branch. Of those only Hubbell and Napoleon survive today. For almost sixty years this was the only public library on New Orleans's West Bank. Although the library came through Katrina relatively well, concerns for the aging structure forced its closing, and a temporary branch was opened behind the Algiers Courthouse.

East New Orleans Branch
5641 Read Blvd.
(504) 596-0200

This replacement branch opened April 12, 2012. The collections include a number of books in Vietnamese, intended to serve the large Vietnamese population of this area (which was the setting for Robert Olen Butler's Pulitzer Prize–winning collection of short stories, *A Good Scent from a Strange Mountain*). Another attraction of this branch is its proximity to Joe Brown Park.

Rosa F. Keller Branch
4300 S. Broad St.
(504) 596-2660

This branch is named in honor of Rosa Freeman Keller, a longtime civil rights activist. In 1953 she became the first woman appointed to the New Orleans Public Library's board of directors, a post she held for the next twenty-six years. One of her priorities was the desegregation of the city's public libraries. The library, located in an historic home, suffered major flooding in 2005 and relocated first to a trailer and then to a temporary facility in nearby Andrew Wilson Charter School. The newly renovated branch opened in April 2012 as a library/community center, the result of an innovative partnership between the New Orleans Public Library and the Broadmoor Improvement Association, headed by Latoya Cantrell. Cantrell's group sought Carnegie funding for the library's renovation and received a two-million-dollar grant. Vartan Gregorian, head of the Carnegie Corporation and former head of the New York Public Library, was present at the reopening. The citizens of

Broadmoor and the neighborhood users of this library are proof of the association's motto: Broadmoor Lives!

Latter Branch
5120 St. Charles Ave.
(504) 596-2625

This 1907 building opened as a library in 1948. Former owners include silent film star Marguerite Clark. Later owners, Mr. and Mrs. Harry Latter, donated the mansion to the city in 1947 as a memorial to their son, Milton, who was lost on Okinawa during World War II. The library was placed on the National Register of Historic Places in 1976. The carriage house in the back is open for the Friends of the New Orleans Public Library book sale, which takes place every Wednesday and Saturday from 10 a.m. to 2 p.m.

Martin Luther King Branch
1611 Caffin Ave.
(504) 596-2695

This branch, inside the Ninth Ward school of the same name, opened in 1995, and like much of the neighborhood (including Fats Domino's home nearby on Caffin Avenue), was completely destroyed by the 2005 flood. It was the site of a temporary branch founded by the Gates Foundation, and it reopened in October 2007.

Norman Mayer Branch
3001 Gentilly Blvd.
(504) 596-3100

Mrs. Norman Mayer, wife of the prominent New Orleans cotton broker, gave a sum for the construction of a building to house the Norman Mayer Memorial Library, which opened in 1949. The branch had to be demolished after the 2005 flood, and a temporary branch was located in a nearby strip mall. The new building was opened in April 2012.

Mid-City Branch
3700 Orleans Ave. (in the American Can Building)
(504) 596-2654

The Mid-City Branch originally opened in June 2007, in a shopping center storefront at 330 N. Carrollton Avenue. Gates Foundation funding made that possible. In 2011 the branch moved to the American Can building on Orleans Avenue, where it nestles snugly in with coffee shops and wine bars, a center for its neighborhood near Bayou St. John.

Nix Branch
1401 S. Carrollton Ave.
(504) 596-2630

This branch in the Carrollton neighborhood originally opened in 1930. It sustained window damage during Hurricane Katrina but reopened in October 2005. It was damaged again by a tornado in February 2007 but reopened shortly thereafter.

Robert E. Smith Branch
6301 Canal Blvd.
(504) 596-2638

This branch in Lakeview was named for a Lakeview resident, and an exhibit on the second floor focuses on his relationship with the library. A branch originally opened at this corner in 1956, but a new, larger building replaced it in 1979 as the community and its need for a library grew. The first floor was completely destroyed by flooding in 2005; temporary libraries operated first in a bookmobile on the site, then in trailers down the street, and the new building opened in 2012.

ARCHIVES AND RESEARCH INSTITUTIONS

Archdiocese of New Orleans
1100 Chartres St.
(504) 529-2651
archives@archdiocese-no.org
By appointment

There are four main sections in the archives in the Old Ursuline convent: sacramental and cemetery records (1718–ca. 1900); archdiocesan historical records (Spanish colonial period–present); several manuscript collections (e.g., the Baudier Collection); and a small research library. The archives serve as the archdiocesan records management office.

Historic New Orleans Collection
533 Royal St.
(504) 523-4662

Williams Research Center
410 Chartres St.
(504) 598-7171
WRC@hnoc.org
hnoc.org

The lovely facility on Royal Street, founded by General and Mrs. L. Kemper Williams in 1966 and housed in elegant French Quarter buildings, is a rich and varied source of information on colonial Louisiana, the Louisiana Purchase, the Battle of New Orleans, the Civil War, Mississippi river life, cartography, transportation, plantations, urban development, Louisiana art and architecture, the French Quarter, Mardi Gras, and many other local and regional topics. The Williams Gallery features changing exhibits and frequent free public lectures; there is a wonderful shop with gift items and books you won't find anywhere else. The Williams Research Center has vast holdings, including an impressive collection of Tennessee Williams material.

The facilities are pretty and comfortable, the staff pleasant and extremely knowledgeable. Well worth a special trip.

Louisiana State Museum Historical Center
P.O. Box 2448
751 Chartres St.
(800) 568-6968, fax: (504) 568-4995
lsm.crt.state.la.us/collections/hcenter.htm

This collection includes records of the French Superior Council (1704–69) and Spanish judicial records (1769–1803) as well as social, political, economic, and medical conditions of Louisiana from the eighteenth century to the present.

Notarial Archives Division
Office of the Clerk of Court for the Parish of Orleans
1340 Poydras St.
(504) 680-9604 (Research Center); (504) 568-8577 (Filing Office)
notarialarchives.org

The Notarial Archives, a division of the Orleans Parish Civil District Court, holds over 35 million pages of notarial contracts (dating from 1731) and also preserves many colorful maps, blueprints, topographical elevations, and design drawings. The records held here increase by about 50,000 acts yearly.

AT LOYOLA UNIVERSITY

J. Edgar and Louise S. Monroe Library
636 St. Charles Ave.
library.loyno.edu

This library was dedicated in 1999, with holdings including the Frère Joseph-Aurelian Cornet archives. Cornet is one of the foremost experts on the arts of the Congo, and his scholarship includes 150 field notebooks and 20,000 photographs. The library's rare book collection consists primarily of books about the Catholic Church, Louisiana, and New Orleans. The Walker Percy and His Circle Collection, begun in 1993 with a donation by Percy biographer Father Patrick Samway, contains books and material related to Walker Percy, Eudora Welty, Mary Lee Settle, Reynolds Price, and other southern writers. The library also has a collection of Lafcadio Hearn correspondence, H. L. Mencken letters, and the archives of the *New Orleans Review,* which is still published by the Loyola English department. The library also houses the Lindy Boggs National Center for Community Literacy, with a focus on combating illiteracy and supporting literacy research and training reading teachers.

AT TULANE UNIVERSITY

Amistad Research Center
Tilton Hall

Tulane University
6823 St. Charles Ave.
(504) 862-3222, fax: (504) 862-8961
reference@amistadresearchcenter.org
amistadresearchcenter.org

Originally part of the Race Relations Department at Fisk University, this archive, founded by the American Missionary Association, moved to New Orleans in 1969 and became an independent repository. This is one of the nation's largest African American history archives, with holdings dating from the 1780s to the present. The collection includes more than ten million documents, twenty thousand volumes, oral histories, and significant art and photographic holdings.

Louisiana Research Collection
Room 202, Jones Hall
Tulane University
(504) 865-5685, fax: (504) 865-5761
larc@tulane.edu

This collection combines one of the more comprehensive research archives (with almost four linear miles of documents from the founding of the city to the present) with a major Louisiana research library, creating a unified resource for archives, books, maps, images, and ephemera. The collection's special strengths are Carnival, colonial Louisiana, Civil War, Ephemera, Jewish studies, Louisiana politics, medical history, social welfare, southern literature, waterways, and women's studies.

Newcomb College Center for Research on Women
Nadine Vorhoff Library
Caroline Richardson Hall
(504) 865-5238, fax: (504) 862-8948
susannah@tulane.edu
tulane.edu/~wc/
Susan Tucker, Archivist

The Nadine Vorhoff Library, located in the Newcomb College Center for Research on Women, is the premier repository of feminist material in the city and has an oral history archive and a large culinary collection. It also serves as the official archives of New-comb College.

Southeastern Architectural Archives
Room 300, Jones Hall
Tulane University
(504) 865-5699, fax: (504) 865-5761
krylance@tulane.edu
http://seaa.tulane.edu/

Plans and drawings, photographs, and office records of architectural firms dating from the 1830s through the 1980s, representing more than two hundred architects.

William Ransom Hogan Archive of New Orleans Jazz
Room 304, Jones Hall
Tulane University
(504) 865-5688
raeburn@tulane.edu
http://jazz.tulane.edu
Bruce Boyd Raeburn, head, Hogan Jazz Archive, and Director, Special Collections

A delight for music researchers, this collection includes primary and secondary material pertaining to jazz, with records and papers, oral histories, recorded music, photographs, sheet music, and clippings.

OTHER UNIVERSITY COLLECTIONS

Center for African and African American Studies
Southern University at New Orleans
Administration Building, Room 209
Southern University at New Orleans
6400 Press Dr.
(504) 284-5550
caaas-suno.weebly.com/index.html

This collection focuses on Africa and the African American experience and has an extensive African art collection.

Dillard University Archives and Special Collections
Will W. Alexander Library
Dillard University
2601 Gentilly Blvd.
(504) 816-4528
http://books.dillard.edu/Archives/Index.htm

The Archives and Special Collections, which is focused primarily on southern African American history and culture, is composed of records and material from New Orleans University, Straight College and Dillard University, Flint-Goodridge Hospital, a United Methodist Church Collection, and the McPherson Memorial Freedom Collection.

University of New Orleans
Louisiana and Special Collections Department
Earl K. Long Library
(504) 280-6544
library.uno.edu/specialcollections/lacol_index.cfm

This collection includes the official archives of the university, the Louisiana State Supreme Court, the Orleans Parish School Board, and the Chamber / New Orleans and the River Region. The main focus of the unit is on twentieth-century ethnic and business records of New Orleans. Another notable collection housed here is devoted to Marcus Christian, who headed the Negro Division of the Louisiana WPA.

AGENCIES

Arts Council of New Orleans
935 Gravier St., Suite 850
(504) 523-1465, fax: (504) 529-2430
artscouncilofneworleans.org

The Arts Council of New Orleans is a private, nonprofit organization designated as the city's official arts agency, one of eight regional distributing agencies for state arts funds, and administers available municipal arts grants and the Percent for Art program for the city of New Orleans.

Louisiana Division of the Arts
P.O. Box 44247
Baton Rouge, LA 70804-4247
(225) 342-8180
crt.state.la.us/arts

This is the state's official arts agency. Write or visit the website for grant details.

Louisiana Endowment for the Humanities
Louisiana Humanities Center at Turners' Hall
938 Lafayette St., Suite 300
Dr. Michael Sartisky, President and Executive Director
(504) 523-4352; (800) 909-7990 (toll-free in La. only)
leh.org

This is the state's primary funding agency for arts and humanities. The LEH publishes the award-winning magazine *Cultural Vistas*; oversees the selection of the state poet laureate; and sponsors the Prime Time Family Literacy Program, Teacher Institutes for Advanced Study, and the RELIC (Readings in Literature and Culture) Program.

LITERACY

The Literacy Alliance
6363 St. Charles Ave., No. 63
gnoliteracy.org

Headquartered at Loyola University, the Literacy Alliance supports adult literacy efforts.

STAIR (Start the Adventure in Reading)
stairnola.org

STAIR is a volunteer-based, nonprofit children's literacy organization that provides reading tutors for public school second grade students. STAIR was founded in New Orleans in 1985. The organization sponsors summer workdays and volunteer training throughout the year.

PUBLISHERS

The Neighborhood Story Project
2202 Lapeyrouse St.
neighborhoodstoryproject.org

In 2004 the Neighborhood Story Project, or NSP, was founded by
Rachel Breunlin and Abram Himelstein as a book-making project
with the mission of publishing "Our stories told by us." The project works with writers in neighborhoods around New Orleans to
create books about their communities. The NSP is a 501 C3 tax-
exempt organization in partnership with the University of New
Orleans. As a fund-raiser, the NSP sponsors the annual Write-A-
Thon in which writers at all levels secure pledges and come together to write.

Pelican Publishing Company
1000 Burmaster St.
Gretna, LA 70053–2246
(504) 368-1175
pelicanpub.com

This mid-sized publishing house has an extensive backlist and
publishes fifty to sixty new titles annually. After the death of her
father, Dr. Milburn Calhoun, in 2012, Kathleen Calhoun Nettleton
became president and publisher as well as co-owner of the company with her mother, Nancy Calhoun, who serves as treasurer
and vice president of special promotions. Dr. and Mrs. Calhoun
began as book collectors and then opened Bayou Books, a mail-or-
der rare and out-of-print book business, then a retail bookstore. In
1970 the Calhouns acquired Pelican Publishing House from Betty
and Hodding Carter and restored its name to Pelican Publishing
Company. Its history includes works by William Faulkner, whose
first trade publication was published by Pelican; Stuart O. Landry,
who ran the company from 1926 to 1966; as well as the Calhoun
family. The company is presently the largest independent trade
book publisher in the South. Among its well-known titles are Zig
Ziglar's best seller *See You at the Top,* the *Cajun Night before Christmas* series illustrated by James Rice, Mary Alice Fontenot's *Clovis
Crawfish* series, and the *Maverick Guide* travel series.

Press Street's Antenna Gallery
3161 Burgundy St.
(504) 298-3161

This community art collective came together in 2005 to promote art and literature in the community through events, publications, and arts education. Press Street produced Intersection / New Orleans, collaboration between twenty-five artists and twenty-five writers, inspired by twenty-five specific New Orleans street corners.

Press Street also produces the annual twenty-four-hour Draw-A-Thon, a round-the-clock, twenty-four-hour drawing extravaganza where multiple forms of drawing are explored by artists and non-artists alike.

In March 2008 Press Street opened the Antenna Gallery, in the Ninth Ward Bywater neighborhood, one of the few small, nonprofit spaces to exhibit visual contemporary art in the city of New Orleans.

Press Street also supports the "Room 220" blog. What started as a literary hub in the former Colton School, Press Street's "Room 220" is now a virtual clearinghouse for news about New Orleans book and literature culture. "Room 220" also hosts a variety of literary events.

UNO Press
University of New Orleans
138 Liberal Arts Building
(504) 280-7457
unopress.uno.edu

The University of New Orleans Press supports the mission of the university. It publishes scholarly as well as trade books and has done fascinating photography books as well as the important Katrina narrative series *Voices Rising 1* and *2*.

LITERARY GROUPS

Melanated Writers Collective
melanola.com

This alliance of writers of color was founded by Jewel Bush in 2010. Check out its website or its Facebook page to see if the collective is having any events while you're in town.

Pirate's Alley Faulkner Society
wordsandmusic.org

The Pirate's Alley Faulkner Society sponsors the William Wisdom Creative Writing competition and the annual conference, "Words and Music."

Society of Children's Book Writers and Illustrators
scbwi.org

This is a state branch of the national organization; the group meets monthly, with meetings staggered between New Orleans and Baton Rouge.

SOLA
The South Louisiana Chapter of the Romance Writers of America
solawriters.org

This group is a local chapter of the national organization and one of the oldest, strongest writers' groups in the city. Members who write in any genre are welcome. The group meets monthly and sponsors the Dixie Kane Memorial Writing Contest.

Women's National Book Association of New Orleans
1030 Dufossat St.

A local chapter of the national organization, the group meets monthly and offers various programs on a variety of literary topics. Membership is open to all who love books. The group meets monthly at various libraries, bookstores, and other locations. In October it sponsors a reading in conjunction with National Reading Group Month. Visit the group's Facebook page for more info.

SCHOLARLY CENTERS

Walker Percy Center for Writing and Publishing
Loyola New Orleans
Box 157
Dr. Mary A. McCay, Director
(504) 865-3389
loyno.edu/wpc

The goal of the Walker Percy Center for Writing and Publishing is to foster literary talent and achievement, to highlight the art of writing as essential to a good education, and to serve the makers, teachers, students, and readers of contemporary writing by providing educational and vocational opportunities in writing and publishing.

LAGNIAPPE

The Reading Life
wwno.org

This weekly radio show airs on the local NPR affiliate, WWNO 89.9 FM, and features interviews with local authors and a weekly events calendar. Listen online anytime.

A New Orleans Reading List

FICTION, POETRY, AND
CHILDREN'S BOOKS

I have spent most of my adult life reading about New Orleans—about every aspect of our culture, our history. I loved the new novels as they came along, cooked from the cookbooks, and shared the children's books with my kids as they were growing up. And I daresay few folks had the *job* of reading the post-Katrina works. So what follows are some deeply personal, idiosyncratic reading lists, culled from the best of my reading life. If I included every book I loved, this book would never be finished—and it's long enough as it is! I hope this will get readers and visitors started on their own reading lists.

THE CORNERSTONES OF NEW ORLEANS'S
LITERARY MYSTIQUE

A Confederacy of Dunces, by John Kennedy Toole. Baton Rouge: Louisiana State University Press, 1980.

This novel won a posthumous Pulitzer Prize for its author, who committed suicide in 1969. Ignatius Reilly, a medievalist who dreamed of philosophy but made his living selling Lucky Dogs, bumbles around New Orleans in this comic odyssey, which reveals the hilarious character of the city. Beyond that, this is a novel that holds out hope for every aspiring writer; after the author's death, his mother flogged the work relentlessly before presenting it to

Walker Percy, who became its champion with Louisiana State University Press.

Interview with the Vampire, by Anne Rice. New York: Knopf, 1976.

This 1976 best seller set Rice firmly on the path to literary fame and fortune, creating a mythic overlay of the city, drawing on its ethereal beauty, its cemeteries, its dark past. Her vampires have continued to talk, joined by witches and werewolves, in her supernatural pantheon. Tourists still drive by Rice's last New Orleans residence at First and Chestnut in the Garden District.

The Moviegoer, by Walker Percy. New York: Knopf, 1961.

This National Book Award winner introduced Walker Percy's basic concerns to the American reading audience—his struggle against despair, his idea of the search for meaning—through the character of Binx Bolling.

A Streetcar Named Desire, by Tennessee Williams. New York: New Directions, 1947.

This is—pardon the expression—the Big Daddy of literary works about New Orleans. The steamy sexiness, the French Quarter languor, the brilliant iconography—all combine to make a perfect literary portrait.

SUSAN'S ESSENTIAL READING LIST

BOSWORTH, SHEILA

Almost Innocent. New York, Simon & Schuster, 1984.
Slow Poison. New York: Knopf, 1992.

No one is better than Sheila Bosworth at evoking the many layers of Catholic life in New Orleans.

BOYDEN, AMANDA

Babylon Rolling. New York: Pantheon, 2008.

This is the second novel (after *Pretty Little Dirty* [2006]) by the University of New Orleans graduate and professor. *Babylon Rolling* captures the lives of the inhabitants of a single block of Orchid Street.

PRIZE WINNERS

Boyden, Joseph. *Through Black Spruce.* [Scotiabank Giller]

Butler, Robert Olen. A Good Scent from a Strange Mountain. [Pulitzer]

Ford, Richard. *Independence Day.* [Pulitzer]

Gaines, Ernest. *A Lesson before Dying.* [MacArthur]

Grau, Shirley Ann. *The Keepers of the House.* [Pulitzer]

Komunyakaa, Yusef. *Neon Vernacular.* [Pulitzer, Kingsley Tufts Award]

Kushner, Tony. *Angels in America.* [Pulitzer]

La Farge, Oliver. *Laughing Boy.* [Pulitzer]

Toole, John Kennedy. *A Confederacy of Dunces.* [Pulitzer]

BUTLER, ROBERT OLEN
A Good Scent from a Strange Mountain. New York: Grove Press, 1991.

This 1993 Pulitzer Prize–winner took its inspiration from the large Vietnamese community in eastern New Orleans, stories of culture clash and adaptation.

CRONE, MOIRA
Dream State: Stories. Jackson: University Press of Mississippi, 1995.

Crone is a former professor in the Louisiana State University creative writing program; her novels and short stories are dreamy, evocative masterpieces of southern life.

GAINES, ERNEST
A Lesson before Dying. New York: Knopf, 1997.

Gaines is truly a Louisiana master. This novel tells the moving story of Grant Wiggins, a young schoolteacher who is tasked with working with a young man in his rural community who is about to be electrocuted. (It's based on an actual case.) *A Lesson before Dying* was the first One Book / One New Orleans selection.

GAUTREAUX, TIM
The Missing. New York: Knopf, 2009.

Gautreaux writes comic short stories of incredible wit and charm (*Welding with Children* [1999] is a marvelous example), and this novel, about a New Orleans department store detective who takes to the Mississippi River in search of a missing child, is a picaresque tale with deep insight into the human desire to fill in our missing parts.

GILCHRIST, ELLEN

In the Land of Dreamy Dreams. Fayetteville: University of Arkansas Press, 1981.

Gilchrist's short stories are brilliant evocations of upper-class life in New Orleans, drawing on her own history here. (She now divides her time between Fayetteville, Arkansas, and Ocean Springs, Mississippi.)

MARTIN, VALERIE

The Great Divorce. New York: Nan A. Talese/Doubleday, 1994.

Martin's best-known work is *Mary Reilly* (1990), a historical novel in which Dr. Jekyll's housemaid is the main character; it was made into a movie starring Julia Roberts in the title role. This underappreciated novel is her version of the story of "Cat People" with a New Orleans setting.

PIAZZA, TOM

City of Refuge. New York: HarperCollins, 2008.

Piazza, also the author of the post-Katrina classic *Why New Orleans Matters*, threw himself into this novel about two families, one white, one African American, and their experiences in the year following Katrina. It was selected for the 2008 One Book / One New Orleans reading initiative.

WILTZ, CHRISTINE

Glass House. Baton Rouge: Louisiana State University Press, 1994.

Christine Wiltz, a New Orleans native, is the author of this literary novel about race relations, three mystery novels featuring Irish Channel detective Neal Rafferty, as well as a biography of New Orleans's last celebrated madam, Norma Wallace, *The Last Madam: A Life in the New Orleans Underworld* (2000). This novel is an unflinching look at race relations in New Orleans.

FICTION—A SURVEY

ALGREN, NELSON
A Walk on the Wild Side. New York: Farrar, Straus & Cudahy, 1956.

Nelson Algren (1909–81) set this picaresque novel in 1930s New Orleans, and its portrayal of the bohemian life is partly responsible for the city's reputation for wickedness. Drifter Dove Linkhorn called New Orleans "the town of the poor-boy sandwich and chicory coffee, where garlic hangs on strings and truckers sleep in their trucks. Where mailmen wore pith helmets and the people burned red candles all night long in old fashioned-lamps."

BARTON, FREDRICK
With Extreme Prejudice. New York: Villard Books, 1993.

Barton, who directs the creative writing program at the University of New Orleans and is the former film critic for *Gambit Weekly,* offers a thriller about a film critic trying to solve his wife's murder.

A New Orleans native, Barton is the author of two other novels—*The El Cholo Feeling Passes* (1985) and *Courting Pandemonium* (1986)—as well as an essay collection, *Rowing to Sweden* (2009), and the musical play *Ash Wednesday,* with composer Jay Weigel.

BATTLE, LOIS
Storyville. New York: Viking, 1993.

Inspired by E. J. Bellocq's photographs of the women of Storyville, Battle's novel weaves the lives of two women, one a Garden District lady, the other a Storyville madam, told during the height of fame of the red-light district.

BERRY, JASON
Last of the Red Hot Poppas. Seattle: Chin Music Press, 2006.

A wonderful spiritual comedy set in the world of Louisiana politics. Berry, a New Orleans native, does it all—music writing (he is the author of *Up from the Cradle of Jazz* [1986]), fiction, cultural coverage (*The Spirit of Black Hawk* [1995]), drama (*Earl Long in Purgatory* [2011]), and hard-hitting journalism. He is perhaps best known for his investigative coverage of corruption in the Catholic Church: *Lead Us Not into Temptation: Catholic Priests and the Sexual*

Abuse of Children (2000) and *Render unto Rome: The Secret Life of Money in the Catholic Church* (2011).

BIGUENET, JOHN
Oyster. New York: Ecco/HarperCollins, 2002.
Rising Water. Play, premiered in 2006.
Shotgun. Play, premiered in 2009.

Rising Water, Shotgun, and *Mold* constitute Biguenet's post-Katrina trilogy. *Oyster* is a fascinating tale of feuding families and star-crossed lovers on the coast.

BLACKWELL, ELISE
The Unnatural History of Cypress Parish. Denver, Colo.: Unbridled Books, 2007.

A novel about an old man remembering the flood of 1927 as he awaits the arrival of Hurricane Katrina.

BOLL, ANDREA
And the Parade Goes On without You. New Orleans: NOLAFugees, 2009.

A vibrant first novel set in the second-line culture.

BRADLEY, JOHN ED
My Juliet. New York: Doubleday, 2000.
Restoration. New York: Doubleday, 2003.

Bradley is an Opelousas, Louisiana, native, who was a football star at LSU and later became a journalist at the *Washington Post* and a contributing editor for *Esquire* magazine. His novels draw on his life's experiences in football and journalism and, in *Restoration,* his experience as an art collector.

BRITE, POPPY Z.
Drawing Blood. New York: Delacorte, 1993.
Exquisite Corpse. New York: Simon & Schuster, 1996.
Lost Souls. New York: Delacorte, 1992.

Brite (now known as Billy Martin), a New Orleans native, is known for her distinctive Gothic and horror novels. Brite/Martin is also the author of several mysteries featuring two rising-star New Orleans chefs—including *Liquor* (2004) and *Prime* (2005)—as well as a 1998 biography of rock star and actress Courtney Love.

BROWN, JOHN GREGORY

Audubon's Watch. Boston: Houghton Mifflin, 2001.
Decorations in a Ruined Cemetery. Boston: Houghton Mifflin, 1994.
The Wrecked, Blessed Body of Shelton Lafleur. Boston: Houghton Mifflin, 1996.

Brown, a native New Orleanian, grew up in a large Catholic family in New Orleans and attended Tulane. He is the author of three gorgeous historical novels set in New Orleans that explore family conflict, Catholicism, and racial dilemmas. He and his wife, novelist Carrie Brown, live in Virginia, where they teach at Sweet Briar College.

BUTLER, ROBERT OLEN

A Small Hotel. New York: Grove Press, 2011.

The story of a marriage coming apart, set partly in the Olivier House in the Quarter.

CABLE, GEORGE WASHINGTON

The Grandissimes. New York: Scribner's, 1880, revised 1883.
Old Creole Days. New York: Scribner's, 1879.
Strange True Stories of Louisiana. New York: Scribner's, 1889.

Cable criticized the racism in Creole society, which eventually made him quite unpopular in New Orleans society. Several of his short stories, most notably "'Tite Poulette" and "'Sieur George," are associated with the French Quarter's historic buildings.

CAPOTE, TRUMAN

A Christmas Memory. New York: Random House, 1966.
The Complete Stories of Truman Capote. With an introduction by Reynolds Price. New York: Random House, 2004.
Music for Chameleons. New York: Random House, 1980.
One Christmas. New York: Random House, 1983.
Other Voices, Other Rooms. New York: Random House, 1948. Reissued in 2009 with a new introduction by John Berendt.
The Thanksgiving Visitor. New York: Random House, 1968.

Of course, Capote's masterpiece, *In Cold Blood* (1966), told a true story of a murder in Kansas. But Capote took a Louisiana plantation as the setting for *Other Voices, Other Rooms,* and *One Christmas* is set in New Orleans. One of his most memorable short stories is "Dazzle," in which an eight-year-old Garden District boy confesses his longing to be a girl.

CAPPS, RONALD EVERETT
Off Magazine Street. San Francisco: MacAdam/Cage, 2004.

This debut novel was the basis for the film *A Love Song for Bobby Long.* Capps is the father of New Orleans musician Grayson Capps.

CHOPIN, KATE
The Awakening. Chicago: H. S. Stone, 1899.
The Complete Works of Kate Chopin. Edited by Per Seyersted. Baton Rouge: Louisiana State University Press, 1969.
Kate Chopin: Complete Novels and Stories. New York: Library of America, 2002.

Finally recognized as an American classic, Chopin's best-known novel, *The Awakening,* is the story of a woman coming to terms with her desires.

CODRESCU, ANDREI
Messiah. New York: Simon & Schuster, 1999.

I love this book, in which Codrescu imagines a millennial Mardi Gras apocalypse with ghosts and humans. Dante is a policeman, Karl Marx works for the Sewerage and Water Board, and Nostradamus is a waiter at the Napoleon House.

CORRINGTON, JOHN WILLIAM
The Collected Stories of John William Corrington. Columbia: University of Missouri Press, 1989.

Corrington, a literary writer and screenwriter, is the author of several novels; his short stories were published posthumously.

CRONE, MOIRA
Dream State. Jackson: University Press of Mississippi, 1995.
The Not Yet. New Orleans: University of New Orleans Press, 2012.

Crone, a North Carolina native, is also the author of *The Winne-bago Mysteries* (1982), *A Period of Confinement* (1987), *The Life of Lucy Fern* (1988), and *What Gets into Us* (2006). She taps into the otherworldly quality of Louisiana with these wonderful stories, many set in New Orleans. And *The Not Yet* offers a futuristic vision of the city, drowned and socially striated, through the character of a young man who must consider whether to seek new opportunities for life extension.

DAVIS, ALBERT BELISLE

Leechtime: A Novel. Baton Rouge: Louisiana State University Press, 1989.

Marquis at Bay: A Novel. Baton Rouge: Louisiana State University Press, 1992.

Davis, a poet and novelist, teaches English and creative writing at Nicholls State University in Thibodaux. These are the first two novels in his projected "Mondebon" trilogy, about life on the bayou and in New Orleans.

DEWBERRY, ELIZABETH

Sacrament of Lies. New York: BlueHen, 2002.

A novel about political corruption in Louisiana told from the point of view of a Louisiana governor's daughter.

DOS PASSOS, JOHN

The Forty-Second Parallel. New York: Harcourt, 1937.

A volume in the *USA* trilogy. Dos Passos also worked on *Manhattan Transfer* while living here.

DUBUS, ANDRE

Selected Stories. Boston: David R. Godine, 1988.

Dubus, a Louisiana native who lived and wrote largely in Massachusetts, received both a MacArthur "genius grant" and the Rea Award for the Short Story. Only a few of his works are set in Louisiana, but every story is a gem.

DURHAM, FRANK

Cain's Version. Nashville: Turner Publishing, 2008.

A small-town Louisiana version of the Cain and Abel story. Durham was a Tulane University professor of physics and a member of the Fellowship of Southern Writers.

EDWARDS, LOUIS

N: A Romantic Mystery. New York: Dutton, 1997.
Oscar Wilde Discovers America. New York: Scribner, 2003.
Ten Seconds. St. Paul, Minn.: Graywolf Press, 1991.

Edwards, a Lake Charles native who now lives in New Orleans and works for the New Orleans Jazz and Heritage Festival, made a great debut with *Ten Seconds,* about a moment in one young African American male's life. In *N,* rooted in the noir tradition, he explores the reasons for so many early deaths among young black men in New Orleans, a problem that continues to this day. His third novel, *Oscar Wilde Discovers America,* follows the great dramatist on his American tour, with a stop in New Orleans, and is told in the voice of Wilde's African American valet.

EFFINGER, GEORGE ALEC

George Alec Effinger Live! From Planet Earth. Urbana, Ill.: Golden Gryphon Press, 2005.

A short story collection by the science fiction writer who won both the Hugo and the Nebula awards.

EHRHARDT, PIA Z.

Famous Fathers and Other Stories. San Francisco: MacAdam/Cage, 2007.

Wonderfully crisp stories set in contemporary New Orleans by the winner of the 2005 Narrative Prize.

FAULKNER, WILLIAM

Absalom, Absalom! New York: Random House, 1936.
Mosquitoes. New York: Boni & Liveright, 1927.
New Orleans Sketches. With an introduction by Carvel Collins. New Brunswick, N.J.: Rutgers University Press, 1958.
Pylon. New York: H. Smith & R. Haas, 1935.
The Wild Palms. New York: Random House, 1939.

Faulkner's brief time in the city was transformative, and the newspaper provided him with steady work at the beginning of his career.

FRIEDMANN, PATTY

Eleanor Rushing. Washington, D.C.: Counterpoint, 1999.
The Exact Image of Mother. New York: Viking, 1991.
A Little Bit Ruined. Washington, D.C.: Counterpoint, 2007.
No Takebacks. Philadelphia: Tiny Satchel Press, 2012.
Odds. Washington, D.C.: Counterpoint, 2000.
Second Hand Smoke. Washington, D.C.: Counterpoint, 2002.

Friedmann, a New Orleans native, writes acerbic, bitterly funny—
and often autobiographical—novels about contemporary Jewish
life in Uptown New Orleans.

GAUTREAUX, TIM

The Clearing. New York: Knopf, 2003.
The Missing. New York: Knopf, 2009.
The Next Step in the Dance. New York: Picador, 1998.
Same Place, Same Things. New York: St. Martin's, 1996.
Welding with Children. New York: Picador, 1999.

Gautreaux, a Louisiana native, brings his sly wit and observant eye
to the essence of small-town Louisiana family life and the disastrous results of the oil bust in the 1980s. *The Missing* is a historical
novel set along the Mississippi in the riverboat days.

GILCHRIST, ELLEN

Collected Stories. Boston: Little, Brown, 2000.
In the Land of Dreamy Dreams. Fayetteville: University of Arkansas
     Press, 1981.
Victory over Japan. Boston: Little, Brown, 1984.

Gilchrist, author of far too many story collections and journals to
list here, won the National Book Award for *Victory over Japan.* One
of her recurring characters, Rhoda, is named for former New Orleans bookseller Rhoda Faust.

Gilchrist moved to the city in 1968. She wrote articles for the
Vieux Carré Courier and then established an abiding friendship
with Faust, then owner of the Maple Street Book Shop. Faust published Gilchrist's second book of poems, *Riding Out the Tropical
Depression,* in 1986. Gilchrist's New Orleans landscape is highly
recognizable to local readers, whether it's the jogging track around
Audubon Park where her characters work out or the buildings at

Tulane where they go to class or the mansions on St. Charles Avenue or State Street where they live. "I think of myself as a New Orleans writer even if I'm not actually there," she said in an interview. Most New Orleanians think of her as a New Orleans writer too.

GRAU, SHIRLEY ANN

The House on Coliseum Street. New York: Knopf, 1964.
The Keepers of the House. New York: Knopf, 1964.
Nine Women. New York: Knopf, 1985.
Roadwalkers. New York: Knopf, 1994.

Grau's short stories and novels treat the grand southern themes of race and family. She won the 1965 Pulitzer Prize for *The Keepers of the House.*

Grau shared a French Quarter apartment with her college roommate, Mary Rohrberger, at 921 Chartres after leaving Newcomb, before her marriage to James K. Feibleman and move to old Metairie.

HARPER, M. A.

For the Love of Robert E. Lee. New York: Soho Press, 1992.
The Worst Day of My Life, So Far: My Mother, Alzheimer's, and Me: A Novel. Athens, Ga.: Hill Street Press, 2001.
The Year of Past Things. Athens, Ga.: Hill Street Press, 2003.

Harper writes funny, observant novels about southern women in impossible situations.

HICKS, ROBERT

A Separate Country: A Story of Redemption in the Aftermath of the Civil War. New York: Grand Central Publishing, 2009.

This wonderful historical novel is centered on the life of Confederate general John Bell Hood in post–Civil War New Orleans.

HORACK, SKIP

The Southern Cross. Boston: Mariner/Houghton Mifflin, 2009.

This brilliant debut collection of short stories has Katrina at its heart, but the stories are equally divided into before and after.

JACKSON, BRIAN KEITH

Walking through Mirrors. New York: Pocket Books, 1999.

This New Orleans native moved to the Big Apple in 1990; he has had two plays produced by Theater for the New City. In 1997 he turned to novel writing with *The View from Here,* set in Mississippi in the 1930s, and followed that up with *Walking through Mirrors,* set in contemporary Louisiana.

JOHNSON, BARB

More of This World or Maybe Another. New York: Harper Perennial, 2009.

This book is composed of linked short stories, some of which are set in Mid-City, where Johnson lives. Johnson worked as a carpenter in New Orleans for more than twenty years before entering the MFA program at the University of New Orleans in 2004. She completed her MFA in 2008, and in 2009 she became the fifth recipient of A Room of Her Own Foundation's $50,000 Gift of Freedom Award, a two-year writing grant. Most of the stories in *More of This World or Maybe Another* were written in 2005, during long nights of sitting on her balcony on Dumaine Street in the post-Katrina landscape, waving off the National Guard patrols, spending her days "trying to make the neighborhood better and trying to find some Wi-Fi."

JOHNSON, DEDRA

Sandrine's Letter to Tomorrow. Brooklyn, N.Y.: IG Publishing, 2007.

A debut novel about a light-skinned African American girl growing up in 1970s New Orleans.

KEYES, FRANCES PARKINSON

Crescent Carnival. New York: Messner, 1942.
Dinner at Antoine's. New York: Messner, 1948.

These are two of the best known of Keyes's historical romances, and dated they are, but with a certain charm of their own. Keyes was also the author of *All This Is Louisiana* (1950), a state history with wonderful photos; she also wrote religious biographies, a cookbook, and *Cost of a Best Seller* (1953), a charming memoir.

KING, GRACE

Balcony Stories. New York: Century, 1893.
Monsieur Motte. New York: A. C. Armstrong and Sons, 1888.

King is also the author of *New Orleans: The Place and the People* (1895) and *Tales of a Time and Place* (1892). Her autobiography, *Memories of a Southern Woman of Letters* (1932), gives a sense of how important she was to the literary life of her time.

LAGASSE, MARY HELEN

The Fifth Sun. Willimantic, Conn.: Curbstone, 2004.

This novel about the lives of Mexican immigrants in New Orleans won the third annual Marmol Prize for a first work of fiction by a Latina writer.

LEMANN, NANCY

The Fiery Pantheon. New York: Scribner's 1998.
Lives of the Saints. New York: Knopf, 1985.
Sportsman's Paradise. New York: Knopf, 1992.

Lemann writes dreamy, almost incantatory novels of southern women falling in and out of love. Also notable is *The Ritz of the Bayou*, a nonfiction work about the first corruption trial of former Louisiana governor Edwin Edwards. (The hotel of the title is Alexandria's Bentley Hotel.)

MAISTROS, LOUIS

The Sound of Building Coffins. New Milford, Conn.: Toby Press, 2009.

Maistros conjures a demonic struggle and the birth of jazz in an otherworldly depiction of New Orleans in 1891.

MARTIN, VALERIE

Alexandria. New York: Farrar, Straus & Giroux, 1979.
The Consolation of Nature and Other Stories. Boston: Houghton Mifflin, 1988.
Love: Short Stories. Amherst: Lynx House, 1976.
Property. New York: Nan A. Talese/Doubleday, 2003.
A Recent Martyr. Boston: Houghton Mifflin, 1987.
Set in Motion. New York: Farrar, Straus & Giroux, 1978.
Trespass. New York: Nan A. Talese/Doubleday, 2007.

Martin's *Property*, a chilling exploration of the effects of slavery on slave owners, won the Orange Prize in 2003. *The Consolation of Nature* and *A Recent Martyr* are two of the most evocative short story collections set in New Orleans, envisioning the city under plague, overrun by nature.

Martin has lived all over New Orleans, from Uptown to the Lakefront to Metairie to the Quarter to the Ninth Ward. She says that it has given her "a sense of nature as both very seductive and very malignant. It's attractive and dangerous. And the city has given me an appreciation for corruption . . . It doesn't change at all. It never changes."

MELMAN, PETER CHARLES

Landsman. New York: Counterpoint, 2007.

A beautiful atmospheric novel about the experiences of a Jewish Confederate during the Civil War.

MILLER, JOHN, and GENEVIEVE ANDERSON, EDS.

New Orleans Stories: Great Writers on the City. San Francisco: Chronicle Books, 1992.

This wonderful anthology offers reading by authors ranging from Twain to Toole, Rice to Thackeray. This is a good sampler of writing about the city.

NERO, CLARENCE

Cheekie: A Child Out of the Desire. Tulsa: Council Oak Books, 1998.

Nero grew up in the notorious Desire housing development, and this autographical tale describes the coming of age of an insouciant young boy. Although it was originally published as a book for young readers, it includes graphic sex scenes and language.

NOLAN, JAMES

Higher Ground: A Novel. Lafayette: University of Louisiana at Lafayette Press, 2011.

Perpetual Care: Stories. Lookout Mountain, Tenn.: Jefferson Press, 2008.

Nolan, a New Orleans native, is a longtime teacher of writing at Loyola University and now at the Arts Council. He is also a poet, translator, and essayist.

O. HENRY

The Collected Stories of O. Henry. Mattituck, N.Y.: American Ltd., 1986.

"Blind Man's Holiday," "Cherchez la Femme," "Renaissance at Charleroi," and "Whistling Dick's Christmas Stocking" are the O. Henry stories with New Orleans settings.

ONDAATJE, MICHAEL

Coming through Slaughter. New York: Norton, 1976.

This impressionistic, lyrical novel centers on the mysterious life of the famous musician Buddy Bolden. Despite many historical inaccuracies, it is still a lovely book.

PASCHAL, DEAN

By the Light of the Jukebox. Princeton, N.J.: Ontario Review Press, 2002.

This is an amazing and very spooky debut collection of short fiction by an emergency room physician.

PERCY, WALKER

Lancelot. New York: Farrar, Straus & Giroux, 1977.
The Last Gentleman. New York: Farrar, Straus & Giroux, 1966.
Love in the Ruins. New York: Farrar, Straus & Giroux, 1971.
The Message in the Bottle. New York: Farrar, Straus & Giroux, 1975.
The Second Coming. New York: Farrar, Straus & Giroux, 1980.
The Thanatos Syndrome. New York: Farrar, Straus & Giroux, 1987.

Percy's novels, complex and philosophical, are explorations of the ongoing struggle between faith and doubt as well as landmarks of the sensibility of the New South. His struggle against despair and illness and toward an authentic Catholic faith struck a responsive chord with a large and fervently devoted readership. *The Moviegoer* (1961) is one of the novels most strongly associated with New Orleans, and Percy tapped into an entire generation's angst when he articulated Binx Bolling's devotion to "the search." In his later years, writing in *The Message in the Bottle* and *Lost in the Cosmos: The Last Self-Help Book* (1983), Percy began to articulate a philosophy of language, asserting that it lies at the very heart of our humanity.

PORTER, KATHERINE ANNE
Collected Stories of Katherine Anne Porter. New York: Harcourt Brace, 1979.
Letters of Katherine Anne Porter. New York: Grove-Atlantic, 1981.

Porter is primarily regarded as a Texas writer, but her time in New Orleans was obviously important to her. She married Albert Erskine here and lived in the Pontalba building.

PORTER, WILLIAM SYDNEY
See O. Henry.

POUSSON, MARTIN
No Place, Louisiana. New York: Riverhead Books, 2002.

An autobiographical novel about growing up gay in small-town Louisiana.

RECHY, JOHN
City of Night. Grove-Atlantic, 1988.

Part of this novel about a homosexual hustler takes place during Mardi Gras.

RHODES, JEWELL PARKER
Voodoo Dreams: A Novel of Marie Laveau. New York: St. Martin's, 1993.
Voodoo Season. New York: Atria Books, 2005.
Yellow Moon. New York: Atria Books, 2008.

Rhodes sets a trilogy in the world of contemporary voodoo in New Orleans.

RICE, ANNE
Series:
Lives of the Mayfair Witches, 1990–94.
New Tales of the Vampires, 1998–99.
The Vampire Chronicles, 1976–2003.

Rice has had a long and varied writing career. It began with the publication of *Interview with the Vampire* in 1976. Her vampires— seductive, worldly, talkative characters—struggled with great questions of morality and immortality; they struck a chord with anyone who has ever felt like an outsider. Later Rice expanded her fictional landscape by creating a New Orleans family of witches called the Mayfairs, which continued for several volumes.

She said that she wrote the Roquelaure books when she couldn't find the kind of pornography that she wanted to read, but most readers will find them fairly conventional. The Anne Rampling books are mainstream contemporary novels, written in what Rice called "her American voice." *Belinda* is a particularly revealing book about what it means to an artist to tell the truth about his work.

Rice has also periodically turned to historical fiction: *The Feast of All Saints* is a novel about the free people of color in New Orleans, and *Cry to Heaven* is a story of the Italian castrati. *Violin,* set in New Orleans, is a highly autobiographical novel about Rice's difficult childhood, set in the house on St. Charles Avenue where she grew up. After the death of her husband, Stan, Rice moved first to a gated community in Kenner, then to California to be near her son, Christopher. She returned for a time to the Catholic Church and wrote several novels fictionalizing the life of Christ. Then, taking a new turn, she began a series of supernatural thrillers featuring angels. A recent book, *The Wolf Gift,* reinvents the myth of the werewolf.

BEST-SELLING WRITERS

Nevada Barr

James Lee Burke

James Carville

Ellen DeGeneres

Walter Isaacson

Nicholas Lemann

Michael Lewis

Laura Lippman

Anne Rice

Cokie Roberts

David Simon

Julie Smith

Erica Spindler

ROBBINS, TOM

Jitterbug Perfume. New York: Bantam, 1984.

The one thing visitors notice immediately is that New Orleans is filled with distinctive scents—seafood frying, coffee roasting, night jasmine, sweet olive, and several less pleasant ones we won't mention here. Robbins makes the most of this olfactory landscape in his charming novel, and you can visit Hové Parfumeur at 434 Chartres for a whiff of the inspiration he found here.

SANCTON, THOMAS

By Starlight. Garden City, N.Y.: Doubleday, 1960.
Count Roller Skates. Garden City, N.Y.: Doubleday, 1956.

These two charming novels by a New Orleans native and a reporter for the *New Orleans Item* capture the underworld of the 1930s and 1940s. In a copy of *Count Roller Skates,* inscribed in May 1971, Sancton wrote. "I look back on those blocks of Canal Street, from 'Carl'ton to the Cemeteries,' in the 1920s and 1930s, as a wondrous imperishable village which had all the elements of the Great Globe itself, and all the human types by which I judged all others through life."

SPENCER, ELIZABETH

The Snare. New York: McGraw-Hill, 1972.

In this novel Spencer draws on her long familiarity with the city to create a young heroine, Julia Garrett, who finds herself drawn to the dark side of New Orleans. New Orleans itself is the snare of the title.

STONE, ROBERT

A Hall of Mirrors. Boston: Houghton Mifflin, 1967.

This novel, about a down-on-his-luck disk jockey named Rheinhardt, trying to get by in the New Orleans of the 1960s, was nominated for a PEN/Faulkner Award and was later made into the movie *WUSA.* Stone touched on his time in New Orleans in the 1960s in his memoir, *Prime Green.*

STRAIGHT, SUSAN

A Million Nightingales. New York: Pantheon, 2006.
Take One Candle Light a Room. New York: Pantheon, 2010.

A Million Nightingales is a lyrical novel about a Louisiana slave girl's quest for freedom, and *Take One Candle Light a Room* is a contemporary novel set partly in Louisiana.

TRAVIS, JOHN, ED.

Something in the Water. New Orleans: Portals Publishing, 2011.

Travis, who has published a wonderful amount of New Orleans poetry, here gathers twenty Louisiana stories from a variety of writers.

TWAIN, MARK

Life on the Mississippi. Boston: J. R. Osgood, 1883.

The classic of river life.

VERNON, OLYMPIA

Eden. New York: Grove, 2003.
A Killing in This Town. New York: Grove, 2006.
Logic. New York: Grove, 2004.

Vernon, a former New Orleanian, is one of the brightest stars in African American writing, with a distinctive voice and language all her own; she studied creative writing at LSU.

WELLS, KEN

Crawfish Mountain. New York: Random House, 2007.
Junior's Leg. New York: Random House, 2001.
Meely Labauve. New York: Random House, 2000.

Wells, an editor at the *Wall Street Journal,* writes wonderful comic capers—usually with an environmental message—set near his native Bayou Black.

WELLS, REBECCA

Divine Secrets of the Ya-Ya Sisterhood. New York: HarperCollins, 1996.
Little Altars Everywhere. Seattle: Broken Moon Press, 1992.
Ya-Yas in Bloom. New York: HarperCollins, 2005.

Wells, from Alexandria, Louisiana, writes about strong southern women. She won the Western States Book Award for *Little Altars Everywhere.* The best-selling *Divine Secrets of the Ya-Ya Sisterhood,* about lifelong female friends, inspired Ya-Ya groups around the country and a best-selling movie starring Sandra Bullock and Ashley Judd.

WYSS, GEOFF

How: Stories. Columbus: Ohio State University Press, 2012.

A wonderful debut collection of short stories, many set in a Catholic school in New Orleans; the author is a teacher.

ZIGAL, THOMAS

The White League. New Milford, Conn.: Toby Press, 2005.

A novel about the way the city's racist history echoes into the present.

MYSTERIES AND THRILLERS–THE BEST SERIES

ATKINS, ACE

Crossroad Blues. New York: St. Martin's Press, 1998.
The Dark End of the Street. New York: William Morrow, 2002.
Dirty South. New York: William Morrow, 2004.
Leavin' Trunk Blues. New York: Thomas Dunne Books, 2000.

Ace Atkins has a huge local following for his series featuring Nick Travers, an ex–New Orleans Saint turned Tulane University blues historian.

BARR, NEVADA

13½. New York: Vanguard Press, 2009.
Burn. New York: Minotaur Books, 2010.

Nevada Barr is the author of the Anna Pigeon series, each one set in a different state park. In *Burn* she finally makes it to Louisiana, and her stand-alone *13½* is also set in New Orleans.

Nevada Barr at Octavia Books
Photo by Tom Lowenburg

RECIPIENTS OF THE LOUISIANA WRITER AWARD
(presented at the Louisiana Book Festival beginning in 2002)

John Biguenet, 2012

James Wilcox, 2011

Valerie Martin, 2010

Tim Gautreaux, 2009

William Joyce, 2008

Yusef Komunyakaa, 2007

Elmore Leonard, 2006

Shirley Ann Grau, 2004

Carl Brasseaux, 2003

James Lee Burke, 2002

William J. Smith, 2001

Ernest Gaines, 2000

BURKE, JAMES LEE
Black Cherry Blues. Boston: Little, Brown, 1989.
Burning Angel. New York: Hyperion, 1995.
Cadillac Jukebox. New York: Hyperion, 1996.
Creole Belle. New York: Simon & Schuster, 2012.
Crusader's Cross. New York: Simon & Schuster, 2005.
Dixie City Jam. New York: Hyperion, 1994.
The Glass Rainbow. New York: Simon & Schuster, 2010.
Heaven's Prisoners. New York: Henry Holt, 1988.
In the Electric Mist with Confederate Dead. New York: Hyperion, 1993.
Jolie Blon's Bounce. New York: Simon & Schuster, 2002.
Last Car to Elysian Fields. New York: Simon & Schuster, 2003.
A Morning for Flamingos. Boston: Little, Brown, 1990.
The Neon Rain. New York: Henry Holt, 1987.
Pegasus Descending. New York: Simon & Schuster, 2006.
Purple Cane Road. New York: Doubleday, 2000.
A Stained White Radiance. New York: Hyperion, 1992.
Sunset Limited. New York: Doubleday, 1998.
Swan Peak. New York: Simon & Schuster, 2008.
The Tin Roof Blowdown. New York: Simon & Schuster, 2007.

James Lee Burke is the creator of Cajun detective Dave Robicheaux, who is ensnared in an ongoing struggle against alcoholism and his own propensity for violence. Though Dave is based in New Iberia, his work frequently brings him to New Orleans, where he and his sidekick, Clete Purcel, have a reputation for wreaking havoc. Burke's *Tin Roof Blowdown* was one of the remarkable post-Katrina novels, and *Light of the World* was the twentieth novel in the series.

CORRINGTON, JOHN, and JOYCE CORRINGTON

A Civil Death. New York: Viking, 1987.
A Project Named Desire. New York: Viking, 1987.
So Small a Carnival. New York: Viking, 1986.
The White Zone. New York: Viking, 1990.

CORRINGTON, JOYCE

Fear of Dying. Charleston, S.C.: Createspace, 2011.

John and Joyce Corrington were partners in life and in writing until John's death in 1988. They collaborated on a mystery series featuring Rat Trap, an African American detective.

John Corrington grew up in Shreveport. He wrote novels, short stories, poetry, and screenplays. He taught English at Loyola University and Louisiana State University, and he received a law degree in 1975 and briefly practiced. He was important in the circles of the *New Orleans Review* and the Loujon Press (and had a tempestuous relationship with Charles Bukowski). His best-known works are the novel *And Wait for the Night* (1964), the short story collections *The Actes and Monuments* (1978) and *The Southern Reporter* (1981), and his collection of poetry *Lines to the South and Other Poems* (1965).

In the 1970s Corrington wrote scripts for such films as *Box Car Bertha* and *Battle for the Planet of the Apes.* He and Joyce also had a long career as scriptwriters for such soap operas as *General Hospital, Search for Tomorrow,* and *Texas.* For a time the Corringtons commuted between California and New Orleans but eventually settled out west; while in New Orleans they lived at 1724 Valence Street. Joyce Corrington returned to New Orleans after her husband's death and now lives Uptown. In 2012 she published the fifth in the Rat Trap series of mysteries, *Fear of Dying.*

DUNBAR, TONY

City of Beads. New York: Putnam, 1995.
Crime Czar. New York: Dell, 1998.
Crooked Man. New York: Putnam, 1994.

Lucky Man. New York: Dell, 1999.
Shelter from the Storm. New York: Putnam, 1997.
Trick Question. New York: Putnam, 1996.

Tony Dunbar is a New Orleans lawyer who draws on his legal experience for the Tubby Dubonnet series. Tubby's adventures in *City of Beads* make that book a true Mardi Gras classic. Dunbar is also the author of the 1990 memoir *Delta Time* and other works of commentary on southern politics and history. A graduate of Tulane Law School, he has lived here since 1978.

FULMER, DAVID

Chasing the Devil's Tail. Scottsdale, Ariz.: Poisoned Pen Press, 2001.
Jass. Orlando, Fla.: Harcourt, 2005.
Lost River. Boston: Houghton Mifflin, 2009.
Rampart Street. Orlando, Fla.: Harcourt, 2006.

David Fulmer lives in Atlanta but sets his mysteries featuring Valentin St. Cyr in the Storyville era.

GRAHAM, C. S.

The Archangel Project. New York: Harper, 2008.

C. S. Graham is one of the pseudonyms employed by Candice Proctor, who writes murder mysteries set in Regency England featuring a protagonist named Sebastian St. Cyr. With her husband, Steve Harris, Proctor, as C. S. Graham, writes contemporary thrillers that are often set in New Orleans.

GRAN, SARA

Claire DeWitt and the City of the Dead. Boston: Houghton Mifflin, 2011.

Sara Gran is a former New Orleanian—also the author of *Come Closer, Dope,* and *Saturn's Return to New York*—who began a new series with *Claire DeWitt and the City of the Dead*, a remarkably otherworldly series with an unforgettable heroine.

HAMBLY, BARBARA

Days of the Dead. New York: Bantam Books, 2003.
Dead and Buried. Surrey, UK: Severn House, 2010.
Dead Water. New York: Bantam Books, 2004.

Die upon a Kiss. New York: Bantam Books, 2001.
Fever Season. New York: Bantam Books, 1998.
A Free Man of Color. New York: Bantam Books, 1997.
Graveyard Dust. New York: Bantam Books, 1999.
Ran Away. Surrey, U.K.: Severn House, 2011.
The Shirt on His Back. Surrey, U.K.: Severn House, 2012.
Sold Down the River. New York: Bantam Books, 2000.
Wet Grave. New York: Bantam Books, 2002.

Barbara Hambly has written all kinds of novels, both historical and fantasy and science fiction (she was once married to noted science fiction author and New Orleanian George Alec Effinger), but as a New Orleans writer, she is best known for her Benjamin January series, which features a protagonist who is a free man of color.

HERREN, GREG

Bourbon Street Blues. New York: Kensington Books, 2003.
Jackson Square Jazz. New York: Kensington Books, 2004.
Mardi Gras Mambo. New York: Kensington Books, 2006.
Murder in the Garden District. Los Angeles: Alyson Books, 2009.
Murder in the Rue Chartres. Los Angeles: Alyson Books, 2007.
Murder in the Rue Dauphine. Los Angeles: Alyson Books, 2002.
Murder in the Rue St. Ann. Los Angeles: Alyson Books, 2004.

Greg Herren works for the NO/AIDS Task Force by day and writes every other minute. He celebrates gay life in New Orleans with his two series featuring detectives Scotty Bradley and Chanse McLeod.

REDMANN, J. M.

Death by the Riverside. Norwich, Vt.: New Victoria Publishers, 1990.
Deaths of Jocasta. Norwich, Vt.: New Victoria Publishers, 1992.
The Intersection of Law and Desire. New York: Norton, 1995.
Lost Daughters. New York: Norton, 1999.
Water Mark. Valley Falls, N.Y.: Bold Strokes Books, 2010.

Jean Redmann grew up in Ocean Springs, Mississippi, and moved to New Orleans in 1989. By day she works for the NO/AIDS Task Force as the director of prevention, and in her spare time she writes a mystery series featuring lesbian detective Mickey Knight. *Deaths of Jocasta* was nominated for the prestigious Lambda Literary Award in 1982. Her third book, *The Intersection of Law and Desire,* won the Lambda for best lesbian mystery. She lives in the Faubourg Marigny.

RICE, CHRISTOPHER

A Density of Souls. New York: Hyperion, 2000.

Rice follows in the footsteps of his writing parents, poet Stan and vampire novelist Anne, and writes contemporary thrillers. This one, his first, is set in New Orleans.

SALLIS, JAMES

Black Hornet. New York: Carroll & Graf, 1994.
Bluebottle. New York: Walker & Co., 1999.
Eye of the Cricket. New York: Walker & Co., 1997.
Ghost of a Flea. New York: Walker & Co., 2001.
The Long-Legged Fly. New York: Carroll & Graf, 1992.
Moth. New York: Carroll & Graf, 1993.

James Sallis lived for a time in New Orleans, when he began his wonderful literary series featuring protagonist Lew Griffin, an African American who's a literature professor at Tulane University.

SKINNER, ROBERT

Blood to Drink. Scottsdale, Ariz.: Poisoned Pen Press, 2000.
Cat-Eyed Trouble. New York: Kensington Books, 1998.
Daddy's Gone A-Hunting. Scottsdale, Ariz.: Poisoned Pen Press, 1999.
Pale Shadow. Scottsdale, Ariz.: Poisoned Pen Press, 2001.
The Righteous Cut. Scottsdale, Ariz.: Poisoned Pen Press, 2002.
Skin Deep, Blood Red. New York: Kensington Books, 1997.

Robert Skinner came to New Orleans in 1979; he has been the librarian at Xavier University since 1987 and coeditor of the *Xavier Review* since 1989. His novels, set in the 1930s, feature detective Wesley Farrell. Skinner is also a scholar of hard-boiled fiction and the work of Chester Himes, the African American detective novelist best known for *Cotton Comes to Harlem* (1965).

SMITH, JULIE

82 Desire. New York: Fawcett Columbine, 1998.
The Axeman's Jazz. New York: St. Martin's Press, 1991.
Crescent City Kill. New York: Fawcett Columbine, 1997.
House of Blues. New York: Fawcett Columbine, 1995.
Jazz Funeral. New York: Fawcett Columbine, 1993.
The Kindness of Strangers. New York: Fawcett Columbine, 1996.

Mean Woman Blues. New York: Forge, 2003.
New Orleans Beat. New York: Fawcett Columbine, 1994.
New Orleans Mourning. New York: St. Martin's Press, 1990.

Julie Smith is the creator of Skip Langdon, that New Orleans police detective who is larger than life and who lives outside conventional society mores, to the dismay of her Uptown parents. Smith won the Edgar Award for *New Orleans Mourning*, which centered on the murder of the King of Carnival. Smith came here after college and worked at the *Times-Picayune* for a year. She is also the editor of the landmark anthology *New Orleans Noir*. She has written more than twenty books, some for young readers, and runs her own e-book publishing company, booksbnimble.

Smith has lived in the Quarter as well as Uptown and now lives in the Faubourg Marigny. "In a lot of ways, New Orleans is the soul of my stories," she said. "It's a character as important as any of the human ones, and it's also an integral part of the soul of the human characters. Everywhere you turn, there it is, a kind of funky mortar sticking the story together."

SPINDLER, ERICA
Killer Takes All. Don Mills, Ont.: MIRA Books, 2005.
Last Known Victim. Detroit: Thorndike Press, 2007.

Erica Spindler began her career as a romance novelist but made a name for herself as the author of best-selling suspense novels. Though she lives in Mandeville, she frequently sets her work in New Orleans.

WILTZ, CHRISTINE
A Diamond before You Die. New York: Mysterious Press, 1987.
The Emerald Lizard. New York: Dutton, 1991.
The Killing Circle. New York: Macmillan, 1981.

Christine Wiltz has had a wide-ranging writing career in both fiction and nonfiction but got her start with the Neal Rafferty series featuring a detective based in the Irish Channel. In her fiction Wiltz has written about virtually every part of the city, from the French Quarter to the Garden District to the Westwego. She lives in Uptown New Orleans.

STATE POETS LAUREATE

Emma Wilson Emery [1942–70]

Ethel Green Russell [1970–73]

Dr. George William Noel Cooper [1973–76]

Henry Thomas Voltz [1976–80]

Jean McGivney Boese [1980–88]

Pinkie Gordon Lane [1988–92]

Sylvia Davison Lott Buckley [1992–96]

Jean McGivney Boese [1996–2004]

Brenda Marie Osbey [2005–7]

Darrell Bourque [2009–11]

Julie Kane [2011–13]

POETRY

Anthologies

The *Maple Leaf Rag* series, published by Portals Press, celebrates the longest-running poetry series in the South.

Individual Volumes

ADAMO, RALPH

The End of the World. Fayetteville, Ark.: Lost Roads, 1979.

Sadness at the Private University. Fayetteville, Ark.: Lost Roads, 1977.

Waterblind. New Orleans: Portals Press, 2002.

BOURQUE, DARRELL

The Blue Boat. Lafayette: Center for Louisiana Studies, 2004.

In Ordinary Light. Lafayette: University of Louisiana at Lafayette Press, 2010.

Bourque is a former state poet laureate.

BRINKS, DAVE

The Caveat Onus. Boston: Black Widow Press, 2009.

BROSMAN, CATHARINE

Breakwater. Macon, Ga.: Mercer University Press, 2009.

Journeying from Canyon de Chelly. Baton Rouge: Louisiana State University Press, 1990.

The Muscled Truce. Baton Rouge: Louisiana State University Press, 2003.

On the North Slope. Macon, Ga.: Mercer University Press, 2012.

Passages. Baton Rouge: Louisiana State University Press, 1996.

Places in Mind. Baton Rouge: Louisiana State University Press, 2000.

Under the Pergola. Baton Rouge: Louisiana State University Press, 2011.

Watering. Athens, Ga.: University of Georgia Press, 1972.

BURNS, MEGAN

Memorial + Sight Lines. New Orleans: Lavender Ink, 2008.

CASSIN, MAXINE

Against the Clock. New Orleans: Portals Press, 2003.
The Other Side of Sleep. New Orleans: Portals Press, 1995.
A Touch of Recognition. New York: AMS Press, 1962.
Turnip's Blood. Baton Rouge: Sisters Grim Press, 1985.

CHAMPAGNE, CHRIS

Roach Opera. New Orleans: Portals Press, 2007.

CHRISTIAN, MARCUS B., edited by RUDOLPH LEWIS and AMIN SHARIF

I Am New Orleans and Other Poems. New Orleans: Xavier University Press, 1999.

Born in Mechanicsville (now Houma), Louisiana, Christian (1900–1976) came to New Orleans when he was a teen and set about establishing a dry cleaning business and a printing press. He was a contributing poet and a reporter for the *Louisiana Weekly,* a black newspaper, when Lyle Saxon asked him to head the Negro Unit of the Louisiana Writers' Project in 1936. Christian's papers—more than a thousand poems as well as unpublished manuscripts on the history of black Louisiana—are in the archives at UNO's Earl K. Long Library. Christian wrote *The Negro Ironworkers of Louisiana, 1718–1900* (2002).

CODRESCU, ANDREI

It Was Today. Minneapolis: Coffee House Press, 2003.

Jealous Witness. Minneapolis: Coffee House Press, 2008.

So Recently Rent a World: New and Selected Poems, 1968–2012. Minneapolis: Coffee House Press, 2012.

Andrei Codrescu was born in Transylvania but has lived in the United States since 1966, and he lived in New Orleans for many years, commuting to his teaching job at LSU in Baton Rouge. He is known for his commentary on National Public Radio's *All Things Considered.* One of the city's most versatile writers, he is a poet, editor, essayist, and novelist, the author of more than twenty-five books.

COOLEY, NICOLE

The Afflicted Girls. Baton Rouge: Louisiana State University Press, 2004.

Breach. Baton Rouge: Louisiana State University Press, 2010.

Milk Dress. Farmington, Maine: Alice James Books, 2010.

Resurrection. Baton Rouge: Louisiana State University Press, 1996.

Nicole Cooley is the daughter of Tulane faculty member and poet Peter Cooley. She attended the New Orleans Center for Creative Arts and won the Walt Whitman Prize from the Academy of American Poets for her debut volume, *Resurrection.*

COOLEY, PETER

The Company of Strangers. Columbia, Mo.: University of Missouri Press, 1975.

Divine Margins. Pittsburgh: Carnegie-Mellon University Press, 2009.

Nightseasons. Pittsburgh: Carnegie-Mellon University Press, 1983.

A Place Made of Starlight. Pittsburgh: Carnegie-Mellon University Press, 2003.

The Room Where Summer Ends. Pittsburgh: Carnegie-Mellon University Press, 1979.

The Van Gogh Notebook. Pittsburgh: Carnegie Mellon University Press, 2004.

Peter Cooley came to the city in 1975 to teach at Tulane, where he can number among his students such writers as children's author-illustrator Berthe Amoss, novelist Ellen Gilchrist, and poets Susan Prospere, Katherine Soniat, and Eric Trethewey.

DAILEY, JOEL

Lower 48. New Orleans: Lavender Ink, 1998.

DENT, TOM

Blue Lights and River Songs. Detroit: Lotus Press, 1982.

Magnolia Street. New Orleans: Thomas C. Dent, 1976.

FERRARA, GINA

Ethereal Avalanche. New Orleans: Trembling Pillow Press, 2009.

FONTENOT, KEN

After the Days of Miami. Meraux, La.: Long Measure Press, 1980.

All My Animals and Stars. Austin: Slough Press, 1988.

GERY, JOHN

The Burning of New Orleans. Bakersfield, Calif.: Amelia, 1988.

Charlemagne: A Song of Gestures. Cerrillos, N.M.: Plumbers Ink Books, 1983.

Davenport's Version. New Orleans: Portals Press, 2003.

The Enemies of Leisure. Brownsville, Ore.: Story Line Press, 1995.

A Gallery of Ghosts. Ashland, Ore.: Story Line Press, 2005.

Gery teaches in the creative writing program at the University of New Orleans.

GRUE, LEE MEITZEN

Downtown. New Orleans: Trembling Pillow Press, 2011.

French Quarter Poems. N.p.: Long Measure Press, 1979.

Lee Meitzen Grue lives in a beautiful home in Bywater, the neighborhood between Faubourg Marigny and the Mississippi; for many years she hosted the meetings of the New Orleans Poetry Forum in a backyard theater. She edits the *New Laurel Review* and is also the author of a short story collection, *Goodbye, Silver, Silver Cloud.*

HARRIS, NANCY

The Ape Woman Story. Paradis, La.: Pirogue Publishing, 1989.

Mirror Wars. New Orleans: Portals Press; 1999.

Harris keeps the Maple Leaf Bar reading series running.

JACKSON, MAJOR
Holding Company. New York: Norton, 2010.
Hoops. New York: Norton, 2006.
Leaving Saturn. Athens, Ga.: University of Georgia Press, 2002.

KAMENETZ, RODGER
The Lowercase Jew. Evanston, Ill.: Northwestern University Press, 2003.
The Missing Jew. St. Louis, Mo.: Time Being Books, 1992.
Nympholepsy. Washington, D.C.: Dryad Press, 1985.
Stuck: Poems Midlife. St. Louis, Mo.: Time Being Books, 1997.

KANE, JULIE
The Bartender Poems. Chapbook. Emscote Lawn, Warwick, UK: Greville Press, 1991.
Body and Soul. Paradis, La.: Pirogue Publishing, 1987.
Jazz Funeral. West Chester, Pa.: Story Line Press, 2009.
Rhythm & Booze. Urbana: University of Illinois Press, 2003.
Two into One. With Ruth Adatia. London: Only Poetry Press, 1982.
Umpteen Ways of Looking at a Possum: Critical and Creative Responses to Everette Maddox. Edited with Grace Bauer. New Orleans: Xavier Review Press, 2006.

Julie Kane was the Louisiana poet laureate from 2011 through 2013.

KAUFMAN, BOB
Abomunist Manifesto. San Francisco: City Lights Books, 1959.
Cranial Guitar. Minneapolis: Coffee House Press, 1996.
Golden Sardine. San Francisco: City Lights Books, 1967.
Second April. San Francisco: City Lights Books, 1959.

KERWICK, DANIEL
Attach It to Earth. New Orleans: Foothills Publishing, 2011.

KOMUNYAKAA, YUSEF
Blue Notes: Essays, Interviews, and Commentaries. Ann Arbor: University of Michigan Press, 2000.
The Chameleon Couch. New York: Farrar, Straus & Giroux, 2011.
Copacetic. Middletown, Conn.: Wesleyan University Press, 1984.

Dien Cai Dau. Middletown, Conn.: Wesleyan University Press, 1988.
I Apologize for the Eyes in My Head. Middletown, Conn.: Wesleyan
    University Press, 1986.
Magic City. Middletown, Conn.: Wesleyan University Press, 1992.
Neon Vernacular. Middletown, Conn.: Wesleyan University Press,
    1993.
Pleasure Dome. Middletown, Conn.: Wesleyan University Press,
    2001.
Taboo. New York: Farrar, Straus & Giroux, 2004.
Talking Dirty to the Gods. New York: Farrar, Straus & Giroux, 2000.
Thieves of Paradise. Middletown, Conn.: Wesleyan University Press,
    2000.
Warhorses. New York: Farrar, Straus & Giroux, 2008.

Komunyakaa, the son of a carpenter, was born in Bogalusa, Louisiana, where he was raised during the beginning of the civil rights
movement. He served in the army from 1969 to 1970 as a correspondent and as managing editor of the *Southern Cross* during the
Vietnam War, earning him a Bronze Star. He is best known for
Thieves of Paradise (1998), which was a finalist for the National
Book Critics Circle Award; and *Neon Vernacular: New & Selected
Poems 1977–1989* (1994), for which he received the Pulitzer Prize
and the Kingsley Tufts Poetry Award. When he lived in New Or-
leans in the mid-1980s, he taught elementary grades in the New
Orleans public schools and English and poetry at the University of
New Orleans. His poems draw on his southern background and
Louisiana childhood as well as his experiences in the Vietnam War.

LAVENDER, BILL

A Field Guide to Trees. New Orleans: Foothills Publishing, 2011.
I of the Storm. New Orleans: Trembling Pillow Press, 2006.
Memory Wing. Boston: Black Widow, 2011.
Transfixion. New Orleans: Trembling Pillow Press, 2010.

Lavender is a stalwart of the New Orleans poetry scene and the
former director of the University of New Orleans Press.

MADDOX, EVERETTE

American Waste. New Orleans: Portals Press, 1993.
Bar Scotch. Paradis, La.: Pirogue Publishing, 1988.

I Hope It's Not Over, and Good-by: Selected Poems of Everette Maddox.
    Edited by Ralph Adamo. New Orleans: UNO Press, 2009.
Rette's Last Stand. Mobile, Ala.: Tensaw Press, 2004.
Songbook. New Orleans: New Orleans Poetry Journal Press, 1982.
The Thirteen Original Poems. New Orleans: Xavier University Press,
    1976.

Maddox, a native of Alabama who died in 1989, was a beloved
fixture of the Maple Leaf Bar scene.

McFERREN, MARTHA
Archaeology at Midnight. Montrose, Colo.: Pinyon, 2011.
Contours for Ritual. Baton Rouge: Louisiana State University Press,
    1988.
Women in Cars. Kansas City, Mo.: Helicon Nine Editions, 1992.

MULLEN, LAURA
After I Was Dead. Athens: University of Georgia Press, 1999.
Dark Archive. Berkeley: University of California Press, 2011.
Subject. Berkeley: University of California Press, 2005.
The Surface. Urbana: University of Illinois Press, 1991.

MURPHY, KAY
Autopsy. Peoria, Ill.: Spoon River Poetry Press, 1985.
Belief Blues. New Orleans: Portals Press, 1998.

NOLAN, JAMES
What Moves Is Not the Wind. Middletown, Conn.: Wesleyan Uni-
    versity Press, 1980.
Why I Live in the Forest. Middletown, Conn.: Wesleyan University
    Press, 1974.

OBRADOVIC, BILJANA
Frozen Embraces. Belgrade: Center of Emigrants from Serbia, 1997.

Obradovic teaches at Xavier University.

OSBEY, BRENDA MARIE
All Saints. Baton Rouge: Louisiana State University Press, 1997.
Ceremony for Minneconjoux. Lexington: University of Kentucky, 1983.

Desperate Circumstances, Dangerous Woman. Brownsville, Ore.: Story
    Line Press, 1991.

History and Other Poems. St. Louis: Time Being Books, 2012.

In These Houses. Middletown, Conn.: Wesleyan University Press,
    1988.

Osbey, a New Orleans native, has lived in Tremé and now lives in
Bayou St. John. *All Saints* received the 1998 American Book Award.
She is a former state poet laureate.

OSUNDARE, NIYI

City without People: The Katrina Poems. Boston: Black Widow Press,
    2011.

Pages from the Book of the Sun: New and Selected Poems. Trenton,
    N.J.: Africa World Press, 2002.

Niyi Osundare, born in western Nigeria, is Distinguished Professor
of English at the University of New Orleans. He is the author of
more than fifteen books of poetry, two books of selected poems, four
plays, two books of essays, and many scholarly articles and reviews.
In 2004 his book *The Eye of the Earth* was named "One of Nigeria's
Best 25 Books in the Past 25 Years." During the flood of 2005, Osundare and his wife were trapped in the attic of their Lakeview
home and had to be rescued by boat. He lost everything. In *City
without People: The Katrina Poems*, he draws on this experience.

PFISTER, ARTHUR

My Name Is New Orleans: 40 Years of Poetry and Other Jazz. Donald-
    sonville, La.: Margaret Media, 2009.

Pfister, who performs as Professor Arturo, is known for his epic
poem "I Am New Orleans."

PIERCE, VALENTINE

Geometry of the Heart. New Orleans: Portals Press, 2007.

RAMKE, BIN

Aerial. Richmond, Calif.: Omnidawn Publishers, 2012.

Airs, Waters, Places. Iowa City: University of Iowa Press, 2001.

The Difference between Night and Day. New Haven: Yale University
    Press, 1978.

The Erotic Light of Gardens. Middletown, Conn.: Wesleyan University Press, 1989.

The Language Student. Baton Rouge: Louisiana State University Press, 1986.

Massacre of the Innocents. Iowa City: University of Iowa Press, 1995.

Matter. Iowa City: University of Iowa Press, 2004.

Theory of Mind. Richmond, Calif.: Omnidawn Publishers, 2009.

Wake. Iowa City: University of Iowa Press, 1999.

White Monkeys. Athens: University of Georgia Press, 1981.

RICE, STAN

Body of Work. San Francisco: Lost Roads Publishers, 1983.

False Prophet. New York: Knopf, 2003.

Fear Itself. New York: Knopf, 1995.

The Radiance of Pigs. New York: Knopf, 1999.

Red to the Rind. New York: Knopf, 2002.

Singing Yet. New York: Knopf, 1992.

Whiteboy. Berkeley, Calif.: Mudra, 1976.

RICHARD, BRAD

Butcher's Sugar. Alexander, Ariz.: Sibling Rivalry Press, 2012.

Motion Studies. Washington, D.C.: Word Works, 2011.

Richard's wonderful poems in *Motion Studies* grew out of a study of Thomas Eakins's paintings. He directs the creative writing program at Lusher Charter High School.

ROBINSON, KYSHIA BROWN

Spherical Woman: Collected Poems. New Orleans: Runagate Multimedia, 2009.

ROWE, DAVID

Unsolicited Poems. New Orleans: Verna Press, 2010.

SALAAM, KALAMU YA

Iron Flowers: A Poetic Report on a Visit to Haiti. New Orleans: AHIDIANA/Habari, 1979.

Revolutionary Love. New Orleans: AHIDIANA/Habari, 1978.

Kalamu ya Salaam, born Vallery Ferdinand III, changed his name to the Swahili phrase meaning "pen of peace" in a 1970 Kwanzaa ceremony. A poet, dramatist, fiction writer, music critic, and teacher, Salaam is also the former executive director of the New Orleans Jazz and Heritage Festival Foundation and the former editor of *Black Collegian* magazine.

SALOY, MONA LISA
Red Beans and Ricely Yours. Kirksville, Mo.: Truman State University Press, 2005.

Saloy is professor of English and founder of the creative writing program at Dillard University. *Red Beans and Ricely Yours: Poems* won the PEN/Oakland Josephine Miles Prize and the T. S. Eliot Prize in poetry. She is probably the only writer in town who has the distinction of being an official folklorist for the National Football League, researching the origin of the phrase "Who Dat."

SINCLAIR, JOHN
Fattening Frogs for Snakes. New Orleans: Surregional Press, 2002.
Song of Praise: Homage to John Coltrane. New Orleans: Trembling Pillow Press, 2011.

SONIAT, KATHERINE
Alluvial. Lewisburg, Pa.: Bucknell University Press, 2001.
Cracking Eggs. Gainesville: University Press of Florida, 1999.
Notes of Departure. Camden, N.J.: Walt Whitman Center, 1985.
A Shared Life. Iowa City: University of Iowa Press, 1993.
The Swing Girl. Baton Rouge: Louisiana State University Press, 2012.
Winter Toys. Maryville, Mo.: Green Tower Press, 1989.

Soniat, a former New Orleanian, teaches writing at Hollins University in Virginia.

ST. GERMAIN, SHERYL
Let It Be a Dark Roux. Pittsburgh: Autumn House Press, 2007.

TRETHEWEY, NATASHA
Bellocq's Ophelia. Saint Paul, Minn.: Graywolf Press, 2002.
Native Guard. Boston: Mariner, 2007.
Thrall. New York: Houghton Mifflin, 2006.

Trethewey is the U.S. Poet Laureate and a Pulitzer Prize winner; her work has been inspired by Louisiana history. She is also the author of *Beyond Katrina: A Meditation on the Mississippi Gulf Coast* (2010).

YAKICH, MARK

The Importance of Peeling Potatoes in Ukraine. New York: Penguin
    Books, 2008.
The Making of Collateral Beauty. Dorset, Vt.: Tupelo Press, 2006.
Unrelated Individuals Forming a Group Waiting to Cross. New York:
    Penguin Books, 2004.

Yakich teaches at Loyola University and is an editor at the *New
Orleans Review.*

YOUNG, ANDY

All Fires the Fire. New Orleans: Faulkner House Books, 2003.
Mine. New Orleans: Lavender Ink, 2000.
The People Is Singular. New Orleans: Press Street, 2012.

Andy Young is the coeditor of *Meena.*

YOUNG, KEVIN

Black Maria: Being the Adventures of Delilah Redbone and A.K.A. Jones.
    New York: Knopf, 2005.
Dear Darkness. New York: Knopf, 2008.
For the Confederate Dead. New York: Knopf, 2007.
The Grey Album: On the Blackness of Blackness. St. Paul, Minn.: Gray-
    wolf Press, 2012.
Jelly Roll. New York: Knopf, 2003.

ZU-BOLTON, AHMOS

Ain't No Spring Chicken: Selected Poems. New Orleans: Voice Foun-
    dation, 1998.

Zu-Bolton was the founder of the Copacetic Bookstore.

CHILDREN'S PICTURE BOOKS

AMOSS, BERTHE

The Cajun Gingerbread Boy. New Orleans: Cocodrie Press, 2003.
The Three Little Cajun Pigs. New Orleans: MTC Press, 1999.

Berthe Amoss, a New Orleans native and the mother of six sons,
is a children's book writer and illustrator. She wrote a children's
literature column for the *Times-Picayune* and taught children's lit-

erature at Tulane University. She is the coauthor, with Eric Suben, of two books about the craft of writing and illustrating books for children.

ARTELL, MIKE

Jacques and de Beanstalk. Illustrated by Jim Harris. New York: Dial Books, 2010.

Three Little Cajun Pigs. Illustrated by Jim Harris. New York: Dial Books, 2006.

BASS, HESTER

The Secret World of Walter Anderson. Illustrated by E. B. Lewis. Cambridge, Mass.: Candlewick, 2009.

The life of the Mississippi artist, a New Orleans native, for young readers.

BRIDGES, RUBY

Through My Eyes: Ruby Bridges. New York: Scholastic, 1999.

Bridges, who now runs the Ruby Bridges Foundation, was the inspiration for the famous Norman Rockwell painting of school integration.

CASSELS, JEAN

Brer Rabbit Captured! A Dr. David Harleyson Adventure. New York: Walker & Co., 2007.

Twelve Days of Christmas in Louisiana. Illustrated by Lynne Avril. New York: Sterling, 2007.

COLES, ROBERT

The Story of Ruby Bridges. Illustrated by George Ford. New York: Scholastic, 2004.

DE LAS CASAS, DIANNE

The Cajun Cornbread Boy. Illustrated by Marita Gentry. Gretna, La.: Pelican Publishing, 2008.

Dinosaur Mardi Gras. Gretna, La.: Pelican Publishing, 2011.

Madame Poulet and Monsieur Roach. Gretna, La.: Pelican Publishing, 2009.

Mama's Bayou. Illustrated by Holly Stone-Barker. Gretna, La.: Pelican Publishing, 2010.

De Las Casas is the founder of National Storybook Month. Her website is storyconnection.net.

DOWNING, JOHNETTE
Chef Creole. Illustrated by Deborah Ousley Kadair. Gretna, La.: Pelican Publishing, 2008.
Down in Louisiana. Illustrated by Deborah Ousley Kadair. Gretna, La.: Pelican Publishing, 2007.
Today Is Monday in Louisiana. Illustrated by Deborah Ousley Kadair. Gretna, La.: Pelican Publishing, 2006.
Why the Crawfish Lives in the Mud. Illustrated by Deborah Ousley Kadair. Gretna, La.: Pelican Publishing, 2009.
Why the Oyster Has the Pearl. Illustrated by Bethanne Hill. Gretna, La.: Pelican Publishing, 2011.

Downing is an award-winning musician who has performed around the world. Her books are usually inspired by her music and by just-so stories.

EVANS, FREDDI
The Battle of New Orleans: The Drummer's Story. Illustrated by Emile Henriquez. Gretna, La.: Pelican Publishing, 2005.
A Bus of Our Own. Illustrated by Shawn Costello. Morton Grove, Ill.: Albert Whitman & Co., 2001.
Hush Harbor: Praying in Secret. Illustrated by Erin Bennett Banks. Minneapolis: Carolrhoda Books, 2008.

A very talented educator, Freddi Williams Evans draws from episodes in African American history to create her children's books.

FONTENOT, MARY ALICE
The Clovis Crawfish series. Gretna, La.: Pelican Publishing, 1961–2004.

The Eunice native created a world of swamp creatures in her books, some eighteen in all.

HARRISON, KENNETH
How I Became the Champion of the World. San Francisco: Tricycle Press, 2002.

An inspiring book about a young boy named Max.

JOYCE, WILLIAM
The Fantastic Flying Books of Mr. Morris Lessmore. New York: Atheneum, 2012.

Joyce is the author of more than fifty books for children, known for his joyful, elegant animation in film and on the page. This is the Shreveport artist's book that is most concerned with New Orleans, his tribute to the late storyteller Coleen Salley and to the role of story in the city's recovery from Hurricane Katrina. This story inspired his 2012 Oscar-winning film.

LANDRY, CORNELL P.
Good Night, NOLA. Illustrated by Louis J. Schmitt. New Orleans: Ampersand, 2009.
Happy Jazzfest. Illustrated by Sean Gautreaux. New Orleans: Ampersand, 2010.
Happy Mardi Gras. Illustrated by Sean Gautreaux. Gretna, La.: Black Pot Publishing, 2010.
One Dat, Two Dat, Are You a Who Dat? Illustrated by Sean Gautreaux. Gretna, La.: Black Pot Publishing, 2010.

Landry's books grow out of his own experience in the city, and these gentle rhyming stories are a hit with children.

LARSON, KIRBY, and MARY NETHERY
Two Bobbies: A True Story of Hurricane Katrina, Friendship, and Survival. Illustrated by Jean Cassels. New York: Walker & Co., 2008.

The story of a dog and a cat that survived the storm by sticking together.

LESTER, JULIUS, with illustrations by LISA COHEN
The Blues Singers: Ten Who Rocked the World. New York: Hyperion, 2011.

MANNING, PEYTON, ELI MANNING, and ARCHIE MANNING
Family Huddle. New York: Scholastic, 2009.

The Mannings were ambassadors for their publishing company during the fall of 2009 and gave away thousands of books; this is a sweet story of how to resolve family conflict.

McCONDUIT, DENISE

DJ and the Debutante Ball. Illustrated by Emile F. Henriquez. Gretna, La.: Pelican Publishing, 2004.

DJ and the Jazz Fest. Illustrated by Emile F. Henriquez. Gretna, La.: Pelican Publishing, 1997.

DJ and the Saints. Illustrated by Emile F. Henriquez. Gretna, La.: Pelican Publishing, 2012.

DJ and the Zulu Parade. Illustrated by Emile F. Henriquez. Gretna, La.: Pelican Publishing, 1994.

McConduit's young protagonist enjoys many of the pleasures of New Orleans life.

RODRIGUE, GEORGE

Are You Blue Dog's Friend? New York: Stewart, Tabori & Chang, 2002.

Why Is Blue Dog Blue? A Tale of Colors. New York: Stewart, Tabori & Chang, 2001.

It seems almost inevitable that Louisiana's best-selling artist would eventually turn his Blue Dog into a children's book character.

SALLEY, COLEEN

Epossumondas. Illustrated by Janet Stevens. San Diego: Harcourt Children's Books, 2002.

Epossumondas Plays Possum. Illustrated by Janet Stevens. Boston: Harcourt Children's Books, 2009.

Epossumondas Saves the Day. Illustrated by Janet Stevens. Orlando, Fla.: Harcourt Children's Books, 2006.

Why Epossumondas Has No Hair on His Tail. Illustrated by Janet Stevens. Orlando, Fla.: Harcourt Children's Books, 2004.

The late great Coleen Salley was a professor of children's literature at the University of New Orleans and a world-renowned performer. After her "retirement" she began writing her own books centered on a young possum guided by a character who is a dead ringer for Coleen herself.

SHAIK, FATIMA

The Jazz of Our Street. Illustrated by E. B. Lewis. New York: Dial Books, 1998.

On Mardi Gras Day. Illustrated by Floyd Cooper. New York: Dial
    Books, 1999.

Two joyful children's books. *On Mardi Gras Day* is one of the best
books about the celebration. Shaik is a New Orleans native and
the daughter of schoolteachers. Her first book was a collection of
three novellas, *The Mayor of New Orleans: Just Talking Jazz* (1987).
Recently she has turned her attention to writing books for young
readers. She lives and teaches in New York City, but she returns to
New Orleans frequently to visit her family and read from her work.

"I grew up in the 7th Ward," Shaik said. "It's a black community, and it was a black community unlike a lot of the pictures of
black communities and the stereotypes . . . When I grew up it
was magical, because my grandmother lived around the corner,
my aunt lived down the block, and my mother taught in the school
half a block away. There was an opera singer who lived on the corner and the fellow next door to us played jazz music. You couldn't
have painted a nicer picture."

STEWART, WHITNEY

Jammin' on the Avenue. New York: Four Corners Publishing, 2001.

A travel guide in the form of a novel for young visitors. Stewart has
also written biographies of figures such as Edmund Hillary, Aung
San Suu Kyi, and the Dalai Lama for young readers.

"TROSCLAIR," ED. HOWARD JACOBS

Cajun Night before Christmas. Illustrated by James Rice. Gretna, La.:
    Pelican Publishing, 1973.

This is the story that began the best-selling series, a Louisiana classic.

BOOKS FOR YOUNG ADULTS

AMOSS, BERTHE

Chalk Cross. New York: Seabury Press, 1976.
Mockingbird Song. New York: Harper & Row, 1988.
Secret Lives. New York: Dell Yearling, 1981.

Berthe Amoss is an author-illustrator and New Orleans native.
Chalk Cross is a novel of time travel for young readers about Marie

Laveau; the other two are about growing up in New Orleans in the 1930s.

HERLONG, M. H.
Buddy. New York: Viking, 2012.

A moving story of a young boy who survives Katrina and continues to search for his missing dog.

HOLT, KIMBERLY WILLIS
Part of Me: Stories of a Louisiana Family. New York: Henry Holt, 2006.

Part of Me, an exquisite novel by the National Book Award–winning author (*When Zachary Beaver Came to Town* [1999]), traces the history of one Louisiana family through the books they read. Holt, a onetime resident of the state, draws wonderfully on her own childhood experience here.

MORRIS, PAULA
Ruined: A Novel. New York: Point, 2009.

A supernatural romance set in the post-Katrina landscape.

RHODES, JEWELL PARKER
Ninth Ward. New York: Little, Brown, 2010.

This is the story of how a heroic little girl and her Mama Ya-Ya brave the storm, a lovely book despite some historical inaccuracies.

WELLS, KEN
Rascal: A Dog and His Boy. New York: Knopf, 2010.

A sweet coming-of-age story set in bayou country; the cover illustration is by George Rodrigue.

A New Orleans Reading List

NONFICTION

SUSAN'S ESSENTIAL READING LIST

The New Orleans City Guide. New Orleans: Garrett County Press, 2009.

This classic 1938 WPA guide holds up incredibly well. The most recent reprint features an introduction by Tulane University historian Lawrence Powell.

BARRY, JOHN

Rising Tide: The Great Mississippi Flood of 1927 and How It Changed America. New York: Simon & Schuster, 1997.

John M. Barry remembers his first glimpse of the Mississippi River; he was a college student visiting New Orleans for Mardi Gras. Then he became an assistant football coach at Tulane University. But that preoccupation with the river led to *Rising Tide.* Barry currently divides his time between the French Quarter and Washington, D.C. He is also the author of *The Great Influenza: The Epic Story of the Deadliest Plague in History* (2004); and *Roger Williams and the Creation of the American Soul: Church, State and Liberty* (2012).

"When I first came to New Orleans, I realized that Tennessee Williams was writing from life," Barry says. "And when I first encountered the New South, in North Carolina, I realized that Walker Percy was writing from life."

BAUM, DAN

Nine Lives: Death and Life in New Orleans. New York: Spiegel & Grau, 2009.

Baum came here to chronicle post-Katrina New Orleans for the *New Yorker* and stayed to write this book, which is one of the best pictures of New Orleans ever in print. It is not, strictly speaking, a Katrina book but, rather, is bookended by Hurricanes Betsy and Katrina and, through the lives of nine individuals, reveals the reality of life in the Crescent City, from the memories of a Carnival King to a high school band leader and to a bar-owning transsexual. Also adapted as a musical; watch for the soundtrack by Paul Sanchez.

BOOKHARDT, D. ERIC, and JON NEWLIN

Geopsychic Wonders of New Orleans. New Orleans: Temperance Hall Press, 1992.

This is out of print, but see if you can track down a copy of this oversized paperback by two keen observers of the city.

CAMPANELLA, RICHARD

Bienville's Dilemma: A Historical Geography of New Orleans. Lafayette: University of Lafayette at Louisiana Press, 2008.

Campanella, a brilliant geographer-historian who teaches at Tulane University, here looks at the city's history as a series of dilemmas from the beginning to its present.

FLAKE, CAROL

New Orleans: Behind the Masks of America's Most Exotic City. New York: Grove Press, 1994.

One of my favorite books ever written about Carnival. Flake came here in 1992, during a particularly turbulent season, and spent her time experiencing every bit of Carnival, from the elaborately scripted balls to the rowdy street life.

McCAFFETY, KERRI

Obituary Cocktail: The Great Saloons of New Orleans. New Orleans: Vissi d'Arte Press, 2001.

This is a glorious look at the city's celebrated cocktail culture.

POWELL, LAWRENCE N.
The Accidental City: Improvising New Orleans. Cambridge: Harvard
University Press, 2012.

Tulane University professor Powell is one of the go-to guys for New
Orleans history. In this volume devoted to the city's first hundred
years, he sees our history as one of adaptation and improvisation,
of unfortunately responding to problems as they arose rather than
anticipating them. He's a great stylist, so the book is packed with
information and wonderfully readable.

ROAHEN, SARA
Gumbo Tales: Finding My Place at the New Orleans Table. New York:
Norton, 2008.

This lovely book will appeal to all who think of coming to live here—
and to anyone who's ever eaten here! Roahen cooks her way to
the heart of the city. *Gumbo Tales* was a onetime selection for the
community-wide One Book / One New Orleans reading initiative.

SANCTON, TOM
Song for My Fathers: A New Orleans Story in Black and White. New
York: Other Press, 2006.

Sancton, who is the son of a novelist and writer who contributed
much to writing about the civil rights movement, grew up in New
Orleans in the 1950s. When his father discovered Preservation Hall,
he took his family along, and young Tom found himself drawn to
the music of "the mens" who played jazz. This book, another One
Book / One New Orleans selection, is one of the very best New
Orleans memoirs, and it has also been adapted into a successful
staged reading with the Preservation Hall Jazz Band.

SEXTON, RICHARD, photographer, with text by
RANDOLPH DELEHANTY
New Orleans: Elegance and Decadence. San Francisco: Chronicle
Books, 1993.

This gorgeous photographic exploration of New Orleans history
and style gave a catchphrase to our vocabulary with its title; it's an
observant look at New Orleans style from the inside.

ART, ARCHITECTURE, AND PHOTOGRAPHY

BENFEY, CHRISTOPHER

Degas in New Orleans: Encounters in the Creole World of Kate Chopin and George Washington Cable. New York: Knopf, 1997.

An interesting look at New Orleans society in 1872, when Edgar Degas came to New Orleans for a visit between All Saints' Day and Mardi Gras.

BRUNO, R. STEPHANIE

New Orleans Streets: A Walker's Guide to Neighborhood Architecture. Gretna, La.: Pelican Publishing, 2011.

Bruno collects her photographs and weekly *Times-Picayune* columns for a block-by-block guide to the city; she can show you how to read an architectural landscape.

DASPIT, FRED

Louisiana Architecture, 1714–1820. Lafayette: Center for Louisiana Studies, University of Southwestern Louisiana, 2004.
Louisiana Architecture, 1820–1840. Lafayette: Center for Louisiana Studies, University of Southwestern Louisiana, 2005.
Louisiana Architecture, 1840–1860. Lafayette: Center for Louisiana Studies, University of Southwestern Louisiana, 2006.

A multivolume survey of Louisiana architecture.

DELEHANTY, RANDOLPH

Art in the American South: Works from the Ogden Collection. Baton Rouge: Louisiana State University Press, 1996.

A glimpse into the collection that became the foundation of the Ogden Museum of Southern Art.

FAGALY, WILLIAM A.

Tools of Her Ministry: The Art of Sister Gertrude Morgan. New York: Rizzoli, 2004.

A study of the self-taught African American artist.

FEIGENBAUM, GAIL, JEAN SUTHERLAND BOGGS, and CHRISTOPHER BENFEY
Degas and New Orleans: A French Impressionist in America. New York: Rizzoli, 2000.

A lovely book accompanying an exhibit at the New Orleans Museum of Art.

FRAISER, JIM, and WEST FREEMAN
The French Quarter of New Orleans. Jackson: University Press of Mississippi, 2003.
The Garden District of New Orleans. Jackson: University Press of Mississippi, 2012.

Photography collections with brief and useful histories.

FRIENDS OF THE CABILDO
New Orleans Architecture. Gretna, La.: Pelican Publishing, various dates.

This landmark eight-volume series includes *The Lower Garden District,* vol. 1; *The American Sector,* vol. 2; *The Cemeteries,* vol. 3; *The Creole Faubourgs,* vol. 4; *The Esplanade Ridge,* vol. 5; *Faubourg Tremé and the Bayou Road,* vol. 6; *Jefferson City,* vol. 7; and *The University Section,* vol. 8.

GERSIN
New Orleans Sojourn: Premiers pas à la Nouvelle-Orleans. Lafayette: University of Louisiana at Lafayette Press, 2011.

An extraordinary sketchbook by a visiting French artist.

HEARD, MALCOLM
French Quarter Manual: An Architectural Guide to New Orleans' Vieux Carré. Jackson: University Press of Mississippi, 1997.

The late professor of architecture at Tulane University knew the Quarter like no one else; he breaks down all of its architectural elements in this important book.

HOFFMAN, LOUISE
Josephine Crawford: An Artist's Vision. New Orleans: Historic New Orleans Collection, 2009.

This is an exquisitely illustrated biography of a captivating French Quarter artist.

KLINGMAN, JOHN
New in New Orleans Architecture. Gretna, La.: Pelican Publishing, 2012.

When people think of New Orleans architecture, French Quarter balconies come to mind; this Tulane professor showcases some of the city's modern masterpieces.

LASH, MIRANDA
The Sydney and Walda Bestfhoff Sculpture Garden. New Orleans: New Orleans Museum of Art, 2012.

The free sculpture garden in City Park is one of the city's great treasures, not to be missed by visitors. Curator Miranda Lash has edited a volume that celebrates its history and is a useful guide to the art within.

LAWRENCE, JOHN H., and PATRICIA BRADY
Haunter of Ruins: The Photography of Clarence John Laughlin. New York: Bulfinch, 1997.

This book draws on the Historic New Orleans Collection's archive of Laughlin's work, along with essays by Andrei Codrescu, Ellen Gilchrist, Shirley Ann Grau, and Jonathan Williams.

MAURER, CHRISTOPHER
Fortune's Favorite Child: The Uneasy Life of Walter Anderson. Jackson: University Press of Mississippi, 2003.

This is a fascinating biography of the well-known Mississippi artist, a New Orleans native.

MENDES, JOHN T.
Dogs in My Life: The New Orleans Photographs of John Tibule Mendes. New Orleans: University of New Orleans Press, 2009.

This book collects a treasure trove of turn-of-the-century photographs taken by an eccentric recluse.

PALMEDO, PHILIP F.
Lin Emery. Manchester, Vt.: Hudson Hills Press, 2012.

A lavishly illustrated volume of the work of one of New Orleans's preeminent sculptors.

PINSON, PATRICIA
The Art of Walter Anderson. Jackson: University Press of Mississippi, 2003.

A collection of 150 color plates published in honor of Anderson's centennial. Anderson, a New Orleans native, is known for his life in nearby Ocean Springs, Mississippi, and if you have the time, a visit to his home, to Shearwater Pottery, or to the Walter Anderson Museum, is a wonderful side trip.

POESCH, JESSIE J., ED.
Printmaking in New Orleans. Jackson: University Press of Mississippi; New Orleans: Historic New Orleans Collection, 2006.

Poesch, who was a beloved art historian at Newcomb College, surveys the printmaking arts.

POESCH, JESSIE, and BARBARA SoRELLE BACOT, EDS.
Louisiana Buildings, 1720–1940: The Historic American Buildings Survey. Baton Rouge: Louisiana State University Press, 1997.

This survey identities and documents hundreds of buildings of different types, and there are scholarly essays on a number of topics by preservationists, architectural historians, and art historians.

RODRIGUE, GEORGE, and GINGER DANTO
The Art of George Rodrigue. New York: Abrams, 2003.

Cajun artist George Rodrigue was known for his moody landscapes set in the southeast Louisiana countryside before he turned his attention to the amazingly successful Blue Dog, one of the state's iconic images, in a series of gorgeous art books.

SACABO, JOSEPHINE, and DALT WONK
Nocturnes. New Orleans: Luna Press, 2012.

This is only the most recent work by the internationally known photographer, from her own fine arts press, Luna Press. She is also the author of many photographic works inspired by literature, such as *Oyeme con los Ojos* (2011), *Pedro Paramo* (2002), *Duino Elegies* (2002), *Cante Jondo* (2002), and *Une Femme habitée* (1991). To explore her work, visit josephinesacabo.com.

SANDUSKY, PHILIP
New Orleans en Plein Air. Gretna, La.: Pelican Publishing. 2003.

If you see a group of outdoor painters as you travel the city, they're probably Sandusky's students; this volume collects 150 scenes he painted out in the open.

SARTISKY, MICHAEL, GRUBER J. RICHARD, and JOHN R. KEMP, EDS.
A Unique Slant of Light: The Bicentennial History of Art in Louisiana. New Orleans: Louisiana Endowment for the Humanities, 2012.

This is a lavishly illustrated survey of the state's art—paintings, sculpture, photography, folk art, decorative art, and furniture—from all periods of history. Truly a landmark publication, it is also supported by extensive online resources.

TOLEDANO, ROULHAC
The National Trust Guide to New Orleans. New York: Wiley, 1996.

One of the most interesting and useful guides to city buildings, written by one of the editors of the Friends of the Cabildo series.

TRAVIESA, JONATHAN
Portraits: Photographs in New Orleans, 1998–2009. New Orleans: University of New Orleans Press, 2009.

Revealing portraits of New Orleanians.

VERDERBER, STEPHEN
Delirious New Orleans: Manifesto for an Extraordinary American City. Austin: University of Texas Press, 2009.

A fascinating examination of pre- and post-Katrina New Orleans architecture, with great photos.

BELLES LETTRES AND ESSAYS

BARCLAY, LEE, with photographs by CHRISTOPHER PORCHE WEST

New Orleans: What Can't Be Lost: 88 Stories and Traditions from the Sacred City. Lafayette: University of Louisiana at Lafayette Press, 2010.

Part elegy, part celebration, this post-Katrina anthology offers wide-ranging personal essays by many writers on what makes New Orleans New Orleans.

CODRESCU, ANDREI

New Orleans, Mon Amour. Chapel Hill: Algonquin Books, 2006.

Codrescu celebrates twenty years of writing about the city with this collection.

GAINES, ERNEST

Mozart and Leadbelly: Stories and Essays. New York: Knopf, 2005.

A welcome collection of Gaines's shorter works, essays, and short stories.

HARVEY, CHANCE

The Life and Selected Letters of Lyle Saxon. Gretna, La.: Pelican Publishing, 2003.

A biography of one of New Orleans's most fabled literary figures. Lyle Saxon was head of the WPA Writers' Project in New Orleans, author of *Fabulous New Orleans* (1933), and a collaborator on the classic *Gumbo Ya-Ya* (1945).

LABORDE, PEGGY SCOTT, with JOHN MAGILL

Christmas in New Orleans. Gretna, La.: Pelican Publishing, 2009.

A wonderful look—with lots of charming photos—at the Crescent City celebration. Peggy, a senior producer for the New Orleans PBS station WYES, is well-known for her documentaries on local history. She hosts *Steppin' Out,* New Orleans's only weekly arts and entertainment review program. She is the author of three books:

Canal Street: New Orleans' Great Wide Way (2006); *Christmas in New Orleans;* and *Lost Restaurants of New Orleans and the Recipes That Made Them Famous* (2011), written with Tom Fitzmorris.

LaBARRE, DELIA, ED.
The New Orleans of Lafcadio Hearn: Illustrated Sketches from the "Daily City Item." Baton Rouge: Louisiana State University Press, 2007.

These are the charming observations of the *Item's* first literary critic and the well-known observer of local culture.

LOWE, JOHN
Louisiana Culture from the Colonial Era to Katrina. Baton Rouge: Louisiana State University Press, 2008.

Many of these essays touch on literary New Orleans.

SALVAGGIO, RUTH
Hearing Sappho in New Orleans: The Call of Poetry from Congo Square to the Ninth Ward. Baton Rouge: Louisiana State University Press, 2012.

A lovely literary memoir about the way poetry ebbs and flows throughout New Orleans history, inspired when the author found a muddy, post-Katrina copy of Sappho's poetry.

ST. GERMAIN, SHERYL
Navigating Disaster: 16 Essays of Love and a Poem of Despair. Hammond, La.: Louisiana Literature Press, 2012.
Swamp Songs: The Making of an Unruly Woman. Salt Lake City: University of Utah Press, 2003.

St. Germain is a brilliant poet and essayist who draws on her rough family history for her subjects.

BIOGRAPHY AND MEMOIR

ADLER, CONSTANCE
My Bayou: New Orleans through the Eyes of a Lover. East Lansing: Michigan State University Press, 2012.

When Adler moved from New York to New Orleans, she settled on Bayou St. John, in the old heart of the city. This memoir is a startlingly honest account of a woman's life and loves.

BATT, BRYAN

She Ain't Heavy, She's My Mother: A Memoir. New York: Crown, 2010.

A lovely, lovely memoir of a great New Orleans character and one man's enchanted New Orleans childhood.

Bryan Batt
Photo by Tom Lowenburg

BOGGS, LINDY

Washington through a Purple Veil: Memoirs of a Southern Woman. New
York: Harcourt Brace, 1994.

The former congresswoman and ambassador to the Vatican recalls
a life that touches on many of the important moments in Louisiana history as well as the history of the nation.

BRADY, PATRICIA

*A Being So Gentle: The Frontier Romance of Rachel and Andrew Jack-
son.* New York: Palgrave Macmillan, 2011.

Patricia Brady came to New Orleans in 1961 to attend Newcomb
College; today she is a distinguished biographer of First Ladies Rachel Jackson and Martha Washington. She is the former director
of publications for the Historic New Orleans Collection and the
former president of the Tennessee Williams / New Orleans Literary Festival. In 2012 the Louisiana Endowment for the Humanities
named her the Humanist of the Year.

BRAZILE, DONNA

Cooking with Grease: Stirring the Pots in American Politics. New York:
Simon & Schuster, 2005.

Brazile's memoir combines her charming memories of growing up
in New Orleans with a hard-nosed look at the American political
scene, including Brazile's tenure as manager of Al Gore's presidential campaign. Today she is a commentator for CNN and a columnist for *O Magazine.*

BROYARD, BLISS

One Drop: My Father's Hidden Life: A Story of Race and Family Secrets.
New York: Little, Brown, 2007.

This is a memoir by the daughter of literary critic Anatole Broyard,
a New Orleans native (1920–90). Two months before his death,
Broyard revealed to his grown children the secret he had kept his
whole life—his true racial identity. This memoir traces Bliss Broyard's attempt to come to terms with this knowledge as she uncovers
her family's history.

COHEN, RICH

The Fish That Ate the Whale: The Life and Times of America's Banana King. New York: Farrar, Straus, & Giroux, 2012.

A fantastic biography of Samuel Zemurray, who for a long time was the head of United Fruit as it turned into a corporate global power.

COTT, JONATHAN

Wandering Ghost: The Odyssey of Lafcadio Hearn. New York: Knopf, 1990.

My favorite Hearn biography.

DeGENERES, ELLEN

The Funny Thing Is . . . . New York: Simon & Schuster, 2003.

This is a comic memoir by the New Orleans native and Emmy-winning talk show host.

DENT, TOM

Southern Journey: A Return to the Civil Rights Movement. New York: William Morrow, 1997.

Dent (1932–98), a poet and founder of the Free Southern Theater and a former aide to United Nations ambassador Andrew Young (also a New Orleans native), revisits many of the sites of the civil rights moment throughout the South, describing progress or lack of it.

DUBUS, ANDRE

Meditations from a Moveable Chair: Essays. New York: Knopf, 1998.

Dubus spent much of his adult life in Massachusetts, but these twelve essays touch a bit on his experiences in his native Louisiana. "Digging" describes working on a construction crew in Lafayette the summer he was sixteen. Other essays describe his life after a hit-and-run driver crippled him in 1986 when he stopped to help stranded motorists.

FEIBLEMAN, PETER

Lilly: Reminiscences of Lillian Hellman. New York: William Morrow, 1988.

Feibleman discusses the years he spent with the playwright, late in her life.

FERTEL, RANDY
The Gorilla Man and the Empress of Steak: A New Orleans Family Memoir. Jackson: University Press of Mississippi, 2011.

A revealing memoir about Fertel's family. His mother was the founder of Ruth's Chris Steak House empire, and his father once ran for mayor of the city on the platform of a gorilla for the city zoo.

FLETCHER, JOEL L.
Ken and Thelma: The Story of "A Confederacy of Dunces." Gretna, La.: Pelican Publishing, 2005.

Fletcher was a friend of John Kennedy Toole in the 1960s.

FOSTER, KEN
The Dogs Who Found Me: What I've Learned from Pets Who Were Left Behind. Guilford, Conn.: Lyons Press, 2006.

Foster, a local writer who moved here from New York, is also a bookseller and founder of Silence Is Violence as well as the Sula Foundation, which provides education and support to owners of pit bulls as well as education about the breed. The Sula Foundation also publishes an annual *Pit Bulls of New Orleans* calendar. This moving memoir describes his love of pit bulls and the way in which they saved his life. Foster is also the author of *The Kind I'm Likely to Get* (1999), *Dogs I Have Met* (2007), and *I'm a Good Dog* (2012).

HOLDITCH, KENNETH, and RICHARD FREEMAN LEAVITT
Tennessee Williams and the South. Jackson: University Press of Mississippi, 2002.
The World of Tennessee Williams. East Brunswick, N.J.: Hansen Publishing Group, 2011.

Holditch is an Emeritus Research Professor of English at the University of New Orleans, He is an acknowledged authority on New Orleans literature in general and Tennessee Williams and John Kennedy Toole in particular. Since 1974 he has been known for conducting literary walking tours of the French Quarter clad in a seersucker suit and straw hat, but he is much more than a tour guide; he is a serious scholar. He is the editor of *In Old New Orleans* (1983), a collection of essays about nineteenth-century New Orleans literature; with Mel Gussow he edited Williams's plays for the Library of America edition. He is the editor of the *Tennessee Williams Journal* and one of the founders of the Tennessee Williams / New Orleans Literary Festival and the Pirate's Alley Faulkner Society.

KAMENETZ, RODGER

The Jew in the Lotus: A Poet's Rediscovery of Jewish Identity in Buddhist India. Northvale, N.J.: Jason Aronson, 1998.

Kamenetz, a poet and scholar who lives in the Uptown university area with his wife, novelist Moira Crone, taught creative writing and Jewish studies at Louisiana State University for nearly three decades. He has written three books about his spiritual search: *The Jew in the Lotus,* the story of his meeting with the Dalai Lama, which was made into a 1998 documentary; *Stalking Elijah: Adventures with Today's Jewish Mystical Masters* (1997); and *The History of Last Night's Dream* (2007), which launched his career as a dream therapist.

MacLAUCHLIN, CORY

Butterfly in the Typewriter: The Tragic Life of John Kennedy Toole and the Remarkable Story of "A Confederacy of Dunces." New York: Da Capo, 2012.

MacLauchlin worked on the documentary *John Kennedy Toole: The Omega Point;* his biography is the definitive work to date.

MONTANA-LEBLANC, PHYLLIS

Not Just the Levees Broke: My Story during and after Hurricane Katrina. Foreword by Spike Lee. New York: Atria Books, 2008.

A rough, raw memoir by the woman who stole the show in Spike Lee's documentary *When the Levees Broke,* then went on to a role in the HBO series *Treme.*

NEVILS, RENÉ POL, and DEBORAH GEORGE HARDY

Ignatius Rising: The Life of John Kennedy Toole. Baton Rouge: Louisiana State University Press, 2001.

The first biography of the eccentric author.

PREJEAN, HELEN

Dead Man Walking: An Eyewitness Account of the Death Penalty in the United States. New York: Random House, 1993.

Sister Helen Prejean achieved national prominence with her 1993 best seller *Dead Man Walking,* which was later made into a film starring Susan Sarandon. In 1980 Prejean began working with residents of the St. Thomas Housing Development. Because many of those people had relatives in prison, she became aware of the need for spiritual counseling for prisoners and in 1982 became a spiritual counselor to a death row inmate named Patrick Sonnier. Those experiences led to her subsequent activism against the death penalty and to her writing career. She is the author of a second book, *The Death of Innocents: An Eyewitness Account of Wrongful Executions* (2004).

REED, JULIA

The House on First Street: My New Orleans Story. New York: Ecco, 2008.

The Queen of the Turtle Derby and Other Southern Phenomena. New York: Random House, 2004.

The journalist purchased the house of the title of *The House on First Street* four weeks before Hurricane Katrina; it was quite a road back. *The Queen of the Turtle Derby and Other Southern Phenomena* is a charming memoir in essays.

RICE, ANNE

Called Out of Darkness: A Spiritual Confession. New York: Knopf, 2008.

A remarkable memoir of growing up Catholic in New Orleans and a chronicle of Rice's relationship with the Catholic Church.

ROBERTS, COKIE

We Are Our Mother's Daughters. New York: William Morrow, 1998.

A series of essays about women who have been pioneers and a tribute to Roberts's own mother, Lindy Boggs.

SCOTT, JOHN W.

Natalie Scott: A Magnificent Life. Gretna, La.: Pelican Publishing, 2008.

The first biography of the writer and journalist, who was a contemporary of Sherwood Anderson, William Faulkner, and William Spratling.

SPOTO, DONALD

The Kindness of Strangers: The Life of Tennessee Williams. Boston: Little, Brown, 1985.

One of the early biographies of Williams by a celebrity journalist.

STONE, ROBERT

Prime Green: Remembering the Sixties. New York: Ecco, 2007.

Stone's experience living and working in New Orleans in the 1960s was the basis for his novel *Hall of Mirrors* (1981).

STRAHAN, JERRY E.

Managing Ignatius: The Lunacy of Lucky Dogs and Life in the Quarter. Baton Rouge: Louisiana State University Press, 1998.

The longtime manager of Lucky Dogs, Inc., gives the real picture behind the imaginary life of Ignatius Reilly. Better read it before you pick up one of those dogs.

SUBLETTE, NED

The Year before the Flood. Chicago: Chicago Review Press, 2009.

A memoir of life in Uptown New Orleans during a violent, turbulent year Sublette spent researching his work of history, *The World That Made New Orleans: From Spanish Silver to Congo Square* (2008).

SUNÉE, KIM

Trail of Crumbs: Hunger, Love, and the Search for Home. New York: Grand Central Publishing, 2007.

A memoir by a woman who was born in South Korea, was adopted and raised in New Orleans, and is now an executive with L'Occitane.

TOLSON, JAY

Pilgrim in the Ruins: A Life of Walker Percy. New York: Simon & Schuster, 1992.

One of the first biographies of Percy.

TOTH, EMILY

Kate Chopin. New York: William Morrow, 1990.

The definitive biography of this important literary figure.

VELLA, CHRISTINA

Intimate Enemies: The Two Worlds of the Baroness de Pontalba. Baton
    Rouge: Louisiana State University Press, 1997.

The fascinating life of the woman who built the famous Pontalba
buildings—she survived a murder attempt by her father-in-law and
a disastrous marriage to pursue a career and a life on the world
stage.

WEDDLE, JEFF

Bohemian New Orleans: The Story of the Outsider and Loujon Press.
    Jackson: University Press of Mississippi, 2007.

A study of the Loujon Press, run in New Orleans in the 1960s by
Jon Edgar and "Gypsy" Lou Webb, who published the literary review the *Outsider* as well as beautiful books by Charles Bukowski
and Henry Miller.

WILLIAMS, TENNESSEE

Memoirs. Garden City, N.Y.: Doubleday, 1975.

Williams wrote this book for some quick cash, but it does have
interesting passages about his experiences in New Orleans.

WYATT-BROWN, BERTRAM

*The House of Percy: Honor, Melancholy, and Imagination in a South-
    ern Family.* New York: Oxford University Press, 1994.

The life and times of one of the most prominent of southern families, dogged by a sense of duty and haunted by family tragedy.

ZONANA, JOYCE

Dream Homes: From Cairo to Katrina: An Exile's Journey. New York:
    Feminist Press, 2008.

A former professor at the University of New Orleans tells of her
search to find a home.

CREOLE HISTORY AND CULTURE

EDWARDS, JAY DEARBORN, and NICOLAS KARIOUK PECQUET DU BELLAY DE VERTON
A Creole Lexicon: Architecture, Landscape, People. Baton Rouge: Louisiana State University Press, 2004.

A primer to the Creole world.

HIRSCH, ARNOLD R., and JOSEPH LOGSDON
Creole New Orleans: Race and Americanization. Baton Rouge: Louisiana State University Press, 1992.

Six essays exploring the ethnic composition and history of the city.

KEIN, SYBIL, ED.
Creole: The History and Legacy of Louisiana's Free People of Color. Baton Rouge: Louisiana State University Press, 2000.

Longtime Creole scholar Kein, who is a poet and the sister of musician Deacon John, edits essays on selected topics.

TORRES-TAMA, JOSÉ, and DAVID HOUSTON
New Orleans Free People of Color and Their Legacy: The Artwork of José Torres-Tama. New Orleans: Ogden Museum of Southern Art, 2009.

A catalog accompanying an exhibit of Torres-Tama's works, *Creoles of Color.*

THOMPSON, SHIRLEY ELIZABETH
Exiles at Home: The Struggle to Become American in Creole New Orleans. Cambridge: Harvard University Press, 2009.

This scholarly work traces the lives of French-speaking Creoles of color in the mid-nineteenth century.

FOLKLORE, CARNIVAL, AND THE SPIRITUAL LIFE

ABRAHAMS, ROGER D., with NICK SPITZER, JOHN F. SZWED, and ROBERT FARRIS THOMPSON
Blues for New Orleans: Mardi Gras and America's Creole Soul. Philadelphia: University of Pennsylvania Press, 2006.

Nick Spitzer, known for his public radio program, *American Routes*, is part of a company of distinguished scholars examining the importance of Carnival culture in the city's recovery.

BERRY, JASON
The Spirit of Black Hawk: A Mystery of Africans and Indians. Jackson: University Press of Mississippi, 1995.

A study of the origins of Spiritual churches in New Orleans. Berry, a New Orleans native, does it all—music writing (he's the author of *Up from the Cradle of Jazz* [1986]), fiction (*Last of the Red Hot Poppas* [2006]), cultural coverage (*The Spirit of Black Hawk*), drama (*Earl Long in Purgatory* [2011]), and hard-hitting journalism. He is perhaps best known for his investigative coverage of corruption in the Catholic Church: *Lead Us Not into Temptation: Catholic Priests and the Sexual Abuse of Children* (1992); *Render unto Rome: The Secret Life of Money in the Catholic Church* (2011); as well as the 2008 film *Vows of Silence: The Abuse of Power in the Papacy of John Paul II.*

CLARK, EMILY
Voices from an Early American Convent: Marie Madeleine Hachard and the New Orleans Ursulines, 1727–1760. Baton Rouge: Louisiana State University Press, 2007.

This book collects firsthand accounts from New Orleans's earliest missionary nuns, revealing their work in forging community among the diverse inhabitants, enslaved and free, who occupied eighteenth-century New Orleans.

GILL, JAMES
Lords of Misrule: Mardi Gras and the Politics of Race in New Orleans. Jackson: University Press of Mississippi, 1997.

Gill, a *Times-Picayune* editorial columnist, explores the tangled history of racial unrest and Carnival.

HARDY, ARTHUR
Mardi Gras in New Orleans: An Illustrated History. New Orleans: Arthur Hardy Enterprises, 2001.

The creator of *Arthur Hardy's Mardi Gras Guide,* a former high school band director turned beloved Carnival commentator and historian, puts together a fascinating and useful compendium of the celebration. There are several editions.

HEARN, LAFCADIO
"Ghumbo zhèbes": A Little Dictionary of Creole Proverbs. New Orleans: Temperance Hall Press, 1991.

A reissue of the 1885 edition of Hearn's collected proverbs.

HURSTON, ZORA NEALE
Of Mules and Men. Philadelphia: Lippincott, 1935.

Folklore collection.

KENNEDY, AL, with a foreword by HERREAST HARRISON
Big Chief Harrison and the Mardi Gras Indians. Gretna, La.: Pelican Publishing, 2009.

A history of the Big Chief, with a foreword by his wife; this really gives an inside look at what it takes to make one of those gorgeous suits.

LABORDE, ERROL
I Never Danced with an Eggplant (On a Streetcar Before): Chronicles of Life and Adventures in New Orleans. Gretna, La.: Pelican Publishing, 2000.
Krewe: The Early New Orleans Carnival, Comus to Zulu. New Orleans: Carnival Press, 2007.

Longtime Mardi Gras scholar and aficionado Laborde is a native and a University of New Orleans graduate, who wrote his dissertation on Mardi Gras, and the former president of the Tennessee Williams / New Orleans Literary Festival. He and his wife, Peggy, are a literary couple, two of the founders of the Tennessee Williams / New Orleans Literary Festival. Errol, editor of *New Orleans Magazine* and *Louisiana Life,* is the head of Renaissance Publishing. *Krewe* is a look at the first sixty years of the celebration.

LEWIS, RONALD
The House of Dance and Feathers. New Orleans: UNO Press / Neighborhood Story Project, 2009.

Ronald Lewis, a Ninth Ward activist, began collecting African American memorabilia, particularly the great suits of the Mardi Gras Indians, only to have his wife throw his collection out of the house; this led him to construct a backyard museum. This wonderful volume tells that story as well as the House of Dance and Feathers's comeback after Hurricane Katrina.

McCAFFETY, KERRI

St. Joseph's Altars. Gretna, La.: Pelican Publishing, 2003.

St. Joseph's Day is observed every March 19; if you're in town, be sure to visit one of the public altars. This book includes a history and 141 gorgeous color photos.

SAXON, LYLE, ED.

Fabulous New Orleans. New York: Appleton-Century, 1928.
Gumbo Ya-Ya: The Folklore of Louisiana. Boston: Houghton Mifflin, 1945.

Two of the classic works that came out of the WPA Writers' Project in New Orleans.

SCHINDLER, HENRI

Mardi Gras New Orleans. Paris: Flammarion, 1997.
Mardi Gras Treasures: Costume Designs of the Golden Age. Gretna, La.: Pelican Publishing, 2002.
Mardi Gras Treasures: Float Designs of the Golden Age. Gretna, La.: Pelican Publishing, 2001.
Mardi Gras Treasures: Invitations of the Golden Age. Gretna, La.: Pelican Publishing, 2000.
Mardi Gras Treasures: Jewelry of the Golden Age. Gretna, La.: Pelican Publishing, 2006.

Schindler, a Carnival historian and designer, collects the best of Carnival-related art in these volumes.

SMITH, MICHAEL P.

Mardi Gras Indians. Gretna, La.: Pelican Publishing, 1994.
Spirit World: Pattern in the Expressive Folk Culture of Afro-American New Orleans. New Orleans: New Orleans Urban Folklife Society, 1984.

Smith's words and images document two important cultural traditions.

TALLANT, ROBERT

Mardi Gras . . . as It Was. Garden City, N.Y.: Doubleday, 1948.

VAZ, KIM MARIE

The "Baby Dolls": Breaking the Race and Gender Barriers of the New Orleans Mardi Gras Tradition. Baton Rouge: Louisiana State University Press, 2013.

Explores the hundred-year history of the women's marching group.

GEOGRAPHY

CAMPANELLA, RICHARD

Geographies of New Orleans: Urban Fabrics before the Storm. Lafayette: Center for Louisiana Studies, 2006.
Time and Place in New Orleans: Past Geographies in the Present Day. Gretna, La.: Pelican Publishing, 2002.

The Tulane geographer and historian provides invaluable information about the city in every one of his books. *Geographies of New Orleans* is a fascinating look at the ethnic communities that make up the city.

COLTEN, CRAIG E.

Perilous Place, Powerful Storms: Hurricane Protection in Coastal Louisiana. Jackson: University Press of Mississippi, 2009.

The LSU geographer once suggested, after the storm, that the water lines should be marked on every street sign so that we should never forget.

LEMMON, ALFRED, JOHN T. MAGILL, and JASON R. WIESE, EDS.

Charting Louisiana: Five Hundred Years of Maps. New Orleans: Historic New Orleans Collection, 2003.

Published to coincide with the Louisiana Purchase Bicentennial, this volume depicts state history through maps from the Historic New Orleans Collection.

LEWIS, PEIRCE F.

New Orleans: The Making of an Urban Landscape. Cambridge, Mass.:
Ballinger, 1976.

The classic guide to New Orleans geography.

HISTORY AND GENERAL NONFICTION

ALEXANDER, S. L., ED.

Courtroom Carnival: Famous New Orleans Trials. Gretna, La.: Pelican Publishing, 2011.

A terrific collection of essays about courtroom shenanigans edited
by a Loyola University professor.

ALLURED, JANET, and JUDITH GENTRY, EDS.

Louisiana Women. Athens: University of Georgia Press, 2009.

Biographical essays.

CAMPANELLA, RICHARD

*Lincoln in New Orleans: The 1828–1831 Flatboat Voyages and Their
Place in History.* Lafayette: University of Louisiana at Lafayette
Press, 2010.

An account of Lincoln's transformative journeys to the city.

DAWDY, SHANNON

Building the Devil's Empire: French Colonial New Orleans. Chicago:
University of Chicago Press, 2008.

A breakthrough work in colonial history; Dawdy, a MacArthur
"genius grant" winner, teaches anthropology at the University of
Chicago.

EVANS, FREDDI WILLIAMS

Congo Square: African Roots in New Orleans. Lafayette: University of
Louisiana at Lafayette Press, 2011.

A history of so much that is crucial in New Orleans culture and
history; this book was selected as the 2012 Humanities Book of the
Year by the Louisiana Endowment for the Humanities.

GAYARRÉ, CHARLES
History of Louisiana. Gretna, La.: Pelican Publishing, 1974.

A reprint of the classic four-volume history, originally published in the mid-1800s.

HARRIS-PERRY, MELISSA
Sister Citizen: Shame, Stereotypes, and Black Women in America. New Haven: Yale University Press, 2011.

The MSNBC commentator teaches at Tulane University.

HORNE, JED
Desire Street: A True Story of Death and Deliverance in New Orleans. New York: Farrar, Straus & Giroux, 2005.

Horne, formerly an editor at the *Times-Picayune,* makes a compelling page-turner out of the circumstances surrounding the murder of Delores Dye in 1984 and the questionable guilt of Curtis Kyles, who served fourteen years for the crime and was later set free.

KUKLA, JON
A Wilderness So Immense: The Louisiana Purchase and the Destiny of America. New York: Knopf, 2003.

Kukla published this compelling history for the bicentennial of the Louisiana Purchase.

LANDAU, EMILY EPSTEIN
Spectacular Wickedness: Sex, Race, and Memory in Storyville, New Orleans. Baton Rouge: Louisiana State University Press, 2013.

The real story behind the notorious red-light district.

LEMANN, NICHOLAS
The Promised Land: The Great Black Migration and How It Changed America. New York: Knopf, 1991.

Nicholas Lemann, a New Orleans native and brother of novelist Nancy Lemann, is a serious social commentator in his books and in his journalism. He is the former dean of the Columbia School of Journalism and a staff writer for the *New Yorker.* He is also the author of *The Fast Track: Texans and Other Strivers* (1981) and *Out of the Forties* (1983) as well as books about the Civil War and standardized testing.

LEWIS, MICHAEL

Coach: Lessons on the Game of Life. New York: Norton, 2005.

Home Game: An Accidental Guide to Fatherhood. New York: Norton, 2009.

Liar's Poker: Rising through the Wreckage on Wall Street. New York: Norton, 1989.

Ever since his first memoir, the New Orleans native has achieved best-sellerdom with his witty writing about the economy, politics, the world of professional sports, even his life as a father. Like his friends Walter Isaacson and Nicholas Lemann, Lewis is the son of a prominent New Orleans family. He became a best-selling author before he was thirty, capturing the spirit of the 1980s in his memoir *Liar's Poker,* about his experiences as an investment broker. He followed that with *The Money Culture* (1991). He achieved even greater fame, and a larger readership, with the film adaptations of two of his later books, *The Blind Side* (2006) and *Moneyball* (2003).

MEDLEY, KEITH WELDON

We as Freemen: Plessy v. Ferguson. Gretna, La.: Pelican Publishing, 2003.

A look at the landmark case that mandated separate but equal treatment.

PATTERSON, BENTON RAIN

The Generals: Andrew Jackson, Sir Edward Pakenham, and the Road to the Battle of New Orleans. New York: New York University Press, 2005.

Patterson sets the conflict in terms of the biographies of the two seminal figures.

PEREZ, FRANK

In Exile: The History and Lore Surrounding New Orleans Gay Culture and Its Oldest Gay Bar. Hurlford, Scotland: LL Publications, 2012.

A beginning look at gay history in New Orleans, centered on the landmark bar Lafitte in Exile.

POWELL, LAWRENCE

Troubled Memory: Anne Levy, the Holocaust, and David Duke's Louisiana. Chapel Hill: University of North Carolina Press, 2000.

The Tulane University history professor describes the long journey of Anne Levy, a hidden child during the Holocaust, to her role as a spokeswoman for the movement against Nazi David Duke.

SUBLETTE, NED

The World That Made New Orleans: From Spanish Silver to Congo Square. Chicago: Lawrence Hill Books, 2008.

A breakthrough work of colonial history, influence, and music.

TUCKER, SUSAN, and BETH WILLINGER, EDS.

Newcomb College, 1886–2006: Higher Education for Women in New Orleans. Baton Rouge: Louisiana State University Press, 2012.

A wide-ranging collection of essays about the college, its history, and its well-known alumnae.

VAN ZANDT, GARY A.

New Orleans 1867: Photographs by Theodore Lilienthal. New York: Merrell, 2008.

A collection of 126 images from the Civil War era, the first municipally sponsored portfolio of a city.

WIDMER, MARY LOU

New Orleans, 1900–1920. Gretna, La.: Pelican Publishing, 2007.
New Orleans in the Twenties. Gretna, La.: Pelican Publishing, 1993.
New Orleans in the Thirties. Gretna, La: Pelican Publishing, 1989.
New Orleans in the Forties. Gretna, La: Pelican Publishing, 2007.
New Orleans in the Fifties. Gretna, La.: Pelican Publishing, 2004.
New Orleans in the Sixties. Gretna, La.: Pelican Publishing, 2008.

These anecdotal, deeply personal histories are locally beloved for their nostalgia.

FURNITURE, INTERIOR DESIGN, AND LIFESTYLE

BATT, BRYAN
Big Easy Style: Creating Rooms You Love to Live In. Written with Katy Danos, with photographs by Kerri McCaffety. New York: Clarkson Potter, 2011.

Batt, who played Salvatore Romano on the series *Mad Men,* operates a stylish home boutique on Magazine Street called Hazelnut. This gorgeous book is an inspiring look at homes and interiors he admires, along with charming reminiscences of his life in New Orleans and New York.

GROSS, STEVE, and SUE DALEY
Creole Houses: Traditional Homes of Old Louisiana. New York: Abrams, 2007.

A gorgeous book, filled with architecture and history.

HOLDEN, JACK D., H. PARROTT BACOT, and CYBÈLE T. GONTAR; with BRIAN J. COSTELLO and FRANCIS J. PUIG
Furnishing Louisiana: Creole and Acadian Furniture, 1735–1835. New Orleans: Historic New Orleans Collection, 2010.

A lavishly illustrated—more than twelve hundred photographs— survey of the history of furniture. It makes for fascinating reading about what these objects reveal about history and lifestyle.

McCAFFETY, KERRI
New Orleans, New Elegance. New York: Monacelli, 2012.

McCaffety is one of New Orleans's finest interior photographers; this is a gorgeous look at contemporary interior design.

PARLANGE, ANGELE, with photographs by WILLIAM WALDRON
Creole Thrift: Southern Living without Spending a Mint. New York: Collins Design, 2006.

Parlange suggests clever decorating on a budget.

SHRIVER, DEBRA
Stealing Magnolias: Tales from a New Orleans Courtyard. New York: Glitterati, 2010.

When high-powered media exec Debra Shriver bought a New Orleans house, she made it a thing of beauty. She shares secrets—and recipes!—in this gorgeous book.

VOODOO

FANDRICH, INA JOHANNA

The Mysterious Voodoo Queen, Marie Laveaux: A Study of Powerful Female Leadership in Nineteenth-Century New Orleans. New York: Routledge, 2004.

A study of how female leadership emerged in voodoo culture.

GLASSMAN, SALLIE ANN

Vodou Visions: An Encounter with Divine Mystery. New York: Villard, 2000.

Voodoo priestess Glassman owns the Island of Salvation Botanica in the New Orleans Healing Center. This book describes the basic tenets of voodoo as well as her personal spiritual odyssey.

LONG, CAROLYN MORROW

Spiritual Merchants: Religion, Magic, and Commerce. Knoxville: University of Tennessee Press, 2001.

A look at the culture of voodoo shops around the United States, including New Orleans.

TALLANT, ROBERT

Voodoo in New Orleans. New York: Macmillan, 1946.
The Voodoo Queen. New York: Putnam, 1956.

Dated books about voodoo informed by the attitudes of the 1940s and 1950s.

WARD, MARTHA

Voodoo Queen: The Spirited Lives of Marie Laveau. Jackson: University Press of Mississippi, 2004.

A well-researched biography by a retired professor of anthropology at the University of New Orleans.

MUSIC

ABBOTT, LYNN, and DOUG SEROFF
Ragged but Right: Traveling Shows, "Coon Songs," and the Dark Pathway to Blues and Jazz. Jackson: University Press of Mississippi, 2007.

An examination of ragtime and minstrel shows and their role in musical history. Lynn Abbott works at Tulane University's Hogan Jazz Archive.

ANCELET, BARRY
Cajun Music: Its Origins and Development. Lafayette: Center for Louisiana Studies, University of Southwestern Louisiana, 1989.

Ancelet is an authority on all things Cajun.

ARMSTRONG, LOUIS
Satchmo: My Life in New Orleans. New York: Prentice-Hall 1954.

A classic of American autobiography. Never forget that Armstrong wrote all of his life, owned and traveled with a typewriter, and signed his letters, "Red beans and ricely yours."

ASWELL, TOM
Louisiana Rocks! The True Genesis of Rock and Roll. Gretna, La.: Pelican Publishing, 2009.

A wonderfully lively tale of the state's contributions to rock and roll.

BATTISTE, HAROLD, JR., with KAREN CELESTIN
Unfinished Blues: Memories of a New Orleans Music Man. New Orleans: Historic New Orleans Collection, 2010.

A beautifully illustrated musical memoir of the great Harold Battiste.

BECHET, SIDNEY
Treat It Gentle. New York: Hill & Wang, 1960.

The autobiography of the great jazz clarinetist.

BERRY, JASON, JONATHAN FOOSE, and TAD JONES
Up from the Cradle of Jazz: New Orleans Music since World War II. Athens: University of Georgia Press, 1996.

One of the best books ever written on New Orleans music, tracing four decades of the art form and its leading figures, from Fats Domino to Professor Longhair, from the Neville Brothers to the Mardi Gras Indians.

BRINKMAN, SHANNON, photographer, with text by EVE ABRAMS

Preservation Hall. Baton Rouge: Louisiana State University Press, 2011.

A volume celebrating the fiftieth anniversary of the great music venue.

BROTHERS, THOMAS

Louis Armstrong's New Orleans. New York: Norton, 2006.

A lively evocation of the complex social and musical culture of the city during Armstrong's early life here.

BURNS, MICK

Keeping the Beat on the Street: The New Orleans Brass Band Renaissance. Baton Rouge: Louisiana State University Press, 2006.

A British music journalist with deep New Orleans ties chronicles the return to prominence of this important musical form.

COHN, NIK

Triksta: Life and Death in New Orleans Rap. New York: Knopf, 2005.

A veteran music journalist journeys through the local rap scene.

COLEMAN, RICK

Blue Monday: Fats Domino and the Lost Dawn of Rock and Roll. New York: Da Capo, 2007.

The first major biography of the beloved rock and roller.

COOK, ALEX V.

Louisiana Saturday Night: Looking for a Good Time in South Louisiana's Juke Joints, Honky-Tonks, and Dance Halls. Baton Rouge: Louisiana State University Press, 2012.

For a rocking good time, follow Cook's advice.

10TH WARD BUCK, with ALISON FENSTERSTOCK and LUCKY JOHNSON

The Definition of Bounce: Between Ups and Downs in New Orleans. New Orleans: Garrett County Press, 2011.

A lively, wonderfully illustrated guide to one of New Orleans's amazing musical genres.

HANNUSCH, JEFF

I Hear You Knockin': The Sound of New Orleans Rhythm and Blues. Ville Platte, La.: Swallow Publications, 1985.

One of the classic New Orleans music histories.

JOHN, DR. [MAC REBENNACK], with JACK RUMMEL

Under a Hoodoo Moon: The Life of Dr. John, the Night Tripper. New York: St. Martin's Press, 1994.

Autobiography of one of New Orleans's most famous musicians, particularly interesting for its chronicle of musical life in the city in the 1950s and 1960s.

MARQUIS, DONALD M.

In Search of Buddy Bolden: First Man of Jazz. Baton Rouge: Louisiana State University Press, 1978.

A jazz scholar discusses the life of the elusive jazz trumpeter.

MARSALIS, WYNTON

Marsalis on Music. New York: Norton, 1995.

Moving to Higher Ground: How Jazz Can Change Your Life, written with Geoffrey Ward. New York: Random House, 2009.

Marsalis is a wonderfully expressive and poetic writer.

McCAFFREY, KEVIN, ED., with principal writers JAN CLIFFORD and LESLIE BLACKSHEAR SMITH

The Incomplete, Year-by-Year, Selective, Quirky, Prime Facts Edition of the History of the New Orleans Jazz and Heritage Festival. New Orleans: e/Prime Publications, 2005.

The best book yet about Jazz Fest, a true celebration that lives up to its title.

McCUSKER, JOHN

Creole Trombone: Kid Ory and the Early Years of Jazz. Jackson: University Press of Mississippi, 2012.

Longtime *Times-Picayune* photographer McCusker also leads jazz tours of the city; this book springs from his fascination with Kid Ory.

OLIVIER, RICK, photographer, with text by BEN SANDMEL

Zydeco! Jackson: University Press of Mississippi, 1999.

A great introduction to zydeco, the music and the culture; gorgeous photos with informative text by Sandmel.

RITZ, DAVID, with ART, AARON, CHARLES, and CYRIL NEVILLE

The Brothers. Boston: Little, Brown, 2000.

A biography of one of New Orleans's preeminent musical families.

ROSE, AL

I Remember Jazz. Baton Rouge: Louisiana State University Press, 1997.

Storyville, New Orleans, Being an Authentic, Illustrated Account of the Notorious Red-Light District. University: University of Alabama Press, 1974.

Two classics by one of the deans of New Orleans music history.

SANDMEL, BEN

Ernie K-Doe: The R & B Emperor of New Orleans. New Orleans: Historic New Orleans Collection, 2012.

A smart, beautifully illustrated biography of the R & B singer best known not only for his hit song "Mother-in-Law" but also for his Mother-in-Law Lounge, a great New Orleans musical landmark.

SMITH, MICHAEL

New Orleans Jazz Fest: A Pictorial History. Gretna, La.: Pelican Publishing, 1991.

Smith was one of the best photographers of musicians in performance.

SPERA, KEITH

Groove Interrupted: Loss, Renewal, and the Music of New Orleans. New York: St. Martin's, 2011.

A series of profiles of musicians by the *Times-Picayune* music critic.

Allen Toussaint with Keith Spera, author of *Groove Interrupted*
Photo by Tom Lowenburg

STARR, S. FREDERICK

Bamboula! The Life and Times of Louis Moreau Gottschalk. New York: Oxford University Press, 1995.

Biography of the New Orleans–born musician, who was America's first internationally recognized composer.

SWENSON, JOHN

The New Atlantis: Musicians Battle for the Survival of New Orleans. New York: Oxford University Press, 2011.

A veteran music journalist describes how musicians have led the fight for recovery after Katrina.

TEACHOUT, TERRY

Pops: A Life of Louis Armstrong. New York: Houghton Mifflin Harcourt, 2009.

A detailed biography of the great jazzman.

TISSERAND, MICHAEL
The Kingdom of Zydeco. New York: Arcade, 1998.

The definitive work on this distinctive music.

WEIN, GEORGE, with NATE CHINEN
Myself among Others. New York: Da Capo, 2003.

The autobiography of the founder of the New Orleans Jazz and Heritage Festival.

NATURE AND ENVIRONMENTALISM

DOUGLAS, LAKE
Public Spaces, Private Gardens: A History of Designed Landscapes in New Orleans. Baton Rouge: Louisiana State University Press, 2011.

A fascinating and wonderfully illustrated history of gardens past and present.

GOMEZ, GAY
The Louisiana Coast: Guide to an American Wetland. College Station: Texas A&M University Press, 2008.

Part history, part field guide.

HARDY, JEANNETTE, and LAKE DOUGLAS, with photographs by RICHARD SEXTON
New Orleans Gardens: Exquisite Excess. San Francisco: Chronicle Books, 2001.

A lavishly illustrated, beautifully written book by two of the best garden writers and one of the best photographers in the city.

HEITMAN, DANNY
A Summer of Birds: John James Audubon at Oakley House. Baton Rouge: Louisiana State University Press, 2008.

Audubon's transformative time at the plantation in the summer of 1821.

KELMAN, ARI
A River and Its City: The Nature of Landscape in New Orleans. Berkeley: University of California Press, 2003.

An environmental history of our public landscape.

REEVES, SALLY KITTREDGE, translator
Jacques-Felix Lelièvre's New Louisiana Gardener. Baton Rouge: Louisiana State University Press, 2000.

A new translation of the first book on Louisiana gardening, written in the nineteenth century.

STEINBERG, MICHAEL
Stalking the Ghost Bird: The Elusive Ivory-Billed Woodpecker in Louisiana. Baton Rouge: Louisiana State University Press, 2008.

Efforts to find the rare bird in our state.

STREEVER, BILL
Saving Louisiana? The Battle for Coastal Wetlands. Jackson: University Press of Mississippi, 2001.

A look at ecological problems facing south Louisiana.

TIDWELL, MIKE
Bayou Farewell: The Rich Life and Tragic Death of Louisiana's Cajun Coast. New York: Pantheon, 2003.

A look at the state's endangered wetlands.

THE SPICIEST COOKBOOKS AND FOOD WRITING

BESH, JOHN
My New Orleans, the Cookbook: 200 of My Favorite Recipes and Stories from My Hometown. Kansas City, Mo.: Andrews McMeel, 2009.

The James Beard Award–winning chef heads a group of restaurants that includes August, Besh Steak, La Provence, Lüke, Domenica, Borgne, and the American Sector and Soda Shop (both in the National World War II Museum). This cookbook is worth every penny for the shrimp creole recipe.

BIENVENU, MARCELLE
Who's Your Mama, Are You Catholic, and Can You Make a Roux? Lafayette, La.: Times of Acadiana Press, 1991.

This is an authentic look at the cuisine and culture of the people of south Louisiana.

CHASE, LEAH
And Still I Cook. Gretna, La.: Pelican Publishing, 2003.
The Dooky Chase Cookbook. Gretna, La.: Pelican Publishing, 1990.

The Queen of New Orleans soul food describes her life—and fine dishes—at Dooky Chase Restaurant.

COLLIN, RIMA, and RICHARD COLLIN
The New Orleans Cookbook: Creole, Cajun, and Louisiana French Recipes Past and Present. New York: Knopf, 1975.

Richard Collin was New Orleans's Underground Gourmet, and this cookbook is a must.

CURRY, DALE
New Orleans Home Cooking. Gretna, La.: Pelican Publishing, 2008.

The longtime food editor of the *New Orleans Times-Picayune* shares her secrets.

CURTIS, WAYNE
And a Bottle of Rum: A History of the New World in Ten Cocktails. New York: Crown, 2006.

The veteran mixologist interprets history through booze.

FOLSE, JOHN
Encyclopedia of Cajun and Creole Cuisine. Gonzales, La.: Chef John Folse & Co., 2004.

The book features more than 850 full-color pages, dynamic historical Louisiana photographs, and more than seven hundred recipes. Chef Folse, pictured on the cover, has chosen the best of the best. It's a hefty tome, to be sure.

GILBERT, TROY, and CHEF GREG PICCOLO
Dinner with Tennessee Williams: Recipes and Stories Inspired by America's Southern Playwright. Layton, Utah: Gibbs Smith, 2011.

Imagine the fun of dining with Tennessee!

HAHNE, ELSA
You Are Where You Eat: Stories and Recipes from the Neighborhoods of New Orleans. Jackson: University Press of Mississippi, 2008.

This is a beautifully photographed exploration of neighborhood food culture, which gives a real taste of the variety here.

HARRIS, JESSICA
Beyond Gumbo: Creole Fusion Food from the Atlantic Rim. New York: Simon & Schuster, 2003.
High on the Hog: A Culinary Journey from Africa to America. New York: Bloomsbury, 2011.

Dr. Harris was the first scholar to hold the Ray Charles Chair in African American Material Culture at Dillard University in New Orleans. She specializes in the food and folklore of the African diaspora.

JUNIOR LEAGUE OF BATON ROUGE
River Road Recipes I–IV. Baton Rouge: Junior League of Baton Rouge, 1959–2005.

Don't miss these classics!

JUNIOR LEAGUE OF NEW ORLEANS
Crescent City Collection: A Taste of New Orleans. New Orleans: Junior League of New Orleans, 2000.

This one's a beauty, with gorgeous photography.

LABORDE, PEGGY SCOTT
Lost Restaurants of New Orleans. Gretna, La.: Pelican Publishing, 2011.

You'll mourn for these restaurants, especially if you're lucky enough to remember some of them. And especially after you taste Spaghetti à la Turci!

LAGASSE, EMERIL, with JESSIE TIRSCH
Emeril's New New Orleans Cooking. New York: William Morrow, 1993.
From Emeril's Kitchens: Favorite Recipes from Emeril's Restaurants.
    New York: William Morrow, 2003.
Louisiana Real and Rustic. New York: William Morrow, 1996.

Bam! Emeril is one of the great voices in Louisiana cuisine, with his flagship restaurants here.

LINK, DONALD, with PAULA DISBROWE, with photographs by CHRIS GRANGER
Real Cajun: Rustic Home Cooking from Donald Link's Louisiana. New
    York: Clarkson Potter, 2009.

This James Beard Award–winning chef owns Cochon and Herbsaint.

MARTIN, TI ADELAIDE, and JAMIE SHANNON
*Commander's Kitchen: Take Home the True Tastes of New Orleans with
    More than 150 Recipes from Commander's Palace Restaurant.* New
    York: Broadway Books, 2000.

A collection of two hundred recipes from the famed Commander's Palace. Eggs Armstrong, anyone?

MARTIN, TI ADELAIDE, and LALLY BRENNAN
*In the Land of Cocktails: Recipes and Adventures from the Cocktail
    Chicks.* New York: William Morrow, 2007.

This is a memoir with a twist of recipes from two local favorites, owners of Commander's Palace, Café Adelaide, and the Swizzle Stick Bar in the Loews New Orleans Hotel.

McCAFFETY, KERRI
Etouffée, Mon Amour: The Great Restaurants of New Orleans. Gretna,
    La.: Pelican Publishing, 2002.
Obituary Cocktail: The Great Saloons of New Orleans. New Orleans:
    Pontalba Press, 1999.

Photographer McCaffety's training as an anthropologist has stood her well in her second career. These gorgeous books celebrate drinking and dining as art.

PRUDHOMME, PAUL

Chef Paul Prudhomme's Louisiana Kitchen. New York: William Morrow, 1984.

The Prudhomme Family Cookbook: Old-Time Louisiana Recipes by the Eleven Prudhomme Brothers and Sisters and Chef Paul Prudhomme. New York: William Morrow, 1987.

From the chef who created blackened redfish—and serves up some wicked martinis.

ROAHEN, SARA, and JOHN T. EDGE

The Southern Foodways Alliance Community Cookbook. Athens: University of Georgia Press. 2010.

All of southern cooking is well presented in this cookbook, edited by Roahen, also the author of *Gumbo Tales: Finding My Place at the New Orleans Table.*

SIMMER, JOE

Joe Simmer's Creole Slow Cooking. New Orleans: 2 Martini Press, 2006.

Joe Simmer is the alias for former restaurateur Richard Stewart and artist Michael Ledet. This book is a hoot!

SPICER, SUSAN, with PAULA DISBROWE

Crescent City Cooking: Unforgettable Recipes from Susan Spicer's New Orleans. New York: Knopf, 2007.

Susan Spicer is the owner of Bayona and Mondo.

STEWART, RICHARD

Gumbo Shop: A New Orleans Restaurant Cookbook. New Orleans: Gumbo Shop, 1999.

More than fifty recipes from the beloved French Quarter restaurant.

THERIOT, JUDE

La Meilleure de la Louisiane: The Best of Louisiana. Gretna, La.: Pelican Publishing, 1990.

True confession: my favorite cookbook. My red beans and rice and jambalaya recipes are from this cookbook.

TUCKER, SUSAN, ED.

New Orleans Cuisine: Fourteen Signature Dishes and Their Histories. Jackson: University Press of Mississippi, 2009.

Imagine how daunting it was to come up with a mere fourteen dishes and then to put together the definitive recipes!

WALKER, JUDY, and MARCELLE BIENVENU, EDS.

Cooking Up a Storm: Recipes Lost and Found from the Times-Picayune *of New Orleans.* San Francisco: Chronicle Books, 2008.

One of the great casualties of Hurricane Katrina was family cookbooks; cookbooks were one of the best-selling category of books after the storm. Encouraged by readers, the *Times-Picayune,* under the leadership of food editor Judy Walker, began a recipe recovery project; this cookbook is the result.

WOHL, KIT, with photographs by DAVID SPIELMAN, foreword by LINDA ELLERBEE

Arnaud's Restaurant Cookbook: New Orleans Legendary Creole Cuisine. Gretna, La.: Pelican Publishing, 2005.
New Orleans Classic Appetizers. Gretna, La.: Pelican Publishing, 2008.
New Orleans Classic Brunches. Gretna, La.: Pelican Publishing, 2012.
New Orleans Classic Desserts. Gretna, La.: Pelican Publishing, 2007.
New Orleans Classic Gumbos & Soups. Gretna, La.: Pelican Publishing, 2009.
New Orleans Classic Seafood. Gretna, La.: Pelican Publishing, 2008.

Kit Wohl's beautifully photographed cookbooks draw from the best restaurant recipes.

SPORTS

BREES, DREW, with CHRIS FABRY

Coming Back Stronger: Unleashing the Hidden Power of Adversity. Carol Stream, Ill.: Tyndale House, 2010.

The beloved Saints quarterback remembers that winning season.

DIXON, DAVE

The Saints, the Superdome, and the Scandal. Gretna, La.: Pelican Publishing, 2008.

One of the city's late great movers and shakers tells how NFL football came to New Orleans.

DONNES, ALAN
Patron Saints: How the Saints Gave New Orleans a Reason to Believe. New York: Center Street, 2007.

Another tale of that memorable first post-Katrina season.

DUNCAN, JEFF
From Bags to Riches: How the New Orleans Saints and the People of Their Hometown Rose from the Depths Together. Lafayette, La.: Acadian House Publishing, 2011.

The *Times-Picayune* sports columnist offers a vibrant history of the franchise and its post-Katrina recovery.

PAYTON, SEAN, with ELLIS HENICAN
Home Team: Coaching the Saints and New Orleans Back to Life. New York: New America Library, 2010.

The coach describes the events leading up to the 2010 Super Bowl victory.

OTHER GUIDES

McNULTY, IAN
Louisiana Rambles: Exploring America's Cajun and Creole Heartland. Jackson: University Press of Mississippi, 2011.

McNulty takes you to wonderful spots you might ordinarily miss— a zydeco trail ride or a houseboat on the bayou. This book is a blast!

STERNBERG, MARY ANN
Along the River Road: Past and Present on Louisiana's Historic Byway, revised and expanded. Baton Rouge: Louisiana State University Press, 2001.

A wonderful mile-by-mile companion.

WELCH, MICHAEL PATRICK, with ALLISON FENSTERSTOCK
New Orleans: The Underground Guide. New Orleans: UNO Press, 2010.

One of the most entertaining guides for the adventuresome, perhaps younger, tourist.

IN A CLASS BY THEMSELVES

Books of the Neighborhood Story Project:
Our Stories Told by Us

Before the Storm: Oral Histories of New Orleans, March 1, 2006, neighborhoodstoryproject.org.

Books by Young Authors

BOLDING, EBONY
Before and after North Dorgenois. New York: Soft Skull Press, 2005.

A young woman reconstructs her life in the Sixth by talking to her neighbors on North Dorgenois and exploring the changing lives of folks on her street and in her neighborhood.

CRAWFORD, DARON, and PERNELL RUSSELL
Beyond the Bricks. New Orleans: University of New Orleans Press, 2010.

Remembrances of childhood in the communities of the Calliope and St. Bernard housing developments, a look at the real lives of teenagers in New Orleans.

HENRY, SUSAN STEPHANIE
From My Mother's House of Beauty. New Orleans: University of New Orleans Press, 2010.

This is a lyrical exploration of the life of a young black Honduran woman living in New Orleans.

JACKSON, WAUKESHA
What Would the World Be without Women: Stories from the 9th Ward. New York: Soft Skull Press, 2005.

This is a young woman's look at the lives of women in the Ninth Ward.

KENNEDY, KAREEM

Aunt Alice vs. Bob Marley: My Education in New Orleans. New Orleans: University of New Orleans Press, 2009.

How one young man survived Katrina, the violence of the streets, and the "heavy hands and hard shoes" of his life.

NELSON, ASHLEY

The Combination. New York: Soft Skull Press, 2005.

Ashley Nelson describes life in one of downtown New Orleans's oldest public housing complexes, the Lafitte.

NELSON, JANA

Palmyra Street. New York: Soft Skull Press, 2005.

Palymra Street is in Mid-City, and Nelson explores the diversity to be found in a single block in words and photographs.

PHILLIPS, KENNETH

Signed, the President. New Orleans: University of New Orleans Press, 2010.

Phillips, the "President" of the title, interviews members of his own family to reconstruct his coming of age.

WYLIE, ARLET, and SAM WYLIE

Between Piety and Desire. New Orleans: University of New Orleans Press, 2010.

Brother and sister Arlet and Sam Wylie talk about their life living above a neighborhood store.

Books about Cultural Institutions

LEWIS, RONALD

The House of Dance and Feathers. New Orleans: University of New Orleans Press, 2009.

This is the story of Ronald Lewis's backyard museum in the Ninth Ward. Based on extensive interviews with Lewis, this book gives us all great insight into the workings of such institutions as Mardi

Gras Indians, Social Aid and Pleasure Clubs, Bone Gangs, and parade krewes.

NINE TIMES SOCIAL AND PLEASURE CLUB, and RACHEL BREUNLIN, EDS.

Coming Out the Door for the Ninth Ward. New Orleans: University of New Orleans Press, 2009.

This is one of the most fascinating books I've ever read about New Orleans; it is the first oral history of a social and pleasure club. Written by the members during that first post-Katrina year, it provides an important oral history of the lives of Nine Times and the life of the city through the rebuilding process. This book truly explores and celebrates the spirit of the city.

A New Orleans Reading List

KATRINA

NONFICTION

ANTOINE, REBECA

Voices Rising: Stories from the Katrina Narrative Project. And *Voices Rising 2.* New Orleans: UNO Press, 2008 and 2010.

This student-run project at UNO collected Katrina stories that centered on the UNO community and neighborhood.

BRINKLEY, DOUGLAS

The Great Deluge: Hurricane Katrina, New Orleans, and the Mississippi Gulf Coast. New York: William Morrow, 2006.

This is then–Tulane University historian's controversial take on the events of the first week following the levee breaks.

BUUCK, MICHELLE MAHL

The St. Bernard Fire Department in Hurricane Katrina. Gretna, La.: Pelican Publishing, 2008.

Buuck's father and son were members of the St. Bernard Fire Department when Katrina hit; this is an amazing account of their heroism.

CLARK, JOSHUA

Heart like Water: Surviving Katrina and Life in Its Disaster Zone. New York: Free Press, 2007.

Clark, the founder of Light of New Orleans Publishing, stayed in the French Quarter during the storm and the flood; this memoir tells what it was really like. "I'll take New Orleans with no electricity and no water and 95 degrees over any other city in America any day," Clark writes.

COOPER, ANDERSON
Dispatches from the Edge: A Memoir of War, Disasters, and Survival. New York: HarperCollins, 2006.

The last third of this book concerns Cooper's Katrina reporting. Cooper is famous for giving New Orleanians a new mantra: "Hope is not a plan," taken from his interview with former mayor Ray Nagin.

COOPER, CHRISTOPHER, and ROBERT BLOCK
Disaster: Hurricane Katrina and the Failure of Homeland Security. New York: Times Books, 2006.

Two *Wall Street Journal* reporters (Cooper at one time worked for the *Times-Picayune*) describe the failure of relief efforts from the top down.

EGGERS, DAVE
Zeitoun. San Francisco: McSweeney's, 2009.

This is the story of a survivor jailed in the aftermath of the storm and his family's struggle to rescue him from unfair imprisonment.

HORNE, JED
Breach of Faith: Hurricane Katrina and the Near Death of a Great American City. New York: Random House, 2006.

Horne, then an editor for the *Times-Picayune*, reconstructs the storm through the experiences of a diverse group of people, including an architect and his family as well as the founder of the relief effort Common Ground.

INGLESE, DEMAREE, with DIANA GALLAGHER
No Ordinary Heroes: 8 Doctors, 30 Nurses, 7,000 Prisoners, and a Category 5 Hurricane. New York: Citadel, 2007.

A memoir by the medical director of the Orleans Parish Criminal Sheriff's Office during the storm.

LONGO, JOE, and JARRET LOFSTEAD, EDS.

Soul Is Bulletproof: Reports from Reconstruction New Orleans. New Orleans: NOLAFugees Press, 2008.

This anthology includes the work of twenty-three writers; the writing is a mix of investigative journalism, first-person reportage, political analysis, and satire.

McNULTY, IAN

A Season of Night: New Orleans Life after Katrina. Jackson: University Press of Mississippi, 2008.

A memoir of that first fall after the storm: McNulty describes how his Mid-City neighborhood came back to life. This memoir provides a fascinating look at what the city was like when so few people were actually here.

McQUAID, JOHN, and MARK SCHLEIFSTEIN

Path of Destruction: The Devastation of New Orleans and the Coming Age of Superstorms. New York: Little, Brown, 2006.

Two *Times-Picayune* reporters get at the science behind the coming age of superstorms.

MOONEY, CHRIS

Storm World: Hurricanes, Politics, and the Battle over Global Warming. Orlando: Houghton Mifflin Harcourt, 2007.

Science writer Mooney grew up in New Orleans and is also the author of *The Republican War on Science.*

NOLAFUGEES.COM

Year Zero: A Year of Reporting from Post-Katrina New Orleans. New Orleans: Lavender Ink, 2006.

This volume collects the best writing from the first year of that satirical website, nolafugees.com.

PENNER, D'ANN R., and KEITH C. FERDINAND, EDS., foreword by JIMMY CARTER

Overcoming Katrina: African American Voices from the Crescent City and Beyond. New York: Palgrave Macmillan, 2009.

Twenty-seven oral histories.

PIAZZA, TOM

Why New Orleans Matters. New York: ReganBooks, 2005.

This was written during Piazza's diaspora as a response to Speaker Dennis Hastert's query about whether or not the city should be rebuilt.

ROSE, CHRIS

1 Dead in Attic. New Orleans: Chris Rose Books, 2005.
1 Dead in Attic: After Katrina. New York: Simon & Schuster, 2007.

A collection of columns from the *Times-Picayune* reporter who became the voice of many New Orleanians after the flood. Rose was nominated for a Pulitzer Prize for his work. The second edition was expanded.

RUTLEDGE, DAVID, ET AL.

Do You Know What It Means to Miss New Orleans? A Collection of Stories and Essays Set in the Big Easy. Seattle: Chin Music Press, 2006.

A beautifully designed anthology of all kinds of writing, this gorgeous small book is designed as a literary jazz funeral for the city.

SOTHERN, BILLY, with photographs by NIKKI PAGE

Down in New Orleans: Reflections from a Drowned City. Berkeley: University of California Press, 2007.

Essays by an attorney who works for the Justice Project, many previously published in the *Nation.* My very favorite essay is about that first post-K Mardi Gras, when Sothern describes listening to the Ninth Ward Marching Band play "Rock Me like a Hurricane" under an overpass during the Muses parade, thunderously echoing to "the mad joy of a city who knew exactly what that meant."

THIBODEAUX, RON

Hell or High Water: How Cajun Fortitude Withstood Hurricanes Rita and Ike. Lafayette: University of Louisiana at Lafayette Press, 2012.

The veteran *Times-Picayune* writer travels throughout south Louisiana to tell the largely untold story of that region's comeback after the devastating storms in the fall of 2005 and 2008.

TIMES-PICAYUNE

The Times Picayune Katrina: The Ruin and Recovery of New Orleans.
New Orleans: Times-Picayune, 2006.

The official publication of the *New Orleans Times-Picayune*, with coverage, analysis, and great photography.

TISSERAND, MICHAEL

Sugarcane Academy: How a New Orleans Teacher and His Storm-Struck Students Created a School to Remember. New York: Harcourt, 2007.

The inspiring story of how Paul Reynaud, a teacher at New Orleans's Lusher school, began a school in New Iberia for displaced New Orleans students during their 2005 exile from the city.

TROUTT, DAVID DANTE, ED.

After the Storm: Black Intellectuals Explore the Meaning of Hurricane Katrina. New York: New Press, 2006.

A collection of essays by thirteen scholars.

VAN HEERDEN, IVOR

The Storm: What Went Wrong and Why during Hurricane Katrina: The Inside Story from One Louisiana Scientist. New York: Viking, 2006.

Van Heerden was the deputy director of the LSU Hurricane Center: his book explains the levee failures of the Corps of Engineers and the way politicization imperiled the rebuilding process.

VOLLEN, LOLA, ED.

Voices from the Storm: The People of New Orleans on Hurricane Katrina and Its Aftermath. San Francisco: McSweeney's, 2006.

Collection of thirteen first-person accounts, including those of Father Jerome LeDoux of St. Augustine Church in Tremé and Rev. Vien The Nguyen of Mary Queen of Vietnam Church in eastern New Orleans.

WARD, JERRY

The Katrina Papers: A Journal of Trauma and Recovery. New Orleans: University of New Orleans Press, 2008.

Poet, scholar, and Dillard University professor Ward recounts the loss of his home in Gentilly and his recovery, sustained all the while by his scholarly work.

WELLS, KEN

The Good Pirates of Forgotten Bayous: Fighting to Save a Way of Life in the Wake of Hurricane Katrina. New Haven: Yale University Press, 2008.

The *Wall Street Journal* reporter describes the comeback efforts of the good people of St. Bernard Parish, one of the hardest hit by the storm.

ESSENTIAL FICTION

BENISCHEK, BRAD

Revacuation. New Orleans: Press Street, 2007.

A graphic novel depicting the events of the storm taking place in a colony of birds.

BOYDEN, AMANDA

Babylon Rolling. New York: Pantheon, 2008.

Strictly speaking, this is not a Katrina book. Boyden gives us the lives of the inhabitants of fictional Orchid Street, one year before Katrina, during Hurricane Ivan.

BURKE, JAMES LEE

Jesus Out to Sea. New York: Simon & Schuster, 2007.
The Tin Roof Blowdown. New York: Simon & Schuster, 2007.

Only two of the thirteen stories in *Jesus Out to Sea* deal directly with Katrina, but all deal with the unfolding decline of the Gulf Coast and the mixture of crime, politics, and Big Oil that have led us to where we are now.

   The Tin Roof Blowdown marked Dave Robicheaux's first venture into the city post-Katrina, on the trail of criminals who hijacked a boat.

DUNBAR, ANTHONY P.

Tubby Meets Katrina. Montgomery, Ala.: NewSouth Books, 2006.

The lawyer-novelist puts his lawyer-protagonist in post-K New Orleans in a wonderful mix of comic and dark storytelling.

GIFFORD, BARRY

Imagination of the Heart: Book Seven of the Story of Sailor & Lula. New York: Seven Stories Press, 2009.

Lula visits New Orleans after the storm, in this final chapter of the story of the lovers from *Wild at Heart.*

LONGO, JOE, and JARRET LOFSTEAD, EDS.

Life in the Wake: Fiction from Post-Katrina New Orleans. New Orleans: NOLAFugees.com, 2007.

This anthology collected fiction from the writers for the satirical website, nolafugees.com, resulting in some beautiful, brutal stories.

PIAZZA, TOM

City of Refuge. New York: HarperCollins, 2008.

Piazza follows the trajectory of two families—one black, one white—through the storm and the following year. This is a balanced, insightful look at the challenges of that period and ends on a wonderful note, looking toward the future.

WARD, JESMYN

Salvage the Bones: A Novel. New York: Bloomsbury, 2011.

Ward, who studied writing at the University of New Orleans, won the National Book Award for this riveting, heartbreaking work, set in her hometown of Delisle, Mississippi.

WILTZ, CHRISTINE

Shoot the Money. Los Angeles: Premier Digital, 2012.

A post-K caper about women and money in a wide-open New Orleans.

ART AND PHOTOGRAPHY

ANDERSON, DAVE

One Block: A New Orleans Neighborhood Rebuilds. New York: Aperture, 2010.

This book collects more than one hundred photographs documenting the before and after of a single block in the Lower Ninth Ward.

ALT, JANE FULTON, with an introduction by MICHAEL A. WEINSTEIN

Look and Leave: Photographs and Stories from New Orleans's Lower Ninth Ward. Chicago: Center for American Places at Columbia College, 2009.

The title refers to the cruel practice of allowing residents to see their damaged homes, then forcing them to leave the devastated area.

Before (During) After: Louisiana Photographers' Visual Reactions to Hurricane Katrina. New Orleans: UNO Press, 2010.

Pictures and essays by thirteen photographers who discuss the way Katrina refocused their work.

COLLIER, PHILLIP, with photographs by DAVID RAE MORRIS

Phillip Collier's Missing New Orleans. New Orleans: Ogden Museum of Southern Art, 2006.

A beautifully designed companion volume to an exhibit at the Ogden, celebrating vanished landmarks, neighborhoods, businesses, and other institutions in the city. This project took on an added urgency after the flood.

HOGUE, CYNTHIA, with photographs by REBECCA ROSS

When the Water Came: Evacuees of Hurricane Katrina. New Orleans: UNO Press, 2010.

Cynthia Hogue turns interviews with evacuees into sheer poetry in this book about thirteen New Orleanians who ended up in Arizona after Katrina. Ross's evocative photos bring them to life.

Katrina Exposed: A Photographic Reckoning. New Orleans: New Orleans Museum of Art, 2006.

This is a catalog accompanying a museum exhibit of work by professional and amateur photographers.

LABORDE, KATHERYN KROTZER

Do Not Open: The Discarded Refrigerators of Post-Katrina New Orleans. Jefferson, N.C.: McFarland, 2010.

After the storm New Orleanians placed their stinky refrigerators on the curb, often duct-taped shut. And they turned those fridges into messages of hope, despair, and humor. This book collects hundreds of photos.

NEFF, THOMAS

Holding Out and Hanging On: Surviving Hurricane Katrina. Columbia: University of Missouri Press, 2007.

Neff teaches photography at LSU; these are his collected portraits of people who stayed through the storm. He came to the city as a rescuer and returned as an artist.

NEUFELD, JOSH

A.D.: New Orleans after the Deluge. New York: Pantheon, 2009.

Graphic novelist Neufeld tells the story from the vantage point of five groups of people—whether to evacuate, how to survive, and what happened to them after the storm.

POLIDORI, ROBERT

After the Flood. Göttingen: Steidl, 2006.

A rather relentless documentation of the city, made up of five hundred photos taken between September 2005 and April 2006.

SHAW, JENNIFER

Hurricane Story. Seattle: Broken Levee Books, 2011.

Shaw, a fine arts photographer, reenacts her Katrina journey, staging it with toys and miniatures in a dreamy light; the result is unexpectedly moving and lovely and certainly unique.

SPIELMAN, DAVID

The Katrinaville Chronicles: Images and Observations from a New Orleans Photographer. Baton Rouge: Louisiana State University Press, 2007.

Longtime Orleanian Spielman stayed in New Orleans for the storm and began sending out e-mails to friends, which are collected in this book. It is a valuable documentation of what life was like in the almost-deserted city as well as a kind of spiritual odyssey. Spielman devoted himself to caring for the convent of the St. Clare nuns at the corner of Henry Clay and Magazine Streets.

POETRY

CODRESCU, ANDREI
Jealous Witness. Minneapolis: Coffee House Press, 2008.

Written to be accompanied by music from the Klezmer Allstars, these poems include "Before the Storm: Geographers in New Orleans." "Conventional geography can't really tell the story of a place like this," Codrescu said.

COOLEY, NICOLE
Breach. Baton Rouge: Louisiana State University Press, 2010.

Cooley's parents (her father is poet Peter Cooley) stayed behind for the storm, and Cooley came down the following spring to see the devastation for herself.

GOMEZ, GABRIEL
The Outer Bands. Notre Dame: University of Notre Dame Press, 2008.

A collection set in the days between Hurricanes Katrina and Rita. Winner of the Andres Montoya Poetry Prize.

KOLIN, PHILIP C., and SUSAN SWARTWOUT
Hurricane Blues. Cape Girardeau: Southeast Missouri State University Press, 2006.

A benefit anthology of work by ninety-four poets from around the nation.

McDANIEL, RAYMOND
Saltwater Empire. Minneapolis: Coffee House Press, 2008.

Amazing collection by a Florida native—especially memorable is a series called "Convention Centers of the World."

NEW ORLEANS HAIKU SOCIETY

Katrina-ku: Storm Poems. Canton, Miss.: Magnolia Press, 2006.

Exquisite little poems.

OSUNDARE, NIYI

City without People: The Katrina Poems. Boston: Black Widow Press, 2011.

The great Nigerian poet, who teaches at the University of New Orleans, had to be rescued from the roof of his Lakeview home. These poems are a moving record of that experience and its aftermath.

SANDERS, ED

Poems for New Orleans. Berkeley: North Atlantic Books, 2008.

A new collection from the 1960s counterculture figure and founding Fug.

SERPAS, MARTHA

The Dirty Side of the Storm. New York: Norton, 2008.

These poems "deal with erosion and disappearing land and loss of home," Serpas said, and many of them were written before Katrina. Eerily prescient.

SMITH, PATRICIA

Blood Dazzler. Minneapolis: Coffee House Press, 2007.

This award-winning collection was based on reading and research. Smith said, "I'm not from New Orleans, but it's good if you think I am."

Lagniappe

LARRY POWELL'S HISTORY HIGHLIGHTS

- The French Quarter, of course, especially the river view of St. Louis Cathedral and its bookended buildings, with Jackson Square in the middle distance.

- Madame John's Legacy, 632 Dumaine Street. Immortalized in a George Washington Cable short story, this home is the best example of what houses in the Vieux Carré must have looked like before catastrophic fires razed much of the Quarter in the late eighteenth century.

- The Haunted House at 1140 Royal Street. Famously haunted by the abused slaves of a Creole aristocrat forced to flee the city after an 1834 blaze gutted her mansion, the building is equally significant for having been an integrated girls' high school during Reconstruction.

- The Pitot House on Bayou St. John, 1440 Moss Street. For more than two centuries this tidal creek served as the watery backdoor to New Orleans. The house is named for one of the city's earliest mayors.

- West End Boulevard and Lafitte Street from N. Claiborne Avenue to Bayou St. John. Their expansive neutral grounds are specters of the man-made canals—New Basin and Old Basin (aka Carondelet)—that once bustled with commerce from the lake trade.

- West End. This neighborhood near the Lakefront is immediately north of the 17th Street Canal levee failure. Ravaged by Katrina, its upended concrete summons memories of the pleasure venues immortalized in Louis Armstrong's rendition of "West End Blues."

- The 400 block of South Rampart Street, especially three derelict buildings: the Eagle Saloon, the Iroquois Theater, and Karnofsky's tailor shop. Here's the heart of the back-of-town area made famous by Buddy Bolden, Kid Ory, and Louis Armstrong, to name just a few of the city's musical greats.

- Public squares, three in particular: Congo Square, in Armstrong Park, with its radial swirl of scalloped stones evoking the ring shouts of West African slaves; Lafayette Square, in the heart of downtown, with its American temple (Gallier Hall); and Coliseum Square, in the heart of the Lower Garden District, especially its trapezoidal park.

- The view of New Orleans from the apex of the Paris Road high rise over the Industrial Canal—a stunning reminder of why early settlers called the city "the isle of Orleans."

- Cemeteries, especially St. Louis 1 and 2. Reckoned on a persquare-foot basis, these two squares probably contain more statuary monuments to historical worthies, black and white, than any comparable plots of land in all of North America. St. Louis No. 1 is bounded by Basin, St. Louis, Conti, and Tremé Streets. St. Louis No. 2 is bounded by Claiborne, Robertson, St. Louis, and Iberville Streets.

Tulane professor Lawrence N. Powell is the author of, among other books, The Accidental City: Improvising New Orleans.

FREDDI EVANS'S BLACK EXPRESSIONS IN THE BIG EASY

- Ashé Cultural Arts Center, 1712 Oretha Castle Haley Boulevard, a gallery and performance space. Check out ashecac.org.

- Backstreet Cultural Museum, 1116 Henriette DeLille Street, backstreetmuseum.org, devoted to second-line culture. Secondline street parades often begin here.

- Bennachin Restaurant, 1212 Royal Street, bennachinrestaurant. com, offering great African food.

- Community Book Center, 2523 Bayou Road, one of the oldest African American bookstores in the country.

- Congo Square, in Armstrong Park, where African Americans gathered to make music and dance, and the Roots of Music Cultural Sculpture Garden.

- Golden Feather Restaurant and Mardi Gras Indian Museum, 704 N. Rampart Street, goldenfeatherneworleans.com, offering fine dining in a gallery space filled with Mardi Gras Indian memorabilia.

- Jazz funerals, one of the great traditions of New Orleans life. Check out listings in the paper, but be considerate of observing someone's loss.

- Maze featuring Frankie Beverly on the Congo Square Stage at Jazz Festival, one of the great closing traditions of the festival.

- Mardi Gras Indians parade on Mardi Gras as well as Super Sunday, usually near the third Sunday in March. Don't miss the spectacle of the rival tribes in all their finery. Check out mardigrasneworleans.com for more info.

- Zulu parades and coconuts, a great Mardi Gras tradition. You'll have to beg hard to get a glittered, painted coconut from one of the floats.

Freddi Evans is the author of Congo Square: African Roots in New Orleans *and three children's books about African American history:* The Battle of New Orleans: The Drummer's Story; A Bus of Our Own; *and* Hush Harbor.

STORYLAND: FUN FOR LITTLE ONES

If you're a booklover who's traveling to New Orleans with children, don't miss Storyland in City Park. This is the place where nursery

Entrance to Storyland
Photo by Dennis Persica

rhymes are life-size! Climb on the web of the spider that frightened Miss Muppet, step into the crooked little house, and watch out for Mother Goose flying overhead. Captain Hook's ship is there too.

One of the most endearing spots in Storyland is a bench honoring the late great New Orleans storyteller Coleen Salley. Settle in next to her and have a chat with her beloved possum character, Epossumondas. Don't forget to take a camera for the wonderful family photo opportunities. City Park offers other attractions: the New Orleans Museum of Art, the Besthoff Sculpture Garden, the New Orleans Botanical Garden, and Carousel Gardens—with a glorious carousel, beautifully restored post-Katrina. Check out neworleanscitypark.com.

—SUSAN LARSON

VIETNAM ON THE BAYOU

Visiting this neighborhood is one of my favorite things to do in New Orleans. Robert Olen Butler's Pulitzer Prize–winning *A Good Scent from a Strange Mountain*, about Vietnamese immigrants, is set partly in the eastern New Orleans enclave called Versailles. A

Robert Olen Butler on familiar ground
Courtesy New Orleans Times-Picayune, *photo by Norman Berteaux*

visit there will bring Butler's literary scene to life. The Saturday open-air market at 14401 Alcee Fortier Boulevard is one of the great pleasures of the city, but beware: it starts at 6 a.m., and it's all over by 9 a.m., so this is for early birds.

To get there, take I-10 east and exit on Chef Menteur Highway, heading east. Take a left on Alcee Fortier Boulevard. You'll notice all the Vietnamese stores and restaurants. In the courtyard of the apartment complex two blocks back on the right, there's an open-air market with local produce, plants and crafts, and *banh mi* for sale (that tasty Vietnamese sandwich). Watch for the truck parked on Alcee Fortier with live chickens and ducks for sale. If you venture down Dwyer Boulevard and over the hill, you will see traditional Vietnamese gardens that will make you think you're in another country. Don't miss the view along the canals as well. On the way back, save time for a bowl of *pho* at nearby Dong Phuong (works wonders for a hangover) and pick up some Vietnamese treats for the road in the fabulous bakery.

—SUSAN LARSON

WHAT JAZZ MAVEN JOHN McCUSKER WOULD TAKE
TO A DESERT ISLAND

If John McCusker, who runs the New Orleans Jazz History Tours, were stuck on a desert island and could only have five recordings of New Orleans jazz to keep the seagulls and himself entertained, he would pick these, in no particular order:

Struttin' with Some Barbeque, Louis Armstrong's Hot Five, 1927. Featuring Kid Ory, Johnny Dodds, and of course the great man himself, this recording is as modern, vital, and awe inspiring today as it was when it was recorded. Boasting signature New Orleans polyphony and collective improvisation, the majesty of this record still gives me goose bumps every time I hear the final chorus.

Blue Horizon, Sidney Bechet, 1944. Known as the "wizard of jazz," Bechet's recording is as blue as blue can be. Though he was known for his fast numbers, nothing pulls at the soul like this slow, low-down blues where every note is like a sentence in a tale of epic proportions. It seethes sensuality like a lover whispering in the ear of the object of his affections.

Black Bottom Stomp: Jelly Roll Morton's Red Hot Peppers, 1926. "Vim" and "vigor" are words that do not begin to describe this all-out, pedal-to-the-floor performance of jazz's first great composer. A seven-piece band that brings all its guns to bear with breaks, breathtaking solos, and an ensemble performance that one best not listen to sitting down.

Burgundy Street Blues, George Lewis, 1944. George Lewis's style was rooted firmly in the New Orleans tradition, but his sound is so personal that it transcends genre. Like Bechet's "Blue Horizon," it has a narrative all its own. But where Bechet's sound is full and round, Lewis's style is gentle, almost delicate in its delivery, like someone telling a tale of woe with resignation, recognizing the fragility of life and the universal human condition.

"Shine," Kid Ory's Creole Jazz Band (Kid Ory at the Beverly Cavern), 1950. This may be the oddball in the group as it is not Ory's

best-known recording and is in fact one that is, to my knowledge, only available on a radio broadcast transcription. Unlike the other recordings that are available on CD and iTunes, one can only find this on an LP record available for sale on eBay. It's worth the price of admission. The band plays at breakneck tempo and features solos by clarinetist Albert "Pud" Brown, trumpeter Teddy Buckner, and Ory himself. Exciting, relentless, and uncompromising, Ory demonstrates his often overlooked genius as a band leader and arranger. The out-chorus will have you clapping along with glee, and you will no doubt punctuate the conclusion with a scream of "Yeah!"

John McCusker is a photographer, the owner of New Orleans Jazz History Tours, and the author of Creole Trombone: Kid Ory and the Early Years of Jazz.

MARDI GRAS MAVEN ARTHUR HARDY'S AIN'T DERE NO MORE REGRETS

- Comus paraded from 1857 to 1991. Comus never threw much, but it didn't matter. The oldest and first krewe presented the final parade each year, providing closure for the Carnival season. With its ancient floats that wobbled as they glided down the avenue, Comus embodied old-world Carnival, with its emphasis on elegance rather than extravagance.

- In 1973 a near-century-old tradition ended when Mardi Gras parades were banned from the French Quarter. For those who watched or participated in them, the parades in the Quarter will always be special. The way lights and sounds bounced off the ancient buildings with their wrought-iron balconies provided an ambiance unmatched anywhere along the parade route.

- When the city's Municipal Auditorium was designed in 1929, special consideration was given to making it Carnival ball–friendly. The expansive floor permitted two balls to be staged simultaneously on different sides of the huge facility. In 1968 some seventy-two balls were presented there. The building was transformed into a temporary casino run by Harrah's from 1994 until 1997. Carnival balls returned in 1998, with the number of events increasing every year until Katrina. Since then the building has remained shuttered.

• Shifting populations and the gradual move toward standardized parade routes, which make it easier for the police department to patrol, have robbed the city of one of its most cherished customs, the neighborhood parade. I remember when Okeanos rolled on St. Claude Avenue, Carrollton on Oak Street, Endymion in Gentilly, Pontchartrain by the lake, Alla on Opelousas, Zeus on Metairie Road, and Mid-City in Mid-City.

• For one hundred years Rex toasted the Queen of Carnival, who sat in the balcony of the Boston Club on Canal Street. The tradition ended in 1992, and one of Carnival's most photographed ceremonial events now takes place at another wonderful and more modern venue, the Hotel Inter-Continental reviewing stands on St. Charles near Poydras.

• Starting in 1857, most major parades not only passed in front of Gallier Hall (old City Hall), but most also stopped there to be toasted by the mayor or other city dignitaries. They were very formal affairs where those fortunate enough to be seated there dressed formally. Starting in the 1980s, however, picnic attire became the norm, and Mardi Gras lost some of its luster.

• In the 1960s legendary broadcaster Mel Leavitt provided parade commentary from the Royal Street balcony of WDSU-TV, which filmed the nighttime parades for delayed broadcast at 10:30 p.m.

• In the 1950s and 1960s, Canal Street was awash in color each Carnival season. Light poles were decorated with painted wooden figurines. Major department stores, such as Maison Blanche and D. H. Holmes, decorated their storefronts as lavishly as they did for Christmas.

• Several parades feature band contests, but from 1963 until 1985 the most famous—the Greatest Bands in Dixie contest—ran as part of the Mid-City parade. The competition was the brainchild of Lloyd Gaubert and Tommy Lupo, and it attracted bands from several states. Each group stopped and performed a three-minute routine before the judges' reviewing stands at Jefferson Davis Parkway and Canal Street. The winning bands were presented their trophies by the mayor at Gallier Hall.

- Until the 1970s the identities of most krewe captains remained secret, adding a certain mystique as the crowds wondered, "Who was that masked man?" Most rode at the head of their processions on horseback, happy in their anonymity.

- Before the advent of generic floats, the daily newspapers (New Orleans had three until 1958) would list the name of every float. For those who paid attention, this made parade viewing more enjoyable.

ARTHUR HARDY'S TOP TWELVE DEAD CELEBRITY GRAND MARSHALS FOR MINOR KREWES

Andy Gibb—Napoleon
Buddy Hackett—Zeus
Evel Knievel—Mecca
Hopalong Cassidy—Elks Orleanians
John Candy—Tucks
Marty Allen—Thor
McLean Stevenson—Vikings
Milton Berle—Grela
Red Buttons—Pontchartrain
Robert Goulet—Iris
Spanky McFarland—Little Rascals
Telly Savalas—Hestia

Arthur Hardy is the publisher of Arthur Hardy Enterprises. He produced Arthur Hardy's Mardi Gras Guide *and is the author of* Arthur Hardy's Mardi Gras: An Illustrated History.

MOIRA CRONE'S "THINGS I LOVE ABOUT NEW ORLEANS"

- A certain kind of Sunday afternoon at the Spotted Cat—one couple is swing dancing, maybe two, the band is playing very old jazz, for a moment the light slants onto the dance floor, and you notice that the weight that usually accompanies life has, for the moment, evaporated.

- The enormous, ancient oak in Audubon Park near the zoo.

- The sweet face of Kermit Ruffins after a set at Vaughn's.

- Gospel on the radio on WWOZ on Sunday mornings.

- This fact: there is nothing unusual in New Orleans about going to a nightclub and seeing the D.A. performing jazz with his combo, or going to a play to see the head of the city council in the lead, or hiring a professional mover and finding out he is a collagist, or going to a life drawing class and seeing physicians and real estate appraisers and tax attorneys dedicating themselves to hours at an easel, or discovering that the sixtyish lady who fund-raises for the hospital has an all-girl band, or that your physical therapist makes a trout amandine better than Galatoire's—for there is a shared recognition that being creative is the same as being alive, in New Orleans—that it is not some detour from the duties that define existence. Art is central to *being* and *celebrating*—unlike anywhere else I have ever been in North America, these two verbs are understood to be essentially synonymous.

Moira Crone is the author of, among many other books, The Not Yet *and* Dream State.

RODGER KAMENETZ'S FAVORITE THINGS ABOUT NEW ORLEANS

- the seasons that should be named for flowers: azalea, gardenia, magnolia

- the cracked sidewalks and potholed roads that suggest the futility of fighting nature

- the storms when the trees outside my house are swaying and a feeling of liberation and fear are in the air

- walking up Oak Street with Moira to do little errands, drugstore, dollar store, bookstore; and purple blossoms are carpeting the sidewalk

- local coffee shops that know how to make damn good coffee and no hint of corporate tyranny

- Dave Brinks and Megan Burns and the fabulous Gold Mine readings on Thursday nights and the community of poets and artists who gather there

- saying "po'boy dressed" and knowing you share a secret code

- the po'boy itself in its magnificence, whether fried oyster, roast beef, whether Parkview or Guy's

- Maple Street Books, Blue Cypress Books, Octavia Books, Faulkner House Books, and the love of books

- Susan Larson!

- eating oysters in the wonderful sonic bathtub of tiled Casamentos on Valentine's Day when a barbershop quarter attending a convention walks in and serenades us

- hearing Irma Thomas in a duet with Paul Simon at Jazz Fest after the storm singing "Bridge over Troubled Waters"

- there are a million more

Rodger Kamenetz is a dream therapist as well as the author of The Jew in the Lotus, Stalking Elijah, The History of Last Night's Dream, *and other works of poetry and memoir.*

SCOTTY BRADLEY'S GUIDE TO GETTING
YOUR GAY ON IN NEW ORLEANS

By Greg Herren
(à la David Letterman)

10. Sunday Tea Dance at the Bourbon Pub, 801 Bourbon Street: classic music, drink specials, the fabled napkin toss to "Love Is in the Air," a video of clips from Mommie Dearest to ABBA's "Mamma Mia," and good-looking guys trying to squeeze every last bit of enjoyment out of the weekend—what's not to love?

9. The Muses, Iris, and Nyx Parades: what would Mardi Gras be without the parades? A bunch of drunk tourists on Bourbon Street, that's what! Everyone has their own favorite parades, but the wom-

en's parades are the best, in my opinion. Nyx rolled in 2012 for the first time and put on a great parade. Muses—well, it just doesn't get any better than the fabulous, irreverent Muses—with dance troupes like the Cameltoe High Steppers and the best high school marching bands in the city! The magnificently decorated shoes they throw are Mardi Gras must-haves! Iris is the oldest ladies' krewe and always rolls on the Saturday afternoon before Fat Tuesday. They're a little more staid than Nyx and Muses but still a good time. And watch the parades on the Uptown St. Charles Avenue route—anything closer to the Quarter than Lee Circle isn't nearly as fun or as true to traditional New Orleans–style Mardi Gras. And it's a lot more fun.

8. The Clover Grill: ah, the Clover Grill, on the corner of Dumaine and Bourbon, just across the street from the oldest continuously operating gay bar in the country, Café Lafitte in Exile. Gay owned and operated, this grill serves a cooked-under-a-hubcap burger that's a late-night staple of any visit to the French Quarter—served with flair and no little sass from the wait staff—who wear shirts reading Clever Girl. The milkshakes are also great, and you can never go wrong with their cheese grits for breakfast, either.

7. Drag Bingo at Oz, 800 Bourbon Street: on Sunday evenings, when the napkins are flying and everyone is singing along with ABBA across the street at the Pub, over at Oz they're playing Drag Bingo, with your fabulous hostess, Blanche Debris. The prizes aren't always the best, but it's really more about the cheap drinks and the comedy show being put on by Miss Blanche and whoever her sidekick is that week as they call out the numbers.

6. Fat Tuesday: everywhere else, it's just Tuesday—but in New Orleans it's Mardi Gras. The primary problem with Fat Tuesday is there's TOO MUCH to do! You can catch the wonderful Zulu and Rex parades as they roll down St. Charles Avenue and Canal Street (and the Zulu coconut is another piece of Mardi Gras booty that everyone wants), or you can get up early and put your costume on to march into the Quarter from the Bywater with the Krewe of St. Ann. There's the wonderful costume contest at the corner of Bourbon and St. Ann—the Bourbon Street Awards—and the entries have to be seen to be believed. The French Quarter is filled with revelers in costumes, every balcony is packed with people drinking and throwing beads to the crowds below, and everyone is just in a marvelous mood. And it all ends with the start of Lent that night when the bells of St. Louis Cathedral begin tolling midnight.

5. Shake your groove thing: I love to dance, and there are two fabulous dance clubs where you can go get your gay on—Oz and the Bourbon Parade (the downstairs bar is the Pub, the upstairs dance club is the Parade). Every Friday and Saturday night the hottest deejays in the city are spinning some of the best dance music you'll ever hear, and the dance floor is packed with sexy shirtless men having a great time . . . the fun starts around eleven, builds to its peak around two in the morning—and goes until six a.m. Our bars never close, chère.

4. But I just wanna soak up the sun: oh, the Country Club! Located in a beautiful renovated home at 634 Louisa Street in the Bywater neighborhood, the Country Club is a clothing-optional private club with a pool, a hot tub, and both an indoor and outdoor bar. They also have a restaurant inside the house, with some of the best grub to be found in the city. So, come have a cocktail, have some lunch, and then catch some rays by the pool in the backyard.

3. The Lazarus Ball: Project Lazarus is an AIDS hospice in the Bywater, and every year at Halloween they hold their big annual fund-raiser: a costume ball—and you know, we all just are looking for another excuse to put on a costume! Thousands of gay men fly in for Gay Halloween, and hundreds of thousands of dollars are raised for a really good cause. The ball is always a blast, with great deejays, free drinks included in the cost of admission, and the costumes—glitter and feathers and sequins, oh my!

2. Ol' Man River: the Mississippi River drains a good two-thirds of the country and runs right through our city. So wide the ships anchored on the other side look like toys, the Father of the Waters has helped shape and define the city of New Orleans since the French landed here in 1718. And there's nothing more relaxing than climbing up the side of the levee and watching the big ships go by—or walking along the Moon Walk at night with a date. Beautiful and always mysterious, the river holds its secrets close—but you might, if you listen closely, hear it whispering one to you after the sun goes down . . .

1. Southern Decadence: the gay Mardi Gras. Every Labor Day weekend thousands and thousands of gay tourists descend upon the French Quarter in the sweltering heat and humidity of the late summer—and it's just too hot to wear much clothing. The party starts on Thursday night and runs through Labor Day—but pace yourself. Remember: everything here is twenty-four hours. And

on Sunday afternoon the drag parade winds its way through the
Quarter on a bar crawl with costumes worthy of Fat Tuesday itself.
Laissez le bon temps rouler, chère.

*Greg Herren works for the NO/AIDS Task Force and is the author of
many, many books in the Scotty Bradley and Chanse McLeod series.*

READING ON THE CHEAP IN MID-CITY:
A DAY WITH BARB JOHNSON

*Some readers might want to hear about active lifestyle things they can
do in New Orleans. I don't know about those things. Those things are
the antithesis of our culture, which is more European than puritanical.
I know about sitting around shooting the breeze, reading and writing.
Mid-City is full of writers. The rent is cheap, and the ambiance is decid-
edly as-is, and all my favorite spots share a single characteristic: they
are not trying to be anything at all. They are only themselves, and what
you will find there is not nearly as interesting as what you will see along
the way, so keep your eyes open.*

1. Start at the Ruby Slipper in the morning (139 S. Cortez). Have
a nice, long breakfast. Bring this story with you: back in the 1980s
I lived down the street from this place. My neighbor was in her late
eighties then, and I used to sit on her porch and get her to tell me
about the neighborhood when it was still new. The Ruby Slipper
is located where there was once a movie theater in the 1930s. My
neighbor made out with her soon-to-be husband in the balcony.
The building was also a corner grocery. My first girlfriend lived a
block from it, and back in the seventies I kissed her outside its then-
shuttered doors. Quelle scandal! You can eat on that spot too—
outdoor dining—and you should definitely kiss someone there.

2. Leave the Ruby Slipper sometime before it closes at 2 p.m.
and walk up to Jeff Davis. Hang a left and go on down to Bayou St.
John, which ends at Lafitte and Jeff Davis. The end is full of gradou and trash. Gradou is a word Cajuns use to describe something
sludgy and gross. Don't even try to look it up. Cajun is not a written language. I mention the gradou because I don't want you to be
discouraged. The whole bayou isn't that way. It rushes out of Lake
Pontchartrain, which is miles away, and then comes to an abrupt

end at Lafitte Street. There's a reason for this. You should look it up. You are nearly in the epicenter of the Mid-City writing world.

3. Stop at the American Can condos at 3700 Orleans Avenue. It used to be a factory that made cans, now it's condos with businesses down below. And a branch of the NOLA public library. Go find you a book or just enjoy reading the list of things you may and may not do in the library. I will warn you: you may not wash your clothes in the library's bathroom. Other than that, things are pretty relaxed there. You are only a matter of yards from both wine and coffee and food. This is true in all of Mid-City.

4. You should wander around the neighborhood. Look at the houses. Read up on shotgun houses, camelbacks. Notice that the porches are used most of the year. They are impromptu barbershops, gathering places for people who are on their way elsewhere, who mean to be moving along, but who stop anyway to talk. Stop and talk. Find out what people are up to. Ask someone what used to be on the corner. Any corner.

5. You'll be going to a bar soon—Parkview Tavern, 910 N. Carrollton, and you'll want to arrive with a full stomach. Go down to Crescent Pie & Sausage on Banks Street or right across from Parkview, there's Toups' Meatery. The Strunk devotees among you should bring a big Sharpie and add an s to Toups's sign. If Sharpie packing is your thing, you will find many, many signs that cry out for your skills. Make a game of finding signs that use boil in the imperative—as in "boil crawfish!" when they really need the adjective form.

6. If it's a Monday and after 9 p.m., go on over to Parkview Tavern (910 N. Carrollton). It will be aswarm with fiction writers. Mostly they will be talking about things that never happened. They will have just gotten out of a fiction workshop over at the University of New Orleans. They will be wound up and good company. Parkview Tavern is the least pretentious place you will ever go. One of the bartenders is a writer. See if you can tell which one. I'll bet you can't. There are a lot of TVs inside and people who are very committed to drinking and smoking without interruption. If you don't like smoke, and you think it will be better outside, you will be wrong. Writers smoking and drinking on a budget—the drinks are cheap as all get-out.

7. When the bar closes down around 2 a.m., folks often head down Dumaine Street, across the bayou and into Pal's Lounge, 949

N. Rendon. Pal's is even smokier. You've been warned. Slightly hipper crowd, younger, but not pretentious at all.

8. If, when Parkview closes, you've had all the drinking that you require, walk down Carrollton until you get to the bayou. Take a right. Walk a couple of blocks to the old (old!) Magnolia Bridge. Sit on the bridge and dangle your feet. Late at night it is beautiful. You may see nutria swimming along. Don't be afraid. They love a party. So do writers. They may have followed you from Parkview. Just go on talking or listening. People will want to know what you're reading. They'll want you to know what they're reading too. Late-night literary differences are solved by way of arm wrestling. Practice before you come if you have strong feelings about books.

Barb Johnson teaches at the University of New Orleans and is the author of More of This World, or Maybe Another.

PLACES TO WRITE

New Orleans has a vibrant caffeine culture, with an abundance of coffee shops that welcome, and are accustomed to, writers who like to sit down and stay a spell. PJ's Coffee, named for founder Phyllis Jordan, has locations all over the city. CC's is another beloved local, named for Community Coffee. A lot of locals favor the Rue de la Course at Oak and Carrollton. In the Quarter there's Café du Monde, of course, which may be too bustling for extended thought—all that powdered sugar flying around! Then there's Croissant d'Or (617 Ursulines Avenue), Royal Blend (621 Royal Street), and Envie (1241 Decatur Street). I like to get out of my Uptown neighborhood for writing (too distracting, running into friends!), and my favorite spots are the Sound Café, 2700 Chartres, and the Cake Café, 2440 Chartres, in Bywater.

Many bookstores have nearby coffee shops: Maple Street Books on Maple Street has a nearby PJ's as well as a Starbuck's; Maple Street in Faubourg St. John is near the Fair Grinds (3133 Ponce de Leon), which often hosts literary events; Garden District Book Shop shares a building with Still Perkin', one of my favorites. Octavia Books has the nearby Laurel Street Bakery.

Of course, libraries are good writing places as well. Latter Library has that historic ambiance, but equally pleasant is the Rosa Keller branch. This is the NEW New Orleans Public Library. The Loyola and Tulane libraries are also lovely places to work, but I tend to doze off in the comfy chairs on the second floor of Tulane's Howard-Tilton.

—SUSAN LARSON

LITERARY BARS

The Gold Mine Saloon
Photo by Dennis Persica

Lost Love Lounge
Photo by Dennis Persica

- Carousel Bar in the Hotel Monteleone, 214 Royal Street, is a must-visit. It really revolves!

- Gold Mine Saloon, 701 Dauphine Street, hosts readings every Thursday night in the 17 Poets! Literary and Performance series.

- Maple Leaf Bar, 8316 Oak Street, is the scene of the longest-running poetry reading series in the South—every Sunday at 3 p.m.

- Lost Love Lounge, 2529 Dauphine Street—there's a library in this bar!

- Napoleon House, 500 Chartres, is one of the all-time great bars, with its signature Pimm's Cup and ancient ambiance.

- Handsome Willy's, 218 S. Robertson, is a NOLAFugees hangout.

- The Columns, 3811 St. Charles Avenue, is the hotel where *Pretty Baby* was filmed; sit on the porch and watch the streetcar pass by.

- BJ's, at 4301 Burgundy, is a Bywater bar owned by poet Lee Meitzen Grue and her son.

- Kajun's Pub is Joann Guidos's bar at 2526 St. Claude Avenue; it was made famous by Dan Baum's *Nine Lives*.

- Finn McCool's in Mid-City is the place to see soccer fans, visiting Irish mystery writers; it was the subject of *Finn McCool's Football Club,* by Stephen Rea.

—SUSAN LARSON

CHRISTINE WILTZ'S SEXIEST PLACES TO READ A BOOK IN NEW ORLEANS

Lafitte's Black Smith Shop. *One of those sudden midafternoon summer rainstorms catches you as you stroll through the French Quarter. You run until you come upon Lafitte's Blacksmith Shop, 941 Bourbon Street. The cool, softly lit, convivial atmosphere welcomes you. With a tall mint-topped drink you sit next to a window looking out into the courtyard and watch the teeming rain. The sculpture of the nude lovers reclines in what was once a fountain nestled against the brick wall of the courtyard. The two lovers lie in each other's arms, their legs entwined, oblivious to the rain. You wish you had your copy of* A Streetcar Named Desire *with you (the Blacksmith Shop was one of Tennessee Williams's haunts), but you don't need it to recall your favorite quote: "Don't you just love these long rainy afternoons in New Orleans when an hour isn't just an hour—but a little piece of eternity dropped into your hands—and who knows what to do with it?"*

You look around the two-and-a-half-centuries-old building and imagine pieces of eternity—the innumerable pairs of lovers who have come through these doors over 250 years. You close your eyes and wish for your lover, who is traveling in distant lands. You sigh and take out the book you are currently reading, A Recent Martyr, *by Valerie Martin, which in spite of its title, is almost too erotic to read in this place with its long and sexy history.*

The Dueling Oaks. *On one of those lush, lovely spring afternoons in New Orleans, you and your lover spread a blanket under the notorious dueling oaks in City Park, near the New Orleans Museum of Art. You have brought only the bare necessities with you—a loaf of French bread, a block of cheese, a bottle of wine, and a copy of* Les Liaisons dangereuses.

You sate yourselves on bread and cheese and top your glasses of wine. You begin to read aloud to each other the letters between the Marquise de Merteuil and the Vicomte de Valmont. The lust and deceit, the secrets and seductions, build as the bottle of wine diminishes. You realize you are each on your edge of the blanket, and you are engaged in your own seductive duel of desire.

Your voices become lower, more urgent, as the afternoon fades into twilight. The songs of the frogs and cicadas fill the air and make it dense. Under the trees the darkness, and the air is closing in; it settles on every inch of your exposed skin.

The wine is gone, you can hardly see the words any longer. As you pass the book to each other, careful not to touch, you ache to move closer. But the game continues as you each try to hold out the longest.

The Marshland. *You and your lover cannot resist spending this glorious October day on the water. You fill an ice chest with delectables and cold drinks, bring along your oyster knife, two small forks, and a couple of fishing poles. You spend the most time selecting the book you will read. Since you are going out into the marsh, it should be a book with a lot of water in it, ideally set in the locale of a river delta; the marshland south of New Orleans sits at the mouth of the Mississippi River. It should have a similar atmosphere of heat and underrated beauty. It needs to be exotic in place and character like the Mississippi Delta. Perhaps other deltas fit that description, but only one book fits it, Marguerite Duras's* Lover, *set at the mouth of the Mekong River. Along with heat and exotica,* The Lover *is an advanced text on longing, desire, love, and sex.*

You rent a boat in Happy Jack and ride along Grand Bayou. You turn into unnamed, narrow waterways that may not exist after the next big storm. The canes and roseaux growing at the edges create walls of privacy that can make you feel you are the only people within miles. You eat, you drink, you cast for fish and even catch a few.

The heat rises; a light sheen covers your skin. You are well into The Lover, each of you taking a turn reading several pages aloud. The novel's power has you gripped in its spell. You decide to stop and let the boat drift. You lounge in the wide bow of the boat and concentrate on reading.

You long to make love, but you run across this passage: "I ask him if it's usual to be sad, as we are. He says it's because we've made love in the daytime, with the heat at its height. He says it's always terrible after. He smiles."

You smile at each other and close the book. This is your little piece of eternity, and you know exactly what to do with it.

Christine Wiltz is the author of, among other books, The Last Madame: A Life in the New Orleans Underworld *and* Shoot the Money.

Acknowledgments

With a book, she would have . . . she was not sure. Something.
A hope.
—FRANCES SHERWOOD, *Vindication*

I always hoped to update my 1999 *Booklover's Guide to New Orleans*,
but it took a long time to do it. When I first wrote that book, I was
just starting out, it seems—a young mother of two, a wife. Now
so much has changed. My daughter, Casey, and my son, Dash, are
launched into the world, and Casey has brought her wonderful
husband, Justin Gorsage, into our lives. Their father, Julian Wasserman, a splendid writer and beloved professor at Loyola University, died in 2003, too soon, one of the very few times he made us
sad after a lifetime of making us happy.

So it took time—and a village—to make me write this book, and
I owe them all my gratitude. First and foremost, Casey and Dash,
who never fail to make me proud and never cut me any slack; I
love you both so much.

Stalwart friends, there when I needed them, gave love and time
to keep me on track. This book is partly dedicated to the memory
of Diana Pinckley, whose long talks and walks with Charlie in the
morning, especially through her own difficult times, enriched my
life in countless ways. I miss her every day. Gratitude to Chris Wiltz,
for life-changing conversations and constant affection over the
years; Marigny Dupuy, for "Lean on me—crash!" and never, ever
crashing; Chris Bynum and Suzanne Stouse, for taking the post-
Picayune leap with me and so many others, sometimes like Thelma
and Louise; Peg Kohlepp, always steady on and level-headed; Susan

Tucker and Mary Ann Travis, for the pleasure of peach parties and Aries birthdays; Mary Lou Atkinson and Millie Ball, and all the Babes. All of you have taught me the joy of long friendship. Thanks to newer friends Judy Walker, Maria Montoya, Judith Lafitte, Karen Kersting, and all the women of the Women's National Book Association of New Orleans. Dennis Persica believed in me all along; thanks for the unexpected joy you have brought to my life. Thanks, too, for our photography expedition.

The fabulous Jenni Lawson, my partner in glitter, has taught me the craft of radio and keeps me focused on *The Reading Life;* Paul Maassen and Ron Biava gave me a welcome opportunity at WWNO. Judith Lafitte and Tom Lowenburg made it all come true.

Near the end of this project, an army of friends and researchers came to my rescue in a difficult time—my deepest thanks to Wayne Everard, Penny Lytle, Suzanne Stouse, Susan Tucker, Casey Wasserman, and Chris Wiltz, but all mistakes are my own. Thanks to all the writers—Moira Crone, Freddi Evans, Arthur Hardy, Greg Herren, Barb Johnson, Rodger Kamenetz, John McCusker, Larry Powell, and Chris Wiltz—for the gift of the "Lagniappe" chapter. Thanks to Paulette Hurdlik and Lauren Graham for the evocative cover photo and a memorable streetcar ride, and to Chris Bynum and Bill Haber for the author photo. Once again, the devoted and talented folks at Louisiana State University Press have made this book possible. Thanks to Margaret Lovecraft for patience and kindness above and beyond; to freelance editor Elizabeth Gratch for her close reading and care; to senior editor Catherine Kadair for guidance during the home stretch; and to Barbara Bourgoyne for her beautiful design.

It is rare to love a city as one loves a person, but New Orleans is just that kind of place. Being here has given me a life I could never have imagined anywhere else. I wrote this book to show not just *my* hope for this city but the hope that is stubborn and strong here in all of us and is bringing New Orleans back, closer to greatness, every day.

Index